# Further Acclaim for *Titanic Survivor*

"Jessop has added a fresh, indispensable chapter to the legend of the *Titanic* that buffs and historians will find invaluable."

—*Publishers Weekly*

"… this unassuming but fascinating memoir … is, in fact, a brisk, no-nonsense account of several decades of oceangoing employment. …But in the end it was her work—exhausting, repetitive and, at times, soul-deadening—that challenged her abilities and defined her life. In that sense, she was a woman ahead of her time."

—*The Women's Review of Books, Wellesley College USA*

"Jessop was poised and graceful as a stewardess. She displays the same qualities as a writer." —*Kirkus Reviews*

"… the recent discovery of Miss Jessop's memoirs gives a new and fascinating insight into the disaster they thought could never happen."

—*Daily Mail, London*

"This is the only book about the sinking of the TITANIC by a member of the ship's crew—Violet Jessop, a stewardess and a survivor. Her story is both charming and simple and yet terrifying. Don't miss it."

— *Clifton Daniel, former Managing Editor of the New York Times*

"This is an amazing book. No, more than that—it's two books: Violet Jessop's vivid memoir, and the inspired, and informative, running commentary of editor John Maxtone-Graham, our dean of maritime historians. If the oceans, and ocean-going palaces and people fascinate you as they do me, this is surely 'must' reading."

—*John Jakes, author of the* Kent Family Chronicles, North and South Trilogy *and other books.*

"… her dramatic experiences produced striking literary touches in her writing…" — *USA Today*

# TITANIC
# SURVIVOR

# TITANIC

Introduced, edited and annotated by
JOHN MAXTONE-GRAHAM

# VIOLET JESSOP

# SURVIVOR

The newly discovered
memoirs of
Violet Jessop who
survived both the
*Titanic* and *Britannic*
disasters

BORONIA PRESS

First published 1997 by
Sheridan House Inc.
145 Palisade Street
Dobbs Ferry, NY 10522 USA

Published in 1998 in Australia
and New Zealand by
Boronia Press
11 Cobby Street
Campbell ACT 2612

Project Editor: Janine Simon
Designer: Jeremiah B. Lighter

Printed in Australia

ISBN    0-646-35277-6

In No. 7 boat I saw one child, a baby boy, with a small woolen cap. After getting all the women that were there they called out three times—Mr. Ismay twice—in a loud voice: "Are there any more women before this boat goes?" and there was no answer. Mr. Murdoch called out, and at that moment, a female came up whom he did not recognize. Mr. Ismay said: "Come along; jump in." She said: "I am only a stewardess." He said: "Never mind—you are a woman; take your place."

*The Truth about the Titanic*
by Col. Archibald Gracie,
Mitchell Kennerley, New York 1913

# To all Violet's Nieces and Nephews

A few years ago I asked my cousins Mary and Margaret Meehan to write notes about our family as I knew they had a great store of knowledge. They remembered our Aunt Vi's manuscript, which she had written in the 1930s, and sent it to Sheridan House, an American publisher in March 1996. Sheridan House engaged John Maxtone-Graham to edit Vi's memoirs and this eminent maritime historian has added much to the enjoyment of the book. *Titanic Survivor* was published in the United States in July 1997.

Inspired by Vi's determination and wanting to bring her story to an Australian audience, I bought the paperback rights for Australia and New Zealand from Sheridan House and established myself as a publisher under the imprint Boronia Press.

I am indeed fortunate that Aunt Vi's memoirs portray not only her life at sea but also her early years in Argentina where she was the first child of Irish immigrants and where my father was born in 1896. So often people tell me the most fascinating stories about their families and I urge them to record their memories. In my own family, my father rarely spoke about his early life and so it is only from Vi's story that I have learnt of experiences in Argentina and England that would have been shared by him.

Although I never met Aunt Vi, I remember as a child receiving the most beautiful cards from her at birthdays and Christmas. My father and his sister corresponded regularly but he did not see her again after he came to Australia with his brothers Will and Jack following World War I. The three brothers had moved to Australia on the recommendation of their brother Phil, who had lived in Cairns with my mother's family, but who had returned to England to serve in the King Edward Light Horse. Phil was killed at the end of the war while manning a crucial machine gun post. With three brothers living in Australia, Vi always held a fondness for this country.

I hope you enjoy my Aunt's story.

Marilyn Skopal
Boronia Press

# ACKNOWLEDGEMENTS

Thanks are due to Walter Lord on three counts. First for suggesting that I edit Violet Jessop's manuscript; second for sharing the resources of his incomparable library; and third, for his generous suggestion to include two hitherto unpublished letters from his files (see following page and Appendix II).

Further thanks are due to three of Violet Jessop's nieces: In London, Margaret and Mary Meehan supplied the original manuscript, photographs and marvelous first-hand remembrance of their lively aunt. From Canberra, Marilyn Skopal provided further illustrations and biographical documentation.

I am grateful to Ian Marshall for his invaluable guidance about the demise of HMS *Audacious*. Also from Maine, my old friend Norman Morse was helpful in providing specifics about turn-of-the-century Royal Mail tonnage. Californian Don Lynch offered extremely useful data about events aboard *Titanic* and *Carpathia*. Jack Eaton filled me in on the ongoing linkage between the White and Red Star Lines. From England, my cousin Robert Maxtone Graham was helpful with some background about the Voluntary Aid Detachment, Jessop's nursing organization. And I remain eternally grateful for Ed and Karen Kamuda's sterling work at the helm of the Titanic Historical Society. My warmest thanks to Lothar Simon of Sheridan House for his faith in my work and the privilege of being involved in bringing Violet Jessop's memoir before the public.

And always, final imperishable thanks to my dearest wife Mary who hears chapters before anyone else, who offers such wise counsel and without whom, this writer's life would be unsupportable.

John Maxtone-Graham
New York, January 1997

The following is an excerpt from a letter by *Titanic* stewardess May Sloan to her sister. Written on board *Lapland* en route from New York, it is a vivid account by another stewardess whose experience mirrors that of Violet Jessop.

S.S. Lapland, April 27th, 1912

My dear Maggie,

I expect you will be glad to hear from me once more and to know I am still in the land of the living. Did you manage to keep the news from Mother? We are now nearing England in the *Lapland*. I hope you got the cablegram all right.

I never lost my head once that dreadful night. When she struck at a quarter to twelve and the engines stopped I knew very well something was wrong. Dr. Simpson came and told me the mails were afloat. Things were pretty bad. He brought Miss Marsden and me into his room and gave us a little whiskey and water. He asked me if I was afraid, I replied I was not. He said: "Well spoken like a true Ulster girl." He had to hurry away to see if there was anyone hurt. I never saw him again.

I got a lifebelt and I went round my rooms to see if my passengers were all up and if they had lifebelts on. Poor Mr. Andrews came along, I read in his face all I wanted to know. He was a brave man. Mr. Andrews met his fate like a true hero realizing the great danger, and gave up his life to save the women and children of the *Titanic*. They will find it hard to replace him.

I got away from all the others and intended to go back to my room for some of my jewellery, but I had no time. I went on deck. I saw Captain Smith getting excited; passengers would not have noticed but I did. I knew then we were soon going. The distress signals were going every second. Then there was a big crush from behind me; at last they realized the danger, so I was pushed into a boat. I believe it was one of the last ones to leave. We had scarcely got clear when she began sinking rapidly.

We were in the boats all night until the *Carpathia* picked us up, about seven in the morning. Mr. Lightoller paid me the compliment of saying I was a sailor.

Your loving sister,
May

# Contents

# Preface

ASTONISHINGLY, WHITE STAR Line stewardess Violet Jessop has reentered my ken. I met her only once, during the last year of her life, in the summer of 1970 while I was researching my first book, *The Only Way to Cross.*

Violet's name had been suggested to me by my mother. Knowing that I was in search of *Titanic* survivors to interview, she recalled that during a crossing she had made on White Star's *Majestic* in the 1920's, her stewardess had left an unforgettable impression. Her name, she remembered clearly over forty years later, was Violet Jessop.

Their brief, mid-ocean friendship had flourished during the crossing, largely due to the state of my mother's health. She was recuperating from surgery and was not sleeping well. So Violet, exhibiting what I would come to learn typified her unfailing dedication to passengers she served, had sat up late with my mother through several nights. The two women talked for hours. Since mother's family had always favored the White Star Line, she and Violet had many ships in common, including my mother's favorite, *Adriatic;* Violet confided that once she had nearly capsized on the ship during a particularly ferocious winter gale.

But the most memorable stories that Violet Jessop shared were those in connection with three later White Star giants: The September 1911 collision of HMS *Hawke* with *Olympic*, the foundering of *Titanic* the following spring and, finally, the sinking of His Majesty's Hospital Ship *Britannic* when the vessel had struck a mine in the Aegean during World War I. Incredibly, Violet had been aboard all three.

With the kind assistance of Ed Kamuda of what was then called the Titanic Enthusiasts of America, I was able to track down Violet Jessop, living in retirement near Bury St. Edmunds in Suffolk. I wrote, telling her that I would be in England the following summer. Would she consent, I inquired, to being interviewed about her experiences with the White Star Line? By return post, she agreed and included careful driving directions.

So one wet July morning, a Sunday, I drove from London up into the Suffolk countryside and, after losing my way several times, finally found her and her diminutive cottage, Maythorn, at the end of a dripping lane.

1

Obviously concerned about my late arrival, Violet was awaiting me outdoors, sheltering from the rain beneath a thatched portico. She was short but erect, with bright eyes and an engaging, direct manner. An Irish lilt colored her voice. She was almost completely bald and wore an auburn wig, legacy, I would learn years later, of a violent head injury received while abandoning *Britannic*. She was genuinely delighted to see me; in common with most pensioners living alone, she had few visitors to Maythorn.

She ushered me at once into her kitchen where on a Tilley lamp—a table top, oil-burning cooker—she brewed me the first of that day's endless cups of tea. In fact, so concerned was I about the possible dangers of that precarious lamp that, the following morning, I went to Harrods and had them send her an electric kettle so that she could brew up without endangering herself or Maythorn's thatched roof.

The remarkable thing about Violet—we became Violet and John instantly—was that she had never talked to a reporter, journalist or historian before. Apparently, she had passed unnoticed on New York's Pier 54 when *Titanic's* 703 survivors sailed into the port aboard *Carpathia*. That young, Irish stewardess had fallen through the cracks, either evading or ignored by an army of pressmen clamoring for stories—any story—during that chaotic but well-documented Manhattan disembarkation. Now, nearly six decades later, I was the first writer of any kind to ask her about her experiences aboard either *Titanic* or *Britannic*.

So, over the course of that rainswept Sunday, seated at her kitchen table, Violet took me back to that cataclysmic April of 1912 with unerring clarity. Some of the stories of her last *Titanic* moments, both on board as well as the overnight ordeal in the lifeboat, have already been shared with readers of *The Only Way to Cross*, published by Macmillan in 1972, and republished by Barnes & Noble in 1997.

Suffusing every moment of Violet Jessop's narrative recall was a wealth of no-nonsense, common sense, delivered in a brisk anecdotal style; one became her captivated friend at once. Though twenty years had passed since her retirement from shipboard, the affable warmth of the practiced stewardess was still effortlessly and gloriously intact. I kept thinking how good Violet must have been at her job.

In mid-afternoon, I thanked her for hours of invaluable talk, kissed her goodbye and drove back to London.

Alas, Violet never saw herself in print. The following year, I received a letter from her niece, Margaret Meehan, advising me that her Auntie Vi had died. I was immensely saddened to hear the news but grateful that I had reached her while she was still so vibrantly alive.

Then, a quarter of a century later, the miracle: In the spring of 1996, Margaret Meehan and her sister Mary submitted the manuscript of an unpublished memoir that their aunt, Violet Jessop, had completed in 1934. The typescript's original title was *Neptune's Greenroom* and the author's pseudonym Constance Ransom (Constance was Violet's middle name). Its yellowing cover sheet indicates that it had been submitted for "a literary competition," nature undisclosed; one can only assume it had been rejected.

Over the succeeding years, Violet had tinkered with her manuscript. By then, it had been retitled *While I Remember* at her sister Eileen's suggestion. Long after Violet died, the sisters Meehan came to the decision that their aunt's memoirs should see the light of day. They sent it to an American maritime publisher in Dobbs Ferry, New York, called Sheridan House.

The publisher, Lothar Simon, in turn passed it along to historian Walter Lord for his opinion. On finding that it was the work of Violet Jessop, Walter was kind enough to tell Lothar that she had been an especial favorite of mine. That was how, long after our only meeting and longer still after its composition, Violet's manuscript ended up on my desk, astonishing resumption, I like to think, of a brief but valued friendship initiated a quarter of a century earlier.

Simon asked if I would accept a commission to edit and annotate Violet's memoir. One swift reading made the project irresistible and I accepted his offer, but only on condition that the Meehan sisters and their cousin Marilyn endorsed his choice.

Curiously enough, in the way these things work, the sisters Meehan had seen on television earlier that spring of 1996 a documentary about Dr. Robert Ballard's exploration of the wreck of the hospital ship *Britannic*; the hour-long film would later be broadcast in the U.S. as part of the *Nova* series on public television. By happenstance, I had been extensively interviewed for the program, in the course of which I had talked at length about Violet Jessop. So, fortuitously, my continuing interest in her life and career had, in effect, preceded my arrival in London that June.

One hot summer's day, I called on Margaret and Mary Meehan in their garden flat near London's Swiss Cottage. The two sisters have lived together throughout their adult lives. Their mother Eileen had been Violet's younger sister; she had married Hubert Meehan. A third Meehan child, John, had emigrated to Australia when he was 21 years old and tragically lost his life four years later in a traffic accident.

His surviving older sisters are a lively, friendly pair, their distinctive Jessop genes very near the surface; both have their aunt Violet's engaging charm. They are retired now, Mary having been an executive secretary and Margaret an art teacher. In 1961, both had also emigrated to Australia; though they very much enjoyed life and work down under, they felt they should live in the United Kingdom to be near their parents. So they returned home in 1965. Their mother, Eileen, died in 1973.

Together with Marilyn Skopal, daughter of their uncle Pat Jessop, they are among their aunt's closest living relatives. Margaret and Mary's mother Eileen had been Violet's only surviving sister, fifteen years younger and, in turn, Violet's closest sibling. All four of Violet's younger brothers had served in the trenches during the Great War. The third brother, Philip, had died on April 10th, 1918, during the final months of hostilities. The trio of surviving brothers emigrated to Australia in the early 1920's.

The Meehan sisters are extremely close and, as with all those who share a compatible life, think very much alike. During the time of my first visit with them, Mary was recovering from an ear infection and confined to bed. However, ear infection or no, I discovered that she was closely following the course of Margaret's and my conversation in the living room; at one point, as we were debating a birth date of one of their uncles, Mary's disembodied voice from the bedroom prompted a brisk correction.

After several hours of conversation with them, I learned invaluable new details about Violet Jessop's long and fascinating career. Prior to reading the manuscript and those conversations in London, I had had no knowledge of Violet's life save for those dramatic hours aboard two doomed White Star vessels; no idea, for example, that she had been born and spent her first sixteen years in Argentina, that she had later attended a French convent school in Kent, that her first job at sea had been with the Royal Mail Line rather than the White Star Line.

Let me share some thoughts about the manuscript that follows. It is largely well-written, dutifully organized and, as any good memoir should be, redolent of the author's spirit and persona. Much of Violet's prose flows beautifully and she knows how to tell a good yarn. It has been my experience that everyone employed aboard passenger vessels—from master to cruise director—inevitably threatens to write their memoirs. But very few do and never before, to my knowledge, has a stewardess. So that is the greatest plus of all, that an articulate witness to memorable maritime events— one of which has fascinated the world ever since—has left an unique record.

Violet did not title her chapters, an omission that I have remedied in the interest of browsers. Moreover, she has provided perhaps more chapter divisions than seem necessary; but, after careful consideration, I came to the conclusion that they should be left as was. This was, after all, the form Violet selected. Sometimes, readers will note that her chapters end abruptly, as though the author may have thought to return and button them up properly at a later date but never did. What also lets down Violet's endings is her reluctance to pause and summarize, reviewing the gist of the preceding chapter and hence sustaining her vital, authorial point of view.

Throughout, she was sometimes tantalizingly selective about what she included. In her defense, she can never have guessed, back in 1934, at our insatiable hunger for ever more detail about the disasters that overtook the last two *Olympic*-class vessels. Though new and fascinating facts emerge in the chapters that follow, one always craves more, not only about *Titanic* and *Britannic* but, indeed, every facet of her shipboard experiences. Often, I wish she had lingered over the kind of detail she either neglects or dismisses with no more than a passing reference.

When Violet Jessop embarks on a ship as employee for the first time, a pivotal moment in her young life, we learn a great deal about her first cabinmate within one page but never share her first passenger summons; she laments about the "dozen and one" components of her uniform but we have been told earlier only that it is gray; no further description is ever forthcoming. And once the ship has sailed, she acknowledges coyly "the little attentions I received from all sides"; from whom, when and of what nature are never divulged. "First impressions," Violet advises us, "are said to be lasting ones"; alas, for my taste, not enough of a novice stewardess' first job impressions memorialize her maiden voyage.

It is a pattern that persists throughout. Perhaps overly familiar with the mundane minutiae of her day-to-day existence, Violet assumes them to be of no interest and concentrates instead on what she considers the high points. Even some high points are conspicuously absent: of HMS *Hawke's* collision with outbound *Olympic* on 20 September 1911, not a mention is made, even though she was on board the White Star liner at the time.

But overall, the pluses far outweigh the minuses. Throughout the manuscript, I have sought to sustain the narrative pace. The childhood chapters about Argentina had to be cut in the interest of space. I not only Americanized the English spelling, I had occasionally to adapt some of her more picturesque usage for Americans. For example, there cannot be many readers on this side of the Atlantic for whom the colloquial admonition "Keep your pecker up," can make any but the direst sense. Similarly, Violet describes her shipboard position as "not a swanker," in place of which I substituted "not prestigious."

Scattered amongst the chapters, I have offered editorial input, clarifying, and occasionally amplifying historical data as they emerge. It is my hope that rather than disrupting the reader's enjoyment, these Maxtone-Graham asides add dimension to Jessop's words.

Throughout the pages that follow, her courage and brisk, no-nonsense persona are never far beneath the surface. Her pejorative of choice is "pathetic" and she hates "cold eyes." Predictably, she has strong feelings about those who throng the pages of her memoir—philandering captains and pursers, loquacious or insufferable fellow stewardesses and an array of sometimes horrifying passengers. She shares them all with us.

Violet Jessop survived not only two great White Star disasters, she was also the remarkable survivor of a demanding childhood. The eldest of six, she became early on a close and supportive companion to her mother, a helpmate very much involved in the care, upbringing and sometimes death of her siblings. And however fondly remembered, one senses that her infancy passed too quickly, that her parents learned early on that little Violet could be relied on as a small but sturdy and extremely competent adult. In truth, her health was fragile and, after several close shaves with death from consumption, one can only admire the way she coped with the physical demands she would encounter in later life.

In sum, Violet Jessop was unquestionably a strong and resourceful woman whose life story sheds riveting light on the era of the great ocean liners. As a marine historian, I feel privileged to have had a part in helping usher that life onto the printed page.

# Introduction

B EFORE WE EMBARK, a brief overview of yesterday's ocean liners is in order. North Atlantic steamships were called liners because they achieved a line voyage, from point A to point B, from Liverpool to New York or, conversely, from New York to Liverpool or Le Havre or Rotterdam or Bremerhaven or Genoa. New York was indisputably the western terminus for all transatlantic lines. In fact, early steamship posters designed to entice emigrants to the New World were never emblazoned with "America" or "United States"; the destination of choice was simply "New York." It stood for liberty and a new life.

Present-day shipboard life revolves largely around cruising, a very different kind of journey from a line voyage. Sailing for pleasure rather than purpose, cruise passengers drift along languid, usually sub-tropical itineraries with no other aim in life than indolence, sun and sightseeing, participants in an essentially fruitless voyage. Having embarked, they call at a succession of exotic destinations before disembarking at their port of origin a week or two later. They achieve no geographical objective whatsoever.

Crossings, on what was sometimes described as the Atlantic Ferry, were quite different, involving year-round adherence to a bruising schedule across the world's most dangerous ocean. And the great weapon with which shipping men surmounted the perils and uncertainties of that dread ocean was the steam engine. Before coal-fired boilers supplemented the gentler press of canvas, it had taken six weeks on sailing packets to cross what was called the Western Ocean to America, aboard vessels that earned the lugubrious appellation "coffin brigs" because so many of them vanished without a trace.

Once steam engines were installed within wooden sailing hulls in the 1830's, crossing time was reduced to an astonishing fortnight. That improved performance came at an emotional price for old-line sailors, typified by a Liverpool gibe of the period to the effect that sailormen might "knock off the sea and go in steam." Steam engines brought on board a host of mechanical intrusions into the ancient, scrubbed ethos of teak, canvas and hemp—the grit and grime of coal dust that pervaded every shipboard space, a distinctive reek combining coal smoke, lubricating oil and steam, the hissing, shuddering resonance of vast working parts, the

7

potential for boiler explosion and a very real danger of fire within hull and rigging alike.

The first steamers were driven by paddle wheels and it was not until the advent of first iron and then steel hulls that those vulnerable and essentially clumsy devices could be replaced by the far more efficient propeller; wooden hulls were inadequate to the relentless thrust of the propeller. But fail-safe sails were still employed until just before the turn of the century when, following the advent of twin propellers—in other words, a spare in case of breakdown—canvas was dispensed with forever. With multiple masts, spars and rigging removed, deckhouses rose amidships and the pure steamer profile emerged.

Despite the advent of supplementary power, pity those earliest steam passengers! We must never forget the appalling shipboard conditions endured by that long-suffering human cargo. Today's cruise passengers, strolling at ease about stabilized hulls sailing through placid waters, can have little conception of the discomfort of early steamship crossings on the North Atlantic. There was only one public room, called the dining saloon; decks were often awash; cabins were crowded, stuffy and sometimes damp, their occupants confined, purposely, within narrow bunks, held fast between bulkhead and restraining leeboard. So too were plates and bowls confined within special racks atop dining saloon tables to prevent them from hurtling into passenger laps.

Year-round, debilitating seasickness was compounded by the effort and exhaustion of simply remaining erect. Merely standing without being hurled to the deck, negotiating heaving alleyways clutching at hand rails or clambering up unpredictably angled companionways; even remaining seated at a dining table demanded unceasing effort. Sea motion aboard the early steamers was seldom the dignified lift and fall of the bows but more akin to the abrupt, unpredictable lurch of the roller coaster. Moreover, a ceaseless cacophony accompanied rough passage: Woodwork creaked and groaned, cabin and cupboard doors slammed, crockery shattered and mountainous seas thundered against deckhouse walls.

And if life for cabin passengers was testing, imagine conditions further below, in what was called steerage, traditional name for the recesses of early sailing vessels given over, literally, to steering the vessel. Those same blighted, working decks were used to accommodate the line's humblest passengers. Here were neither glistening rows of white-painted cabins nor concerned stewards on demand, only bleak, ill-ventilated compartments deep within the hull, devoid of decoration, privacy and any but the meanest amenities—dark, damp and claustrophobic spaces within deafening proximity to stoke hole and boiler rooms.

Owners and masters alike neglected their immigrant berthing compartments. An undercover inspector from America's Immigration Commission of 1908 described typical steerage thus: "It is a congestion so intense, so injurious to the health and morals that there is nothing on land to equal it . . . Everything was dirty, sticky and disagreeable to the touch . . ."

But regardless, the ships steamed on and that most dangerous ocean played host to more traffic than all the other oceans of the world combined. From 1840, Cunard had had the field to themselves for two decades before competition proliferated: French, German, Dutch, American, Italian, Scandinavian and British rivals sailed in their wake. At first, the British retained the leader's complacency and under-estimated the competitive rigors that would shortly prevail. "As things stand now," pontificated The Times of London in the summer of 1852, "it is scarcely possible, in the absence of any remarkable invention, that the speed of our Atlantic voyages can be materially increased."

A cutthroat war in quest of the most advantageous crossings began, the two vital imperatives de luxe and dispatch. Owners, builders and their naval architects discovered that increased speed, comfort and reliability across the North Atlantic inevitably spawned larger hulls. Increased size and sophistication permitted on-board comforts for cabin passengers undreamed of only decades earlier. Passengers could enjoy a choice of decks by day and a choice of public rooms by night and a few—very few—private bathrooms appeared on deck plans. In the first class, passengers were encouraged to pack evening clothes in their steamer trunks. Wrote an American in 1905: "Fashionable travelers are gradually turning ocean voyages into social festivities and millinery shows . . . They come to dinner in full dress also, with low necks and bare arms and diamonds and flowers until the dining room on a big steamer is as gay as a banquet hall."

Tonnage escalation was given further impetus towards the end of the 19th century when the westward flow of immigrants turned into a flood. A seemingly infinite demand for inexpensive berths prompted the North Atlantic's ultimate tonnage aggrandizement, elevating ships' size and displacement to record heights. Hordes of Europe's persecuted, dispossessed or merely ambitious trekked to the continent's ports and embarked within the steerage compartments of huge liners. Once on board, neglected, underfed and abused, they endured a week's transatlantic purgatory. Yet however ghastly the conditions of passage between old world and new, stoic acceptance of that heaving, noisome odium was their only choice; in compensation, incomparable reward lay just over the western horizon, the promise of limitless possibilities within these burgeoning United States.

By the time Violet Jessop went to sea in 1908, more than a million immigrants a year were passing through Ellis Island. They arrived in the port of New York packed within hulls over 800 feet in length and displacing more than 50,000 tons. Ponder this socio-maritime irony: The hulls were built larger to accommodate more immigrants but, because they were larger, even more dazzling interiors could be created for cabin passengers.

Absorbed within those black steel hulls and glistening white upperworks was a spectrum of Edwardian society. Let us examine the passenger class spread, for example, throughout the Olympic, the vessel on board which Violet Jessop spent most of her sea-going days. Of the total passenger complement, 689 could be accommodated in first class atop the vessel, about the same number in second class slightly aft and, far below, over a thousand within a combination of cabins housing either couples or up to ten passengers. By 1911, the year of *Olympic*'s debut, the term steerage had been abolished in favor of third class. The notorious berthing compartments of old had been supplanted by humble yet private cabins along every lower deck. The first emigrant families ushered into these modest accommodations thought themselves interlopers into the second class.

This was the shipping world into which young Violet Jessop sought admission, entering a specialized life of service aboard steamers catering to rich and poor alike. Though initially assigned to the second class, she soon graduated into the first and found that those complacent souls inhabiting a steamer's most rarefied decks expected—nay, demanded!—the best accommodations, food and service the shipping companies could provide. Jessop was among thousands who toiled in response.

A very bright journalist, unfamiliar with shipboard, once asked me exactly what it was that a steward or stewardess did. Since readers of this volume may be similarly uninformed, a steward's primer follows.

Within every passenger vessel's crew, there are three clearly defined divisions: Deck department, engineering department and what was called in Violet Jessop's day aboard British vessels, the victualing department. On board today's cruise ships, that third division of the crew is called the hotel department, headed by a hotel manager rather than a chief purser.

The victualing department was always the largest in number, made up of a chief purser and his staff, chief steward and his second-in-command, chef and sous-chefs in the galley, deck stewards, smoking room stewards, bath stewards and a large corps of stewards grouped into one of two categories: Either bedroom stewards, who looked after passengers and their cabins, or saloon stewards who served them meals in the dining saloon. Those latter stewards and their assistant commis were the equivalent of what are called waiters and busboys today.

Violet Jessop was assigned to cabin service because, in those days, women never served in the dining saloon. Contemporary cruise ship dining rooms, save on board Cunarders, also employ exclusively male waiters despite the recent inclusion of some female sommeliers.

What were her duties? She made beds, cleaned the cabin and, if there was one, its adjoining bathroom; she kept the alleyways vacuumed, swept and dusted; she brought trays for breakfast or tea (or, indeed, any meal requested), answered summonses, ran errands, arranged flowers, turned down beds at night, put away clothing and, invariably, comforted and cosseted the seasick. The only thing she never tells us is how many cabins there were in the section for which she and a male colleague were responsible. On cruise ships today, one steward generally looks after a dozen.

In sum, throughout Violet's long days and evenings, it would be safe to say that there was no aspect of service that was not her or her colleagues' responsibility. It has always been my contention that there exists on board ship an unique relationship between passenger and steward: Passengers will say, without thinking, "my steward" just as stewards will automatically refer to "one of my passengers." Those instinctive possessives distinguish shipboard service in a way seldom duplicated ashore. Hotel maids, by and large, remain anonymous, enjoying scant communion with the guests they serve. But aboard ship, the very opposite holds true: The passenger/steward relationship is as complex as it is symbiotic, an interdependency that flourishes within the peculiar exigencies of shipboard; if not consistently congenial, it must involve discreet, social intimacy. Stewards were more—far more—than mere company servants: They were factotums who lived aboard year-round, knew everything about everybody and suffered passengers as only temporary intruders into their hectic lives. First and foremost, the ship was their home.

One pierside caveat remains before we cross the gangplank. I think it mandatory that we pause to evaluate the present-day *Titanic* phenomenon. At the time Violet wrote her memoirs, more than six decades ago, she was, chronologically and emotionally, close to the event. Yet by 1934, both impact and memory of the notorious shipwreck had receded. Nowadays, *Titanic* is once again on every lip; I think that Violet would have been astonished at the contemporary world's inexhaustible preoccupation with the lost White Star liner.

Ever since *A Night to Remember*, Walter Lord's incomparable recreation of 1955, an unstoppable *Titanic* juggernaut has gathered momentum. After a slight lull in the seventies, the juggernaut regained speed in 1985 when Dr. Robert Ballard found the wreck two and a half miles down at the bottom of the North Atlantic. Though rent in twain, the hull was in more recognizable shape than any of us had dared hope. With this discovery, *Titanic*'s legend steamed full ahead once more, despite a bitter dispute over the salvage of artifacts from what those who disapprove prefer to call a tomb.

This volume is published in 1997, eighty-five years after that unforgettable maiden voyage, only one of a plethora of offerings commemorating the anniversary. This same period also witnessed a television deluge—several documentaries and one scripted docu-fantasy—a Broadway musical, a megafilm, half a dozen non-fiction works as well as Beryl Bainbridge's *Titanic* novel *Every Man for Himself* (with *Olympic* on its cover) and the English-language version of Erik Fosnes Hansen's haunting *Psalm at Journey's End.*

How to account for this literary and artistic outpouring? Perhaps our angst has something to do with the approaching millennium, as though we cannot bear relinquishing the 20th century without a final orgy of *Titanic* remembrance.

Publishers, producers, librettists, composers, directors, novelists and historians alike can attest to *Titanic*'s durable appeal, combining as it does wonder, splendor, hubris, tragedy and death in one imperishable package. In an attempt to intensify the impact of a gripping saga that surely needs no further embroidery, RMS *Titanic* has been manipulated from a workaday, 45,000-ton Edwardian liner into an apparently inexhaustible literary gold-mine. Ostensibly unsinkable in life, she has proved positively unsinkable posthumously.

The vessel's loss heralded "the end of an era," Walter Lord suggested; "a western apocalypse" declared historian Wyn Craig Wade; only weeks after the tragedy, the Bishop of Winchester thundered from the pulpit of St. Mary's Church in Southampton that "*Titanic*, name and thing, will stand for a monument and warning to human presumption."

Did the vessel's loss really serve as allegorical watershed, separating prewar dream from ugly reality? *Titanic* was a large liner that, because of complacency, bad luck and recklessness, went to the bottom with appalling, preventable loss of life, a new steamer that never reached New York. However extensive, her interiors were no more lavish than those of half a dozen competitors. *Titanic* was a steady, comfortable and, apart from the bridge, well-run vessel. She was certainly not fast. Persistent legend notwithstanding, Captain Smith was not trying for the blue ribbon for a very good reason: stately *Olympic*-class ships were just not competitive with faster Cunard greyhounds like record-holder *Mauretania*.

Save for the addition of more lifeboats, the displacement of steamer tracks further south, and the establishment of an ice patrol, I am not convinced that an era ended with her loss, nor that very much changed on the North Atlantic as a result. White Star passengers still boarded *Olympic* in three classes, ocean liners still raced at sometimes dangerous speed through Grand Banks' fog and, apart from memorial wreaths dropped overboard annually from many vessels south of Cape Race, the impact of *Titanic*'s loss faded.

But nowadays, it seems a tragedy destined never to achieve closure. *Titanic*'s image has been cherished, burnished, distorted and inflated to wring yet more emotional mileage from that foundering back in 1912. My sense is that we should view the vessel as neither symbol nor metaphor but merely an imprudently captained vessel lost at sea. Leave *Titanic* as she was, one of hundreds of wrecks littering the Atlantic depths.

That is the way I choose to perceive *Titanic* and the way Violet did too. In the midst of pursuing her life's work, she was accidentally and inadvertently caught up in maritime tragedies. Herewith, her story.

# 1

# The Early Years

WILLIAM JESSOP HAD emigrated from Dublin in the mid-1880's to try his hand at sheep farming in the Argentine. His fiancée, Katherine Kelly, followed him out there from Dublin, probably in 1886. They were married shortly after her arrival and their first child, Violet, was born on October 2nd, 1887.

A dazzling blue sky, the early morning sun reflecting the innumerable shades of dainty flowers which covered the *campo* like a thick carpet. Three galloping horsemen drew nearer to our *puesto*. My father and two adopted uncles—everyone was an uncle to me then—were returning to breakfast after finishing parting sheep that had strayed. I was standing in my new pink dress, quite conscious of the fact that I was playing hostess for the day, on that my second birthday.

That is my first memory of the pampas. It may have been the compelling beauty of a spring morning in early October or the intense excitement of being feted, that evoked my childish mind to an appreciation of that vast tract of land where we had our home in Argentina.

Nothing could have been humbler than a *puesto*, smaller than a cottage, with earth for a floor. Ours was one large room, built by my father out of adobe bricks using nothing but a wooden chair to stand on. Here he brought my mother as a bride.

She was one of those romantics who put love before anything else. If on chilly nights a fire was lighted with dried cow dung, she preferred not to notice her dresses gradually becoming smoke-streaked; she chose rather to give her attention to the evening meal she was preparing on her stove, an improvised kerosene tin. They were very much in love with one another, in love with life and ready for all adventures. When I arrived one stormy Saturday soon after they had moved into the new home, they were extremely proud and content with life.

Mother had landed in the Argentine well provided with clothes but vague about household effects. Often, in gratitude for some kindness, she gave away some of her nice clothes to native women who had never owned anything but a cotton frock. As she spoke no Spanish, she depended greatly on the goodness of her native neighbors for help in buying necessary articles during their periodical visits to Bahia Blanca, the port south of Buenos Aires, a day's journey on horseback.

Our place was not overburdened with furniture; my cot was a gin box and most of the other articles had a similar beginning. Father's tiny garden beds were bordered with upturned stout bottles, a relic of my arrival, I was told. A high fence protected the house from the *paja voladora*—a high grass which when dry, blew into great drifts, the cause of brush fires. There was not a tree to be seen on that vast stretch of pampa, except down by the arroyo.

Moonlit nights were very often made hideous by the call of the *viscachas*. Rabbit-like animals, their noise resembled a donkey's bray and their burrows were a great danger to horsemen. They stole things left lying around—boots, implements, clothing, would be found at the mouth of their holes in the morning.

Father's day started at dawn, when he left home on horseback to join his two partners and "part" the flock that had mingled with others because of the absence of fencing in those vast spaces. I was never awake when he left, but was eager for his return for breakfast and would wait patiently at the door until Mother ascertained at what distance he was by putting her ear to the ground, an old gaucho custom. She would then put on the kettle and tell me that I could go to meet him.

Galloping over the plain he'd come, waving his big sombrero to me, his lasso by his side, spurs jingling, a trail of dust behind him. It was always my joy to be lifted to the front of his saddle of rugs and sheepskin. I loved the smell of sheep that permeated his clothing, and in this way we made a triumphant arrival home.

He left us after breakfast till sundown, during which time usually not a soul would call or pass our way and the silence seemed immense. I followed Mother about her daily work, chattering and asking questions. She would tell me of her arrival in Buenos Aires to be married; it coincided with a cholera plague, and nobody to meet her because of the failure of the mails to get through in time. She landed on a sweltering November day, knowing no Spanish and dressed in a long cloth coat, trimmed with beaver which the local inhabitants eyed with surprise. Helped by a vivid imagination, I early made the acquaintance of all her folks in Dublin, the foundation of a very intimate relationship between Mother and myself.

The most exciting part of the day was the preparation of the evening meal. It generally meant roasting a side of lamb on a long iron skewer laid across the red embers. My job was to baste it with salt water flavored with garlic. Mother baked huge sponge cakes in a kerosene tin oven let into the ground. From my seat on an old ox skull, I kept an eye on the horizon for my father's return. His homecoming in the evening meant a present, generally a pet, some bird or animal found in distress or perhaps an ostrich egg which Mother converted into delicious omelets or pancakes.

At certain seasons, brush fires were the topic of conjecture and dread. Caused very often by the match of a careless horseman or, more often, the hot rays of the sun striking a flinty stone, they roared for leagues, fed by long grass, dried by the hot summers. In an incredibly short time, the whole plain became a veritable hell. All available men were needed to get them under control. A number of mares were slaughtered, cut open and the wet carcasses dragged a good many times across intervening stretches of land, for water was generally unavailable. This would arrest the passage of the fire which would die down as quickly as it started.

Shearing time I enjoyed most. As gauchos arrived, greetings and news were shouted as they galloped up. They all came to help with the shearing. A shed had been added to our modest place for the purpose, and I was allowed to watch. Hand shearing turned those woolly creatures into sleek naked-looking things, pitted with cuts, where a careless shearer had nicked the skin.

The day's work over, a crowd of helpers would assemble to prepare their meal, *carne con cuero*, "meat with the hide on," a sheep or a heifer. While the meat was cooking, the inevitable *mate* would be sipped. Conversation never flagged, as a gaucho always took a lively interest in his fellows. But horses, his own in particular and its merits, would always open the discussion.

The juicy *carne* was cut into chunks and passed on the end of a fearsome, pointed knife. That and *galletas*, the hardest and most tasteless biscuits in the world, constituted the meal, washed down by the native common red wine. When all appetites were satisfied, a guitar would make its appearance. Gauchos love their guitar and not a few are masters of counterpoint. Sitting round the camp fire, with the light from the still glowing embers fitfully playing on swarthy but fine faces, while a singer and his guitar entertained, the blue-black night sky as a background, they gave an impression of great serenity and ease.

Life was much simpler then: A man was taken at his worth all the time. Our neighbors had all come from different walks in life. Many were British, of good social standing in their own country, who had left home because of some lapse. They had come to Argentina to start afresh. Quite a few had lovely *estancias* where warm hospitality was shown to all friends, irrespective of their worldly means.

On festive occasions when there was a large gathering, a complete levelling of classes was noticeable. People would come long distances on horseback. Everything was put aside to attend these fiestas, for they were looked forward to for months. I had my first ride on horseback at the age of three months in my mother's arms, to attend one, while my father, leading her horse by a halter, recited, I believe, *The Charge of the Light Brigade* to make the distance seem shorter.

As I grew a little older, there were lovely days spent wandering about the *campo* on my own, now that a smaller brother was added to our household and kept my mother busy. Even at that age I was very impressed by some things. I hated the wind, for instance; it made me gloomy and sad, and nothing that anyone could do would alter my mood while it continued. Yet I loved the rain and the smell of the earth after the rain was the loveliest perfume of all.

This carefree *campo* life terminated when my father, not having the means for a full flock of sheep—without which very little headway could be made—accepted a post with the port authority in Bahia Blanca. For the first time I went to live in a real house, made of bricks, with wood floors in place of mud.

# CHAPTER

# 2

# The Railway Interval

IT TOOK ME some time to get used to seeing my father dressed in what was to my mind "visiting clothes," and to people calling at all hours. Above all, having by comparison a big house was the strangest feeling of all.

I was not allowed to wander any more, so I began to spend my time in a funny little make-believe world of my own. My headquarters was the sitting room, where the family portraits were on show. My mother's conversation about the subjects of these pictures made me feel I was in a room full of people I knew well and who were watching me. I held long conversations with them, telling them all the daily happenings. To my grandmother's photograph, I always showed much deference, and would bow to it gracefully whenever I passed it.

Most of Bahia Blanca's sidewalks were unpaved, and to cross a street meant sinking up to one's ankles in soft earth; in contrast, down by the Port where we lived, it was clean and paved. The ships coming in and out were a constant fascination, and their jolly men, in blue suits and brass buttons, seemed to make our home their first calling place on landing, with always a gift, tins of marmalade, something we never tasted in *campo* life, or a box of chocolate creams for me.

Certain ships and their crews were favorites, and once, on the arrival of one of these, a group of officers and engineers serenaded outside the house with all kinds of Irish songs.

Next day Mother presented me with a new brother whom I thought not beautiful, though Mother assured me that he was perfect. Mother told me years afterwards that she could never forget that night, with the pains of labor getting worse and the songs outside becoming more sentimental. On the new baby's arrival, I was put in charge of the house and felt fearfully responsible and serious about it.

17

Reaching things was a problem that I solved by carrying a small stool with me everywhere, and nobody dared separate me from it.

Not long after this, my father came in very jubilantly with the news that he had been offered a post with the Southern Railway; if he took it, he would be sent up the line to open a new station nearing completion.

Soon we were on the move again, on a trolley pulled by our old roan horse Colorado on the railway line itself, after the Buenos Aires express had gone through. Our furniture and ourselves were packed on the trolley, and we set out one beautiful sunny day for the unknown.

On arrival at the station itself, my parents were overjoyed to find all sorts of things we had never had before: A real stove in the kitchen, beautiful wood floors, a patio paved with red tiles and a sink in the corner where I was to spend many hours helping wash babies' diapers.

The whole place looked as if it had sprung up out of a sea of alfalfa, which was at the height of its odorous loveliness just then. The nearest neighbors were leagues away. The only building in sight was the inevitable *bolichi*, a tiny tavern, store and meeting place kept by a stout widow with a squint eye and her old father. She set herself out to be most affable to Don Guillermo, as Father was known; he was consulted at the most extraordinary times about the most trivial matters. My father was station master and sole factotum in a lone place, everything official rolled into one. The two important trains of the day dispatched, the good Doña Rosa would surely need some advice from Don Guillermo.

Mother assiduously dressed every afternoon at four o'clock for all the world as though she expected guests, while Ray, my young brother, and I walked all round her, lavish in our admiration, though it was always the same best dress she wore.

My curiosity took me often into Doña Rosa's *bolichi*, but nothing on earth would induce Ray to come further than the outer gate. He broke his custom one day, however, and came in with me for my father had come with the news that a woman traveler and her child had halted there and appeared to be ill. The nearest doctor was at Bahia Blanca. Would Mother go over and see if she could do anything for her?

Mother went. The fact that she went there at all was so unusual that, unobserved, we followed. Ray came unhesitatingly, eyes wide and wondering. He stood at the door of the room where the sick woman lay before Mother noticed us and hurriedly packed us home.

The woman died of black scarlatina the following day.

As our parents seemed very preoccupied for several days, Ray and I wandered far afield and came upon a heap of half-burnt clothing, some only slightly destroyed and rather nice. We decided to dress up and went proudly to the house to show ourselves off. Mother, however, showed consternation when we explained where we found the clothing and hurriedly got us out of them.

Ray died three days later of black scarlatina, and when I emerged from the stupor of the same disease with close-cropped head and wizened face, everything seemed changed. Mother no longer sang at her work and would sit with a far-away look in her eyes, reciting her rosary.

Promised my first lesson on horseback, I felt rather grand, dressed up in a long black skirt of Mother's, though I could not see why I should sit side-saddle when my father looked so much more comfortable. I was praised for doing very well. Later, when I found I could not sit down because of blisters, I had to pretend I preferred to eat my supper standing.

About this time I developed a cough which often kept me awake at nights. I liked to be awake when all the world seemed asleep and used to creep to the window. I should have loved a little sister but the prayers I sent up in those wakeful nights were answered only by the arrival of a baby brother nearly every year. I always knew the sign when Mother would sit sewing narrow lace onto tiny garments.

On the days when my father had to deliver mail to people living many leagues away (a stationmaster's duty in those days), I was allowed to sit up later and listened to Mother's stories of her childhood and of Ireland.

Then one day something happened that made the sun and *campo* flowers not seem so gay. Doña Rosa's old father invited me in as I was playing near the *bolichi*. He told me Doña Rosa had gone out, then patted my face and told me I was "very simpatica."

He took me to his room—he said he had something to show me—and locked the door. He lifted me in his arms and kissed me and then put me on the bed and started feeling my body and pulling at my clothes. I saw then such a horrible look on his face that I screamed with terror. He went white and terribly angry as Doña Rosa's footsteps could be heard passing the window on her way in.

He unlocked the door and told her we had been chasing a rat in his room. She scolded, with a strange look at him, for allowing me to get so frightened that I should shed tears, and added I must only visit when she was at home. I knew I should never want to visit the house again and that I would not be able to explain my reasons at home, because I could not explain them to myself.

Most of my young days seem to have been spent in bed, getting over some malady or other, not the least and most unpleasant of these was the result of sampling the contents of all the saucers of poison—I did not know it was poison at the time—which my father had placed on high shelves to get rid of flies which made summer time a misery. On my little stool I reached the mysterious saucers to my cost.

It must have been with some degree of relief that my parents heard of their transfer to Buenos Aires and their isolation was at an end.

# CHAPTER

# 3

# Buenos Aires

HELPED BY A vivid imagination that had little to distract it, I regarded Buenos Aires as my dream city. Coming to it from the loneliness of the *campo*, it did not disappoint me.

It was beautiful and sparkling. Its well laid out plazas, its wide Avenida de Mayo were a joy. The most compelling thing was its houses, the better class houses. My greatest treat was to be allowed to stand at the open street door of one of these, with its splendid wrought-iron gates, and look through the wide, cool hall into the patio beyond, filled with palms and flowering plants and a fountain playing in the center.

They looked so inviting, so reposeful and dignified, these houses. I spent many hours weaving imaginary stories around their occupants. Argentine women of that class had such poise, were so beautifully graceful in every detail of their dress and their bearing was one of extraordinary dignity and cool stateliness that seemed to come from an inner calm.

Transplanting a growing family to the expensive town gave my parents many an anxious moment. Things hadn't gone as well as they had hoped, though they kept a cheerful front.

I saw much they did not think I noticed. My father looked thinner, and was absent all day at his work. Sometimes, as a treat, Mother allowed us to remain up late for his supper, at which time a little characteristic by-play took place: She would consent to share the lovely steak she had cooked, telling him she was not hungry as she had eaten with us at midday, while he assured her it gave him a better appetite if she ate with him; all the while she desperately tried to conceal the fact that she was ravenous. There was never enough for her at midday dinner. The latest arrival in the family, whom she nursed as was her custom, did not thrive as the others had done, and she often looked at him anxiously.

Mother occasionally bought a *decimo* in the National Lottery, and generally won a few pesos. This made for a little celebration. Mother would go to collect her winnings in her best blouse and saucy little bonnet that I had adventurously trimmed with pale yellow roses. My father would take her to a *confiteria* on the Avenida to have a *refresco* and cakes, sitting at a little table on the pavement in the cool of the late afternoon, indulging in the delightful pastime of watching people. Then they would wend their way home with a little gift for each of us. No money ever was made to stretch like those winnings of Mother's.

A day came when I felt very ill and was in bed with a raging temperature. The doctor looked grave. Later I was to learn that I had had typhoid fever and congestion of the lungs but my only consciousness of it was a dim awareness of being plunged into a very hot bath, then wrapped in cold wet sheets followed by long periods of nothingness.

One day, however, I was brought to full consciousness. It was the day of crisis, and my parents were anxiously keeping vigil when a neighbor walked in with a huge bunch of honeysuckle and bent over me. The perfume woke me out of the long trance. I remember resenting being brought out of that lovely, softly sinking feeling that we know as death.

Our schooling had been undertaken by my parents. Although I was old enough to go to school, on the advice of a doctor, I was not allowed to start, much to my unhappiness; for it was the one thing I ardently looked forward to, joining the band of *delantales blancos*, or white-overalled scholars at the *Escuela Normal*. As all classes of society sent their children to the normal school, these overalls the juniors wore were great levelers as there was no outward show of station.

My parents had, however, promised that I should take lessons with a certain talented English lady. But recalling many English women I had seen and their cold aspect, the prospect did not thrill me.

I dutifully went, however, having pleaded to be allowed to go alone the first day. The house, set in a beautiful garden where all the plants had the appearance of being pampered and well cared for, cheered me greatly. We evidently had one thing in common, this lady and I, we both loved gardens.

Inside, I was met, and eyed with interest and not a little suspicion by a couple of *teros*, delightfully graceful birds. I always loved *teros*, so decided that this woman must be after my own heart. I found her charming, natural and very kind.

The after-effects of illness, however, were very trying and I found myself constantly having to absent myself from the lessons, which I loved, and visit the doctor, who pounded my chest and made me repeat the Spanish equivalent of "ninety-nine."

Three months later, I had my first hemorrhage due to my lung ailment. Then started our pilgrimages to the British Hospital. I was examined by a big burly man who suggested that I should remain in the hospital for treatment. When he heard from Mother how I had admired the oleanders blossoming in the grounds, as an inducement, he promised to have my bed put in the middle of the gardens.

Lying peacefully amongst banks of sweet-smelling white freesia did not still the ache I had for home so the good doctor would often conduct friends to my bedside, introducing me as "Curly-tops."

One day he marched up with a huge doll, the gift of a lady friend of his. I never in my wildest imaginings thought to have such a beautiful doll; all I could do was cry for joy.

Later my mind was much occupied as the silent witness of a little intrigue. I felt somewhat important as the means by which two people could keep up a correspondence. No word was spoken by them or by me, but every morning when the young house doctor came my way, he slipped a letter under my pillow. Then Nurse Black would find some reason to come to me and quietly remove it; she returned about noon and put another in its place. So it went for several months and not long afterwards they were married.

The hemorrhages continued, and at more frequent intervals. Blood seemed to be on everything, so violent were the attacks at times. I felt humiliated, helpless and angry, angry at the pity I saw on the faces around me and at the look of incredulity when they noticed the little muslin-like pieces of flesh I used to spread on the basin's edge. Mother was sent for, looking ill and terrified. She was probably tired out, no doubt having had to walk because she could not afford a *coche*.

I then determined that this malady was not going to kill me and, strangely enough, the hemorrhage ceased. All appeared to be going so well that I was allowed to accept an invitation to convalesce at the *estancia* of an old friend of my parents away in the pampas.

However, in a month's time I was back at the British Hospital, lying subdued and pale, overhearing the big doctor say: "What a shame! Remarkable child, I shall miss her when she's gone." Gone, indeed! There was to be no "gone" about me, I warranted.

Speaking and moving being out of the question now, I just lay still all day, sucking ice and swallowing creosote, communicating with anybody by writing pad. My father spent as long as he could with me. One evening he told me the result of his interview with the doctor: I had about three months to live but life might be prolonged if I were taken to the mountains. So he had asked to be transferred to Mendoza, in the foothills of the Andes, and we were to go almost at once. I protested that it would mean a lot of expense with perhaps a doubtful return, although my resolution not to die was strong as ever.

He told me cheerfully that he was decided and, besides, where there's a will there is a way!

Autumn had come, torrents of rain fell. In a couple of days the part of Buenos Aires where we lived was under water. All of the city lays low on the La Plata river. Seeing all our worldly possessions stacked out of reach of the water that lapped about the rooms did not dim my delight at homecoming and I entered into the novelty of the topsy-turvydom of the place. Wading about and crossing streets in improvised boats, no place seemed so perfect to me just then as my own home, especially as we were to leave it so soon for the unknown.

The day of our departure came and the last view of our home as the boat turned the corner of our street was spoilt for me by a return of hemorrhage and a long trail of blood on the water. The boys, on the other hand, were having the greatest fun; their spirits could not be dampened, they were so young and full of life.

At the station, the guard of the train, who knew my father well, made us comfortable but looked alarmed at the sight of so much blood. Utter weariness, and the hateful smell of a steam train which has ever since depressed me, were the last things I was conscious of as the train slowly steamed out of Retiro Station for the Province of Mendoza.

# 4

# In the Mountains

A WORD ABOUT NAMES. In her continuing quest for anonymity, Violet, writing as Constance Ransom, felt compelled to disguise the identities of her siblings. In fact, the four younger brothers to survive childhood were christened William, Philip, Jack and Patrick; her only surviving sister, fifteen years younger and born just prior to the family's departure for England, was Eileen. In the original manuscript, although the boys were renamed Harry, Don, Joe and Brian, her adored baby sister—Margaret and Mary Meehan's mother—was never identified by name at all. Since there seems no valid reason to prolong Violet's gentle deception, I have chosen to call all six Jessop children by their real names.

I awakened to a morning of crystalline air. The hemorrhage had miraculously ceased and everyone, including the guard, was tremendously pleased.

The foothills came into sight and beyond them the magnificent Andes, immense peaks with the sun shining on eternal snow; the beauty of it all almost hurt. At our midday meal, never had soup tasted so good.

At Mendoza, we were met by an official of the railway where my father was to work, who introduced us to our new home, an old rambling adobe house. It spread aimlessly with rooms here and there, enclosing a large garden full of most beautiful trees. Behind was a little well-tilled vineyard where white muscatels grew in profusion and the gnarled old vines formed a perfect arbor. Flitting in and out at evening times were bats by the hundred. That night we picnicked by candlelight out in the sprawling kitchen which became later the stronghold of the children and Jack, my pet armadillo, by far the cutest of us all.

The air of Mendoza was wonderful, although it took us some time to get used to the sub-tropical heat which accounted for the people's leisurely mode of life; their gentleness and placidity were restful yet at times aggravating.

I was on the road to recovery from my lung ailment and explored the neighborhood. I was drawn towards the activities of the working people, especially the harvesting of grapes and wine-making. On doctor's orders, I consumed a great quantity of the common red wine. But, when I watched the grapes being trodden down by bare, unwashed feet, I decided that wine was no longer going to be part of my daily fare.

Denis, the baby, was slowly fading. The flood and the journeyings had begun his undoing. Mother's rare outings, when I was left in charge, were always of concern to me. A feeling of estrangement would often creep in between my brothers and myself, obscuring our usual joy of living. No sooner had four innocent looking creatures bidden her goodbye, with reiterated promises to be good, than a fearful uproar would start somewhere, generally in the region of the pigsty, their favorite haunt. Or if their silence was noticeable, I'd find them trying to milk the ass we kept to supply the sick baby with milk.

Later, I would leave my father and mother chatting after the supper I always loved to prepare, and read by the light of the brilliant moon, high up in my old vine. All was peace and silent beauty, broken now and again by the discordant hoot of an owl.

One day and night stand out vividly in my memory. We had just recovered from the nerve-racking effects of a "Sonda wind," a hot scorching wind that howls through the Sonda pass. All was now calm and a late summer day of intense heat was drawing to a close. Though we smelled ripening grapes and apricots, the leaves of the trees had ceased moving. Mother was concerned about the baby's fretfulness, so I persuaded her to come with me for a little drive after sunset when the children were safely in bed. My father would mind house and be glad of the peace.

We found our favorite *cochero* and his decrepit old coach. He was friendly and full of topical information. We felt very luxurious as we rolled placidly down the Avenida, eighteen inches of dust silencing our progress. Groups of people sat talking in gentle undertones at street doors. Mother and I tried to determine their status by the odors as we passed: Perfume meant quality, the pungent the would-bes and garlic the people.

On our return we sat in my bedroom drinking *mate* and eating cakes that my father had thoughtfully provided for us. Then the house, the furniture started to sway and rock in a grotesque manner, and we realized that the stillness had been forerunner of an earth tremor.

Outside a scream broke the silence, there were hurrying feet and a commotion of voices, then a gradual settling down of the earth again.

The children had slept through it, and I went over to look at Denis, the baby. A little smile on his face had erased the wizened expression that ill health had given it. He was dead.

The great problem was how to get round my parents to allow me to start school; I regarded this as the most desirable thing in the world. I had already outlived the period allotted to me by the big doctor in Buenos Aires and I had as good a chance as anyone else to go on living. The two elder boys were about to start school and I felt humiliated to be outdone by them.

At long last came the great day for William and Philip. We waved them off, looking nervous and proud, wearing with pride the new suits Mother had finished at 2 a.m. Then the house settled down into unaccustomed calm.

That evening, a very disheveled figure came running up the Avenida. It was Philip, alone, his face scratched and dirty, his book in tatters, his new slate shattered and cap and white collar gone. Soon William came reluctantly into sight.

Mother's horrified face brought tears of embarrassment to Philip's. He explained that he had fought all the boys who had jeered at the "Ingleses." He had caught sight of a bigger boy chasing William with a penknife. He had used his fists and made for their noses. Argentine boys prefer knives but fists won this time although it was a completely wrecked victor that emerged. During this recital, a tense and white William gazed at his brother with awe and admiration.

The sun was scorching as Father and I went down the Avenida on our way to the *Escuela Normal de Maestras* (Normal School for Teachers) for an interview with its directress. Our doctor had at last given his consent to my starting school. I longed for school life and the sociability of other girls.

The school was a cool, rambling building with many *patios* and lovely shady gardens, the directress a North American lady of kindly manner and ample proportions, whose face seemed to brim with learning and knowledge. The vice-directress, also North American, turned out to be as small as the directress was large; yet she had the same nice way, the same power of making one feel that one was of some consequence. They told me that they were pleased I was coming to their school, and I believed them.

Although there were three weeks before term started, I could not sleep that night. The two most desired things in my life were crowded into those few weeks: School and the sister I had wanted so much, Molly, arrived at last. I felt unequal to cope with so much joy and excitement.

Though babies came at fairly regular intervals, they never lost their novelty for us children, especially the boys. On this occasion, a girl having arrived, Molly, they felt this an unknown quantity, though their hot little perspiring faces beamed as they touched the baby's hand with reverence.

The old rambling kitchen, where the noise would not disturb Mother, was our headquarters. Into its cavernous corners, we brought our personal treasures and pets. By far the most venturesome was Jack, my armadillo who, now that Mother was *hors de combat*, felt free to roam at will. During meals he succeeded by extraordinary maneuvering to scramble up the legs of the table and as a reward get a share of everyone's supper. He kept an eye on the door, as if expecting Mother to appear, for she used to put him under a big flat bathtub at mealtimes. He learned to move about with the strength of his head and, discovering an opening in the boards, he would go down under the foundations into the yard and in by the door again, to the great delight of the boys. One spring day, Jack wandered off, probably in search of a mate. He never returned and left very sad hearts behind.

My baby sister came up to all my expectations, so I entered school in a very contented frame of mind. Everyone's daughters attended the Normal School, government officials', doctors' and lawyers' children, together with those of humbler parents. Snobbishness could not exist. Our directresses had a unique way of making each girl feel her importance.

Of course, certain little groups did form friendships. The Church of England clergyman's daughter and myself were the only two British-born girls among 500 pupils. We both pleased the directresses by being able to follow classes fully in Spanish and skipping a class during the first year.

School gave me such a feeling of elation that I was full of generous impulses. I insisted on tackling a mountain of ironing, my contribution to the big, almost daily washing Mother got up at four-thirty in the morning to do, dry and beautifully white before we got out of bed.

To avoid the hot midday sun, and the long walk home and back, the directresses invited me to take lunch in their beautiful quarters. There I first learnt to appreciate North American cooking and their practical, sane way of approaching life, to be more self-dependent and resourceful.

Hitherto I had been used to the clinging vine, albeit beautiful type of Argentine woman who was not expected to think for herself. I naturally listened in growing wonder to those two very capable women discussing plans for a new house, the layout of a new vineyard and an improved system of irrigation; the knowledge they displayed about materials and the engagement of workmen was remarkable. Indeed, the inhabitants of Mendoza thought those two must belong to a race apart, tackling things quite outside a woman's sphere. One thing they had however in common with their Argentine sisters, they were always beautifully and suitably dressed.

To catch up with my studies, I used to wait for the family to retire and be asleep before quietly creeping back to study. I must have fallen asleep many times, for often my father carried me to bed, scolding me the next morning. But I worked out many problems in peace and so prepared myself for a scholarship.

# 5

# Illness and Death

THE APPROACH OF summer, with its heat, dust and drought, brought its list of fears, not the least the recurrence of dreaded smallpox. We were accustomed to seeing people disfigured by its ravages; nearly every tenth person was pockmarked.

My science teacher—so charming a woman with lovely manners and calm personality—had been greatly disfigured by childhood smallpox and it planted an ever-present fear of the disease in my mind. Whenever the notice VIRUELA was displayed outside a house, I would shun the vicinity and keep a watchful eye for further notices.

On one hot summer morning, I was walking to school, engrossed in my botany book. Mother had asked me to deliver some magazines to an English friend of hers on my way. But the dreaded yellow notice was affixed to the neighboring house. Panic took hold of me and without stopping to give my message, I flew out into the street holding my breath with the idea that germs were in the air.

Arriving at school red-faced, hot and tired, I could not concentrate during class. That night I developed a high fever, with chattering teeth and profuse nose-bleeding which I knew to be a symptom of smallpox. I was quite surprised the next day to find myself back to normal although excessively weak. The doctor told me I had nearly frightened myself into getting what I dreaded most.

About this time our little colony was greatly excited. King Edward VII was about to be crowned and in our own particular way we were going to celebrate it in style. It was a day of glorious revelry and merrymaking; jovial British men clapped each other on the back, repeatedly inviting each other to another drink, as if they had personally taken part in placing this king on England's throne.

We children thought it a fine idea, the occasion providing unlimited quantities of toys and sweets, as well as making our elders so reasonable. My father's day was complete when he saw Patrick win the boys' race. Only seven, he was the youngest in the event, and it was good to see his little flying figure with his fair curls streaming out behind, outdistancing the bigger boys.

On the way home in the evening, tired and proud, we all declared that having kings crowned was a fine idea and Patrick decided his life of sport had started in real earnest.

I came home from school one sweltering day to find Mother's beautiful eyes red-rimmed: My baby sister had a raging fever, moaning pitifully and tossing her head from side to side.

The clever native doctor said meningitis, another dreaded scourge that took toll of infant life at that time. He ordered ordinary tea, freshly made, to be administered in teaspoonfuls every half hour, but gave little hope.

For several weeks I attended classes but left half my mind at home; I was very worried and felt the whole burden on my shoulders. Eighteen days reduced a fat, blue-eyed impudent cherub to a tiny skeleton. When the blue plumbago vine—whose first flower had called forth gleeful shrieks of admiration—was in full flower, we laid her in a tiny white coffin, covered her with its blooms, and for the last time tidied up the little square-toed shoes and the dilapidated one-eyed doll.

The daily round seemed to be more full of pain than joyful hours of study. I failed to obtain my scholarship, a blow to my pride and the death knell to my secret hope of helping the family. To me, it was a calamity which no amount of sympathy helped minimize.

Another little sister [Eileen] arrived and Mother, not being as well as usual under these circumstances, I was allowed to make the baby my particular charge. I made a bad start the first day for, after bathing her carefully, I used pure afenic acid lotion to clean her navel. She screamed all day and I cried most of the time too. I was finally rescued from panic by the kindly doctor at visiting time.

It was a very severe lesson and I decided that when I grew up, I would be a nurse and learn to look after people properly. Mother reassured me and told me I was a good one already. To prove her words and to revive my flagging courage, a week later immediately after an operation on her breast, the doctor was hurriedly summoned to the mountains where an English explorer had suffered a frost-bitten foot which needed amputation. He told me he was leaving me in charge of the dressings on Mother's wound. On his return, he raised my spirits by his wholehearted praise at my efforts.

A day came when the house was very silent. William and Philip, the two older boys, were down with diphtheria. It came on suddenly, so virulently that the doctor despaired for them unless he could get the serum which had just come into prominence and was being sent from France for the treatment of diphtheria.

We worked frantically to keep them alive, swabbing out their throats as one would a dirty milk bottle, while we waited impatiently for the arrival of the express train from Buenos Aires to bring the serum.

That day the train was late. The doctor went to the station himself and, dispensing with formalities, received the package from the guard. We heard his high-stepping horse pounding up the Avenida.

A couple of hours later, what had appeared to be two dead bodies miraculously came to life. That night and long afterwards, we included the Pasteur Institute in our nightly prayers.

A year passed, then one March day our dear, courageous and gay father died.

Two days previously he had come to my bedside where I was confined with a low fever, telling me that he was taking his friend Doctor Gomez's advice to have a thorough examination at his hospital. He said he might have to undergo an operation but promised me that, in a few days' time, I might take a *coche* ride down to see him; it would be his birthday and we loved keeping birthdays in our family.

Mother took so long to return from her first visit to him after the operation, where she had gone laden with all our little gifts, that we were all sleepily keeping supper waiting for her. When she arrived with a stricken look in company with Father's chief and his wife, we guessed the truth. Father was dead.

In my grief, I resented outsiders sharing in this moment of deep sorrow and I could not be natural with them. Visitors were rare anyway and on this sad occasion, I was tongue-tied and stunned. Whenever I tried to speak, I discovered I had lost my voice completely.

They brought Father home and, when all had gone, I tiptoed in alone to look for the last time at the face I loved so well. I remember noticing the bruise on his thumb nail we used to tease him about, because it looked dirty. But death is an ugly thing and it smells. I would rather have remembered him with his twinkling kind blue eyes and his gay manners.

His friends thought it wise for Mother to take us all to England to school, especially the boys, who would be eligible for military duty if they came of age in Argentina. Everybody was most kind, though we were too desperately lonely to fully realize it at the time.

My school directress offered to adopt me, arguing that my lung, now almost healed, would never stand up to the English climate. However tempting, there was never any doubt in my mind that I would remain with Mother and the family.

With heavy heart, I bid goodbye to my beloved mountains, those glorious Andes. I was leaving for a new country whose people, by Argentine standards, seemed cold to me, for a new life where nothing would ever be the same again, and where I felt sure I would often need the reassuring pressure of a hand, now forever stilled.

One glorious autumn day in April, a day so brilliantly blue of sky, with tiny white clouds, that it gave me an ache to look at it, saw us packed into the train for Buenos Aires. That train journey seemed never ending. To Mother it must have appeared like a lifetime.

# Repatriation

IT IS MAY of 1903. Violet Jessop is no more than 16 years old, by any adolescent standards, chronologically young. But several aspects of her testing Argentinean upbringing have not only shaped her forever, they have turned her into a precociously capable young woman as well.

As the eldest of six, Violet enjoyed the firstborn's inevitable intimacy with her parents. Clearly her father's favorite, she became from an early age far more to her mother—companion, confidante and helpmate. "I felt the whole burden on my shoulders," she writes when her first baby sister Molly died. From the moment her first baby brother Ray was born, she coped not only with household chores but also an ordeal of successive childhood ailments. Of the children that William and Katherine Jessop produced, many were either plagued by or succumbed to diphtheria, smallpox, scarlet fever or meningitis, diseases that too often proved fatal to children at the turn of the century.

The eldest Jessop child was herself victim to debilitating tuberculosis. More than once, she had been given up for lost by the doctors. Violet suffered disproportionately throughout childhood, her schooling in jeopardy, her very future in doubt. How ironic that the consumptive older sister should have proved so stalwart! Like all infant invalids conditioned to long hospital stays, she seems to have matured quickly as a result. That she experienced a mountain cure in Mendoza was miracle enough; that she went on to a demanding adult career and lived in apparently vibrant good health to the age of 84 seems remarkable. By the same token, I sense that more than tonic Andean air was at work, that Violet's stubborn, almost fierce will to live healed her remaining lung as well.

Her chronic invalidism as well as the compassion she lavished on siblings and parents fostered an early affinity for nursing, a talent that would serve her and her patients well during World War I. Instinctively, skillfully and enthusiastically, Violet hovered over every sickbed. When William and Philip were at death's door with diphtheria, it was their parents *and* Violet who swabbed out their throats while awaiting the arrival of Pasteur's life-giving serum; awesome and demanding duty for a girl scarcely into her teens.

In addition to those inherent nursing skills, Violet had long been saddled with running much of the Jessop household—cooking, cleaning and ironing as well as becoming surrogate mother to four obstreperous brothers. At sixteen, embarking on the vessel that would carry the Jessop family to a new life in Great Britain, Violet was really an adult, close to her brothers and adored baby sister while at the same time companion to her newly widowed mother. Katherine Jessop was fortunate in her firstborn, a dutiful child/woman who would continue to care for her until she died.

The good ship *Burgundy*, carrying usually cargo and livestock, with room for a few passengers, was the least attractive vessel lying in dock; but she was chosen purely for economic reasons.

For anyone brought up in fresh country air, she proved revolting on first encounter in spite of her novelty. To our uninitiated eyes, she appeared an untidy jumble of ropes and tackle, exuding every kind of disagreeable smell. To me, boarding her was depressing, though the boys invaded her with great glee, so pronounced that I noted a certain amount of anxiety on the faces of the sailors on duty. There were about ten other passengers besides ourselves, mostly elderly, and a good deal of livestock destined for England.

The captain, a jovial man, thought we were great fun. He belonged to a class of captain that is quite human; he had no illusions about himself and remained on the same plane as his fellow men. I believe his sympathy for Mother—who was expecting another baby—had a good deal to do with his patience and good temper with us. He won the boys' hearts when he offered a shilling prize to the one who did not get seasick. Going down the La Plata river was so smooth that each thought it an easy win, having had no experience of the deep sea.

Later, they got greener and greener, vainly attacking the typical ship's fare of the period, which in the end remained untouched. Jack, the second youngest, won the prize in his quiet solid way, possibly because of his deep absorption in a miniature stable he was allowed to construct in a corner he had claimed as his own the moment he set foot on board.

One found him at any moment of the day in that part of the dining saloon into which all the cabins opened, quietly cutting out cardboard horses for his stable, assisted by the steward. Jack made the stable walls with lumps of sugar discarded by the steward as having too many fly marks to be presentable at table; he had a mutual agreement with the steward to hand over any lump with more than three marks.

Rough weather came and went, swaying oil lamps and crashing crockery, all passed unnoticed by Jack. His curiosity was not even roused when William came dashing in from the pantry one day, where the steward, an extremely cadaverous looking man, busy and no doubt wanting to get rid of the boy, dropped his false teeth on to his lower lip, turning on him like a grinning corpse. William fled, white with terror. False teeth were things that he had never even heard of.

The cargo of live bullocks suffered greatly from seasickness and one of our daily pastimes was watching the burial of any of these poor beasts that had succumbed. It seemed strange that anything so healthy could go down through seasickness. I remember feeling very sorry and sentimental about it. As each was dumped overboard, I thought: "There goes another poor Argentino, so far from home!" I was feeling mighty far from home myself at the time.

The captain showed the boys how to climb rope ladders, and all sorts of things sailors know how to do. I felt very much out of it all, so I determined to try secretly some of these accomplishments. I began to slide down companionways, which I had seen them do and for my trouble, landed at the bottom with a badly bruised back.

After that my life was a continual series of jaundice attacks. There was no doctor on board, so I had to obey captain's orders and lie quietly in my chair. I was feeling too ill to care much, registering a thorough distaste for swinging oil lamps—our only means of lighting—and for the song *Rocked in the Cradle of the Deep* which the captain sang nightly in a feeling, if somewhat toneless, voice. It certainly did not seem a matter for song since it was the cause of our discomforts and the daily burial of beasts.

Crossing the equator did not distress us much because we were used to terrific heat but we were not prepared for the intense humidity of the doldrums. I used to sit feeling perfectly miserable.

This part of our journey gave occasion for the age-old ceremony of "crossing the line" and Father Neptune's reception and ministrations, which the youngsters looked forward to and took full advantage of. Not having swimming pools as in modern times, old tubs served the purpose for duckings. The whole affair was very crude, enjoyable and thorough, inasmuch as everyone looked battered to pieces afterwards. Most of that day we were treated to the spectacle of greasy, tar-splashed, feather-beplastered little ruffians crawling everywhere.

I saw for the first time a swarm of flying fish skimming the waters, shimmering in the sun and finally flopping back into the sea. It was fascinating to watch them and I wondered how long they could keep in the air.

As the voyage drew to a close, we bade farewell to the friends we had made among the crew. Suddenly we seemed to renew our liking for some of them, and discovered qualities in them hitherto unappreciated. I realized for the first time that the steward had always stared so hard at me and had brought massive helpings of buttered toast at every opportunity (causing me to hate it ever since) because of his admiration for me which he awkwardly expressed when he presented me with his most treasured possession, a worn copy of *Nuthall's Dictionary*, generously fly-specked.

From my earliest days I had always imagined that Englishmen were not in the least like everyday folk we were used to in Argentina. I thought they were a sort of supermen, aristocrats in bearing, manners, speech and dress. I do not know how I acquired this childish hero-worship; it certainly was not because of the Englishwomen in Mendoza. Perhaps it was through earlier contacts with the exiled Englishmen of the pampas. But I think it was a fancy of my own invention, although to this day, a good many Argentines have the same idea.

So when the ship docked in Liverpool, I could not quite reconcile the men working on the quayside with anything that I had ever imagined. These men were poor and humble, jolly and willing to do anything; and they spoke English very carelessly.

It cheered me up immensely to know they were so human, so full of faults, likable yet English. Our hearts went out to these Bills and 'Arrys, helping us cheerfully with our queer assortment of packages. I fear they regarded us once or twice as if we were extremely odd folk. They stared at the boys especially, at their straw sailor hats, with ribbon falling down the back, short knickerbockers and socks. It was the socks that caught their eye mostly. Every kid stopped to look at us, first with wonder, then amusement, to the lasting humiliation of the boys, who never forgave us for allowing them to land, dressed, as they put it, like girls. Mother also came in for her full share of attention in her widow's weeds, a long cloak and a heavy crepe veil falling to the end of her dress which we found out later only royalty wore in Europe.

It must have been with some trepidation that my aunt—my mother's sister Sadie—and her husband Cecil Ridley met us. Of course, it seemed wonderful to us to have real live relatives to greet us and, to their lasting credit, they hid any qualms they may have felt as we all trooped out to be presented.

At Liverpool's Lime Street Station, we stood in a row and screamed with surprise and delight, pointing at what we called the "tiny" train without a cowcatcher, which we thought extraordinarily small compared to our Argentine trains. We boarded with misgivings about its capacity to take us to the magic city of London.

Violet Jessop poses proudly in her V.A.D. uniform. Inscribed "Your loving sister, Violet," copies of this picture would be treasured in several wartime kit bags. *(Margaret and Mary Meehan)*

William and Katherine Jessop.
The oval photograph of Violet's
father, the only known one in
existence, has been enlarged
from a miniature worn in a locket
by his widow. *(Margaret and
Mary Meehan)*

Young Violet poses with her baby brother William. Her cropped hair betrays a recent bout of scarlet fever. *(Margaret and Mary Meehan)*

Violet's younger brother Patrick, father of Marilyn Skopal who writes from Canberra that he was "the only fair-haired child in the district"; hence, his parents kept his hair long. *(Marilyn Skopal)*

Violet with another brother, poor little Ray who would succumb to black scarlatina. *(Margaret and Mary Meehan)*

Ready to go back to sea, Violet poses with her mother. Both women shared an innate sense for clothes that always made them stand out. *(Margaret and Mary Meehan)*

Smart and trim stewardess Jessop at sea aboard *Orinoco*. She conceals the dressing on her right hand which had a badly infected thumb. *(Margaret and Mary Meehan)*

A wartime group, circa 1915: Katherine Jessop with two of her children, Private Patrick Jessop—blonde curls long since shorn—and his younger sister Eileen, who would give birth to the Meehan sisters. *(Margaret and Mary Meehan)*

## CERTIFICATE 5 · OF DISCHARGE. 6

| No. | *Name of ship and official number, Port of registry, and tonnage.† | *Date and place of engagement. | *Rating; and R.N.R. No. (if any). | Date and place of discharge. | Description of voyage. | Signature of Master. |
|---|---|---|---|---|---|---|
| 1 | Orinoco 91942 London - 2451 | 28 Oct. 1908 Southampton | Stdess. | 28 Dec. 1908 Southampton | West Indies & New York | |
| 2 | Oruba 96310 Liverpool - 3577 | 3 Feb. 1909 Southampton | Stdess. | 5 Apr. 1909 Southampton | Do | |
| 3 | Do | 14 Apr. 1909 Southampton | Stdess. | 14 June 1909 Southampton | Do | |
| 4 | Danube 102868 London - 3120 | 9 July 1909 Southampton | Stdess. | 28 Aug. 1909 Southampton | River Plate | |
| 5 | Clyde 98131 London - 3051 | 15 Sept. 1909 Southampton | Stdess. | 15 Nov. 1909 Southampton | West Indies | |
| 6 | Do | 22 Dec. 1909 Southampton | Stdess. | 21 Feb. 1910 Southampton | Do | |

*Extracted from Agreements*
*Registrar General 15th May 1912*

* These columns are to be filled in at time of engagement.    † In Engineers' Books Insert Horse Power.

680439

The first page of Seaman Jessop's first Certificate of Discharge book. *Orinoco* marked her maiden debut to sea. *(Marilyn Skopal)*

A rather solemn portrait of Violet Jessop taken in the mid-twenties.
*(Margaret and Mary Meehan)*

# In Charge

THE JOURNEY FROM Liverpool to London was a series of delights, everything so different to anything we had seen before. Why were there no mountains about? Mountains seemed to us a necessary part of a landscape.

But the countryside was beautiful. It was the end of May and everything looked magical and miniature to our eyes. Tiny hedges, little fields and small cows and sheep, instead of the vast spaces and big animals we had been used to. The hedges especially intrigued us, for we had no hedges in Argentina.

Our elation dimmed when we approached London. There was a greeny mist enveloping it, but not sufficiently to obliterate the sordidness that surrounds Euston station. By the time we reached it we were thoroughly subdued, not to say a little bit scared.

I suppose anyone used to the smell of Euston would not be affected, but to strangers it strikes with appalling force. It is like the accumulation of all kind of smokes with a strong suspicion that sanitary arrangements have been unattended to for years. For days afterwards, I had the smell in my nose and the taste in my mouth, but above all the depression in my heart.

The boys were not unaware of it either, because it acted as a complete brake on their activities, and for the first time in the long trip they obeyed without question, following us about like mice with big questioning eyes. They did not regain their normal cheerfulness until Uncle deposited us in a nearby hotel; which I think he did to give him time to tactfully prepare his mother for our arrival at her home in the suburbs.

There was nothing about the hotel to justify the boys' return to normal, except at the entrance there was one large palm. This the boys caught sight of and found at last something they were used to.

They revived at once, so that when they spied the flight of stairs to the upper floors (and stairs were things they were totally unused to in Mendoza), they made a concerted rush up them to explore, coinciding with the arrival of the proprietress.

Apparently Uncle Cecil had taken the precaution of engaging the rooms beforehand, but he was not unprepared to hear her say, as her eye traveled anxiously up the stairs in the wake of four little rears, that all her rooms were booked up "after today!" Personally, I was delighted to hear it. One more day in that hotel would have banished for ever my dream picture of London. We were all sitting in a row, polished and waiting, when Uncle called next day, and our exit reminded me of sheep dashing out of a railway truck after a long journey.

We loved Uncle at once, a person of the most charming, kindly manners and an old-world courtliness. This we were not unused to because in Argentina they are a very mannerly people, so we thoroughly appreciated Uncle and decided that our aunt had good taste in selecting him as a husband.

The liking was reciprocated, and whenever we overstepped the mark, he would cover it by a story of his boyhood or an escapade of his young years when he first went traveling to Australia in the "good old woolly days," as he put it.

We had never met any relatives, so we were only too glad to have some claim on these nice people. It sounded grand to be able to call his mother "Grandma" as often as we liked, and her fine sons "Uncle." We at once felt more important. Our pampas exuberance must often have shocked them, as it took time for us to tone down to the restraint of suburban London. I still suffered from the fall on board ship but nothing could have prevented me from exploring London with Uncle and listening spellbound to stories of mighty deeds of history.

Many days I spent with Mother, searching for a permanent home for the family. For the time being we only wanted rooms until her resources were adjusted. At first we all begged to be allowed to go with her on these expeditions but we soon found they ended unhappily. No sooner did a landlady see us, than she would snap out a refusal or shut the door in our faces, muttering, "We don't take children."

Very soon we began to think it must be a crime to have children and felt very sorry for Mother who had so many. Finally, she decided to leave all but me with Grandma, and we contrived by tact and blarney to persuade somebody to let us a few rooms. Not, however, before a promise was extracted that the boys would be soon sent away to school.

I wonder how many people realize how the decisions, sometimes hastily arrived at, that they make about their children's schools cause repercussions in later life. We had little left to live on and, after the baby died at birth, Mother decided to get some kind of employment. But before she did this, she wanted to put the boys in a school. It was essential that they be placed where their faith would be maintained; that, and the fact that her resources were low, decided her on sending them to a Catholic orphanage for the time being.

They were excited about it, although their feelings were mixed because it was our first parting. I think their free, gay hearts must have been staggered by their change of environment, to which was added the vagaries of a climate, the like of which, even in our wildest imaginings, we could never have pictured.

Through influence, Mother obtained a post as stewardess in a well-known shipping company and, although she loved the sea, she was distressed at the long separation from us all.

The shipping line in question was the Royal Mail Line. Katherine Jessop would serve as a stewardess for five years, from 1903 until 1908. Very little documentation about this first Jessop stewardess remains extant save one revealing item of ephemera, a testimonial from a ship's surgeon on a sheet of *Tagus* notepaper, written from Trinidad on October 13th, 1905:

"During the voyage from Southampton to Trinidad, Mrs. Jessop, the stewardess on the RMS *Tagus*, acted as sick nurse to a lady under my charge, who was very ill during the entire journey.

"Mrs. Jessop discharged the duties to not only my, but the invalid's, satisfaction.

"Mrs. Jessop was most attentive and kind, and appears to be familiar with her duties."

It is signed "J.W. Young, M.D." Who the patient was or what became of her, we shall never know; nor is it clear for whom Dr. Young's rather perfunctory testimonial was written. It may have bolstered Katherine Jessop's chance for a promotion. But what it does reveal without question is the Jessop predilection for dedicated and devoted care: Like mother, like daughter.

There were bright reunions, however, on her periodical returns, and we would go to visit the boys, laden with good things.

There would be four eager, well-scrubbed faces with shiny noses to greet her on these occasions. They developed a strange shyness towards Mother and myself after a short time, and would stand in a silent row around her chair, never taking their eyes from her face, anxious to be spoken to but never taking the lead. To any question put to them, would come the quick united answer: "Yes, Mother," or "No, Mother"—nothing more or less.

It was very disconcerting, yet they were obviously well and cheerful, but it was alarming to find that it had been possible in so short a time to reduce such high spirits, to that almost military unison.

Their idea of utter luxury seems to have been governed by the quantity of condensed milk which they could consume. Strangely enough, they did not acquire roughness of character or manner, which one would expect in such schools; on the contrary, their childish simplicity had been preserved.

I spent my first English Christmas in hospital recovering from an operation for gallstones, alarmed at the austerity of that noble institution compared to the friendly atmosphere of our British Hospital in Buenos Aires. I still shudder at the recollection of my first hour as a patient, when I was dumped into a tepid bath. Then the nurse proceeded to give vigorous attention to my long hair with carbolic soap. Having left most of it in my hair, she put me to bed, draping my hair over the pillow to dry, the whole operation taking place with stony silence on her part and growing resentment on mine.

The doctors were regarded as demigods and took that adulation with befitting modesty. It was, therefore, almost a crime to do anything but lie in silence and complete stillness when they were expected in the wards. When they finally did arrive in a group, led by the senior man, they clustered round my bed and demanded my history.

Mentioning my recent, and I hoped complete, recovery from lung hemorrhage, and being duly pounded by the great man all over, I was treated to a tolerant superior smile and the remark that it was "impossible, no trace of that," and he passed on, pausing an instant to say: "You've got a wonderful set of teeth, young lady," with the tone that it was quite unique for people in my station to have teeth at all. By the end of that day I felt more or less apologetic for being alive.

Christmas Day was the one occasion when the stiff hospital formality relaxed. Doctors and nurses smiled and became human, cooperating to do everything to make the patients happy. Everybody was asked to hang up their stocking, and you were naturally expected to be equally surprised to find it filled with delightful gifts. Mine of a leather writing pad gave me great joy, though I suspected it was the gift of a charming young doctor, who, when he could spare the time, liked hearing about my life in the pampas.

But my joy was not complete until I saw Mother appear. All the lights and colors around could not equal for me her loving solicitude. Her hands, soft in spite of all the hard work, timidly put into mine a carefully wrapped packet; a treasure she had cherished for so long, a reminder of days when laughter, not tears and hardship, were for her the order of the day.

Big Ben across the water kept me company during many sleepless, lonely nights. Years later, those chimes, heard in odd corners of the world, revived memories of that first Christmas in England.

I was happy to be back at last with my little sister in the one room where we lived while Mother was away at sea. It was home, though it could have been brighter; its only window looked out on a nightmarish backyard of concrete and sooty bricks. It was the quintessence of sordidness and depression. The only things that seemed to thrive in that environment were the neighborhood cats, always prowling and yowling, scraggy restless things that belonged nowhere.

We lived in an isolated world of our own, my little sister and I, surrounded by strangers whose chief article of diet seemed to be kippers and cabbage; the odor was varied on Mondays by the addition of steamy suds.

We made daily visits to the park to escape into a world of make-believe. I would sit and watch Eileen's childish antics and listen to her stories so seriously told. She would never wander far but dash back, tripping over my foot in her excitement, which she would immediately stoop down to kiss. This habit of hers, which I had never stopped, caused much surprise and not a little amusement at times.

I soon learnt to distinguish the difference between a house and a home. The rich had homes while the poor seemed to exist in dark and ill-ventilated houses, from which the odor of boiled cabbage never fully escaped. Even the wallpaper manufacturers were in on the conspiracy. The most popular wallpaper for lower middle-class houses in 1903 was bilious brown and thickly varnished, as if to preserve it for posterity.

Our landlady, a prim, old-maidish youngish woman, tried hard to convert it into her idea of a home. She had been to America in her early youth and had absorbed some very practical, if not artistic ideas. Her straight, well-corseted figure could be seen daily working out her unvarying routine.

Her place was always clean and neat. Her tightly-closed airless front room, with its three aspidistras and the silver teapot in the place of honor on the piano, which nobody knew how to play, was her pride and joy.

It was peaceful. The only other occupant besides ourselves was her policeman brother, a nice carefree young Irishman. His only drawback, in my eyes, was a determination to master the fiddle in his off-duty time.

Circumstances influenced them to advertise for another lodger and in reply arrived a portly widower, a brass worker by trade, whose practiced eye soon discovered our landlady good to look upon. One day she told me shyly that she was engaged to him, although any sign of joy was absent; she received my congratulations and good wishes in a reserved manner.

From then on followed periods of alternating happiness and ruction. No one looking at the prospective bridegroom could imagine him anything but a staid, fat working man, of sane and well-balanced habits. But apparently love so changed his outlook that he became a jealous, suspicious and temperamental lover.

The lady of his affections appeared to enjoy her power to rouse such emotions. At the culmination of a quarrel, a furniture van appeared at the front door, a sign that her betrothed was removing the furniture he had brought with him, and was finished with romance. But days later, she would greet me with a serene smile, and the van would restore his furniture into her good care.

When later the house became a storm center of dictatorial husband and crying children, I spent as much time as possible sitting in the park with Eileen, where sometimes all the amusement available was counting the number of flat-footed people who passed in one hour.

On one of her visits home, I begged Mother to allow me to go to a convent boarding school where I could still have my sister with me. She needed a change of air after a severe illness, when we had battled with death, all through one hot July in our small room. We both emerged mere ghosts of ourselves. Eileen was too young for most schools but eventually we found a convent that took us both in. Being the youngest child to became a boarder, she became the convent pet.

While her mother was away at sea, Violet was left in sole charge of Eileen, yet again, daunting responsibility for a teenager. Confined within one small room of that dreary boarding house, Eileen battled illness. Thank heavens for the older sister's competence and skill! Violet had had so much first-hand experience with a wide variety of disparate hospital care that she must have known, by example, what would most soothe and comfort her little patient.

# 8

# Convent Days

**D**OWN A PEACEFUL and leafy road in a Kentish town, an old rambling house lay surrounded by beautiful and as yet to me unfamiliar lanes. It was almost hidden from view by the spreading branches of immense cedars and from its top windows, the undulating South Downs could be seen fading into the horizon. This was my new home.

The good Breton nuns, practical, middle-class exiles from France, were so cheerful that it was impossible to remain either homesick or ill at ease in their company. Except during class time, they were all noisy, cheerful and busy as bees, expecting everyone around them to be the same.

At first, I found it strange to sit at meals at a refectory table with dozens of other girls after my isolation in one room; or to sleep in a big dormitory. The pleasure of resuming school life, despite the difficulty of conforming to new teaching methods and a new language, helped me overcome my shyness.

Very soon I felt I had always known them and, if at times I had to face their good-natured badinage because of my "foreign" upbringing, I was able to join in the laugh at my own expense.

Sister Superior, a gentle unassuming little woman from Alsace, ruled over us with great firmness, though she did it more or less in the shadow of our headmistress Sister Juliana, whom she greatly admired and respected. They were great contrasts. The headmistress was clever, gay and witty, with an occasionally reckless humor which one felt to be an outlet for her volatile nature. I felt that it was Sister Juliana's brilliant mind that Sister Superior had so much confidence in, for she herself was of humble origin with no special talent save her saintliness and courage.

We saw her more human side during the hour after supper on winter evenings when we older girls were allowed to gather in the sisters' recreation room. The fire would be built up and we would draw the heavy curtains to keep out the moan of the wind that howled from the Downs. Sister Superior's chair would be placed where we could all sit around it on little petitpoint footstools, cherished possessions from the France that she loved.

We would get her to tell us tales of her life as a young girl, especially during the Franco-Prussian war. During the terrible siege of 1870, her starving people had considered mice a great luxury. We used to try and imagine our dignified little Superior picking the bones of a mouse and finding them savory!

In our wildest escapades, however, we never lost sight of the fact that few could get so angry as she. To see her stalk into a room after hearing of some delinquency and to hear her *mes enfants* spoken in a deep, lingering nasal note—peculiar to the French when roused—would result in deep contrition.

We had great freedom after study time and paid visits to the nuns in different parts of the building, where we found them busy but always welcoming a chat or a bit of news. Sister St. Ange, who was in charge of the laundry, was very popular. Like our headmistress, she retained the gaiety and devil-may-care of her youth, despite her untiring industry at the washtub. Her stories of youthful escapades, in the company of her many brothers—now all in the French Navy—she recalled with pride, including her secret running away from home to become a nun, because she could not face the emotion of saying goodbye to her father.

I remember Sister Superior shaking her head sadly at my deplorable handwriting and foreseeing unending failure because of it; yet she willingly consented to my getting up an hour earlier in the mornings to work quietly and uninterrupted at my painting which she greatly approved of.

In the kitchen, autocratic Sister Marie Bernadine saw through our wiles; though we paid her homage, she knew it was only cupboard love and was unmoved by it. Meal times never came quickly enough and we always seemed hungry. It may have been the good Kentish air, but I suspect it was mostly French frugality: We always left the table feeling we had not nearly had enough to eat. I used to fill up with bread and butter of which we could have an unlimited amount. I often wondered how the nuns could get up so much enthusiasm for their subjects, on the meager fare they allowed for themselves.

Sister Felice was our arts mistress, with her enigmatic aloof smile, gay, noisy but nevertheless saintly. Sister St. Cecilia, the garden expert, wore wooden sabots, the pockets of her checked apron bulging with garden residue—even worms and snails!—because everything superfluous went into those pockets. Sister Marie Sabine was young and plump, with a balanced temper and intelligent face, whose history we were curious but never satisfied about.

When we returned to the convent after the holidays, the whole gay throng would stand in a chattering group around Sister Superior. Gayest of them all would be our headmistress, who could so easily play the child again, but who we all knew next day, at the magic word *mathematics*, would again become the genius, encouraging us to study what for her was the most absorbing subject of her worldly career.

Everything was of interest on our return. Our new dresses and hats were admired and faces keenly scrutinized to see if our holidays had benefited us. Our families were inquired about and, that night in the refectory, we students all put aside the usual meal-time restraint and exchanged news and gossip with the nuns. Later, once their office and rosaries had been said, their chief topic would be us girls, and the chances each one had for success in the coming term. I doubt if loving parents would have spent more anxious hours trying to guide us than did these nice Breton women.

I loved the very smell of the place, the pine-wood corridors, the beeswax in the classroom, and the lingering odor of coffee, so noticeable to us tea drinkers. When the day was over, the rows of white beds in the long dormitories were very inviting. That first night, we were all too tired to remain awake and wait for the coming of the sister who guarded us at night, in order that we might satisfy our curiosity as to whether she had long or short hair under the tight little nightcap she donned when she removed her coif.

Weekends in spring and summer when we explored the countryside were a never-to-be-forgotten pleasure, visiting the cherry orchards, watching the hop-pickers working or roaming the Downs in search of nut-trees. To anyone, like myself, unfamiliar with the English woods, it came as an enchanting revelation to visit Boxley Woods. I remember how impressed I felt as we came under the big trees whose branches met overhead like the arches of a great cathedral.

At six o'clock every evening, study over, I would be reunited with Eileen. A fat little figure with red curls would come staggering down the path, her forget-me-not blue eyes registering as much worship as it was possible for a small person of four to show. She always ran staggeringly when she was excited, this small sister of mine, and she was always happily excited, when that special hour arrived, which we called "our very own."

All through the day she was the convent's idolized plaything, keeping everyone amused by her little songs which I had taught her, or standing on a table in the midst of a crowd of sisters, solemnly reciting the story of the Passion without any sign of embarrassment. But at the hour of six she was mine entirely and would have eyes for nobody else; she gave me all the pent-up news of the day while I prepared her for bed and told her stories.

One can readily understand Jessop's nostalgia for the convent. Quite simply, it was the first time in her young life that she was not burdened with responsibility for others, neither surrogate parent for four younger brothers and a sister nor dutiful companion to a widowed mother. Refreshingly, she became a student, enjoying caring teachers, congenial peers, and flourishing in a benign academic environment. Of course, Eileen continued in her care but it sounds as though there were more than enough willing helpers among the sisters. Violet patently cherished a taste of the normal adolescence of which she had, for too long, been so deprived.

# 9

# Choosing a Career

I HAD A DREAM and a goal.

There was an examination I was studying for and hoped to take. If I passed, it would open many doors; I did not dare think of my chances of passing it, not even where I would obtain the entrance fee. The boys were gradually being drafted to better schools, so Mother needed all she could earn.

One day, Sister Superior told me that a daily governess post was open in a family living a little way out of town. They had asked her if she could supply someone. She suggested I apply for the position and an interview was arranged. I was accepted, but was to continue making the convent my home, fitting in my studies.

The fragrant outdoor smell of fresh apples still comes to me when I recall that mellow Elizabethan house with its heavy beams, low ceilings, and uneven floors. My employers were local tradespeople with three children, two of whom were to be my charges. Their mother, whose outstanding attraction was her beautiful figure, was a most industrious, intelligent and ambitious Devon woman, to whose good example I owe much.

In my opinion, she had only one fault: She felt very much her inability to fit into the local county set, a very exclusive and hard set. This made her otherwise kind nature bitter and critical, raising a barrier between us and leaving me nervous and diffident in her presence.

I loved the children but always felt on parade trying to cope with varying ambitions of the household. Her husband was tall and reserved, and gave the impression of never being very enthusiastic about anything. Looking more at home with a dog and a gun than running a shop, he was a man whose personality one never felt sure of.

A while after I came to them, I was chatting with him one night in the dining room while his wife paid her nightly visit to the nursery.

50

He suddenly came over to me and said in his gentle, drawling voice: "That is beautiful material in your dress," at the same time stroking me with predatory hands, with a sly sort of smile on his face.

He then suddenly dropped his aloofness and became utterly vulgar. I pretended to ignore the whole thing but could never feel comfortable with him again. I was more drawn to his wife, a lonely woman who made herself a slave to home and family. Longing for intellectual company, she only achieved the outer fringes of local society, a patronizing nod from some of the gentry during county cricket week or an invitation to a charity bazaar.

I often wanted to ask her to forget all these artificial, aloof people and just be content with her lovely old home and the few friends of her own set, but felt she would have resented my awareness of her ambitions.

One day news came that Mother was ailing. She had not been really well since my father's death. Now she was advised by the ship's doctor to give up her post at sea and take a complete rest. Suddenly I lost interest in exams and a career seemed of no moment.

So I decided, as money was urgently needed, to try myself for a position as stewardess on a ship. I must confess that in closing my books for good, something completely went out of my life, leaving an ache behind.

The day I told the good sisters that I intended seeking my living at sea stands out in my mind, as well as the consternation my announcement provoked. I remember so well to what trouble they went to point out all the dangers, both spiritual and physical, into which I would be plunging.

My employer was no more encouraging, though that I think was because of an ulterior motive. I was useful to her, and she lived an isolated sort of life which my advent had helped brighten. Certainly we had many interests in common, for she was a home lover, and like most Devon women a splendid housewife.

I was not deterred when she painted lurid pictures of sea life. When she reminded me that all my studying would be wasted, I retorted that there must be many nice women, mentally well-equipped and physically attractive, who had chosen the sea as a career. We parted rather coldly, for which I was very sorry.

Mother, too, was unprepared for my news. She had never told me much about her shipboard life but I gathered that although she loved the sea and had always done so, she was not enthusiastic about her work. However, I could well imagine that, with her Irish "come hither" look and her capacity for friendliness, she might easily make her life at sea bearable.

In those days, there were comparatively few posts at sea for women, therefore the ones who did choose that life were treated with deference and a consideration that is unknown today.

I remember sending off my letter of application with a feeling of exhilaration. In spite of my lost hopes as regards my studies and the little box of books which I had painstakingly collected and might never need again, I felt I was about to explore a field where endeavor might yield a material advantage. Surely some compensation would come in the form of changing scenes and faces, and perhaps romance.

It was one thing to decide to go to sea and quite another to get there. After various preliminaries by letter, I was at long last invited for a personal interview with the man who could give me the position I sought. I was charmed by his friendliness and natural courtesy, but above all, his humanity.

The meeting seemed to go well from the start, until he remarked that he had misgivings. He enumerated his objections: I was far too young, they generally took officers' widows, and then again, I was too attractive.

These outspoken criticisms, even from a charming and obviously sedate, elderly man, embarrassed me. In the year 1908 and especially in a convent, one's good looks were not openly commented on.

He enlarged further on the drawbacks of sea life for a woman, especially a young one, and though I accepted his warnings with due respect, I did so with amusement. I felt sure he was overstressing things a bit, albeit I was grateful he showed so much interest. I could not disassociate his solicitude from a desire to create a good impression, a pardonable vanity even big-minded men indulge in occasionally.

I gave him my word to be most circumspect and careful if he gave me a post as a stewardess. I also made a mental note not to seek too eagerly for my dream hero, that wonderful, chivalrous man of faultless manners and integrity, who was bound to be waiting for me somewhere.

After due consideration on his part and much trembling of the knees on mine, I was promised the first vacancy but warned that it might be some time before one occurred.

I went home to Mother well pleased with my news and we sat down to a specially nice tea in honor of the occasion. We talked a long time, planning ways and means of making my "attractiveness" as inconspicuous as possible without losing zest in life.

My first idea was to prepare a very staid wardrobe. I packed away my prettiest dresses, and introduced the lovely pink La France roses on my best gray hat to a touch of the sun in order to dim their fresh beauty. Mother and I called it a "man-frightening" wardrobe, and we felt sure it would satisfy a paternally inclined shipping company.

In fact, it seemed in keeping with the uniform list I had been requested to obtain from an old, established house and which, on examination, appeared almost archaic. This subdued me from the first, for although in design it was much like a nurse's outfit, its gray—an awful gray—dresses somehow reminded me of those of a prison wardress.

At last everything was ready, but no word came and the days of waiting dragged interminably. My funds were getting very low. I could not possibly expect help from Mother, whose allowance from the sum my father's company had allotted her was considerably diminished because she had been obliged several times to draw on it for various increasing expenses.

The check that arrived every so often was hardly sufficient to meet our needs, and if it missed a day, as sometimes happened, we would find ourselves in great difficulties. As this had occurred several times, we had found a temporary way out. Mother had quite a number of nice things left but not many of intrinsic value when pledged at the pawnshop. However, it was enough to get a few days' groceries, though we used a shop some distance from our own district.

The boys were now at home attending a daily school and I remember one chilly autumn Saturday. We were trying to keep warm with a handful of coals on our small kitchen fire, carefully supported by a brick at the back. We were eagerly awaiting the funds—already long overdue—for the next day's dinner.

On such occasions, Mother would always infuse a hopeful outlook. Every contingency was surmounted by her droll philosophy, though I had noted lately that her unflagging spirit and optimism had weakened a little; but I put this down to indifferent health. On this occasion, however, she was very cheerful and eagerly joined with us in betting whether the money order would arrive in time or not. The subject was discussed at length, alternative preparations for its non-arrival made, and purchases carefully and sparingly listed.

When a "target of mutton" was chosen for the Sunday dinner, a general groan went up, however, for its large size and convenient price created no illusions about the drawback of this joint. We all admitted it was succulent enough but we also knew it was too generous as to bone.

It was arranged that, should the money arrive in time, each boy should take a different shop in order to get through before closing time. I can see them all now, sitting expectantly on the stairs waiting for the postman, their controlled eagerness more for the sake of adventure than because the morrow's dinner was at stake. Tucked down by the stairs was a carefully tied parcel in care of William, the most reliable: Should the postman fail us, he was to grab it and dash to the pawnbroker before he closed. This parcel contained Mother's very best pair of handsewn boots, made of that beautiful Russian leather that gave off such a delightful aroma and which seems to have completely disappeared nowadays.

As dusk fell, four silent, patient outlines could just be distinguished in the hall, for Mother would not allow the gas jet to be lighted for fear the gas would run out before we made our evening meal. Suppressed squeals of laughter would drift up during what seemed to me the longest period I had ever known those boys to remain quiet.

Suddenly, down the road a gate banged and the postman's two knocks sounded. All ears were cocked. How often has that banging with the postman's double knock not failed to bring a certain thrill or dread to the listener's heart?

At last footsteps came nearer; a rustle at the letter-box, dead silence in the hall as a long, familiar envelope dropped onto the mat. Suddenly, with one accord, a roar from darkness. Peeping from an upstairs window, I saw the postman recoil with amazement and make a hasty exit through the gate, giving a mystified backward glance at what had appeared to be a silent, uninhabited house. Had he waited a few moments longer, he would have seen four eager figures bursting through the front door and dashing down the road, each with a basket or bag.

Mother's familiar expressions, either "Ah, well, something good is bound to happen soon," or, more often, "God never shuts one door but He opens another," never failed to give me joyful anticipation of divine intervention in the ups and downs of our existence. All the bitter struggles, the days of care and weariness, had not spoiled her unselfish nature, nor dulled her sense of humor. Teatime was a charmed time in our household. Everything of importance was discussed during this happiest part of the day. Mother would produce some surprise, stored up against a "rainy day," bought out of her meager allowance. This would initiate eager talk and laughter, the laughter of youth that refuses to see the blackness around the corner.

We most enjoyed getting Mother on to the subject of her girlhood in Ireland. It only needed one of us to remark what lovely buns a local firm made or how green a certain field had become, for her to say: "Ah, these are not anything like the grand buns you would get in Dublin," or: "Sure, the green here is nothing like the green in Ireland." Then she would tell us of the wonders over there, where cinnamon buns and fish were the best value and where making a purchase amounted to a social call, so charming to each other were the parties concerned. There would be an exchange of news and enquiries about absent ones, with a little flattery sprinkled in and with smiling "Goodbyes" and "God bless you's" added.

I would try to imagine our little local grocer, he of the cold, inquiring eye and red-tipped aquiline nose, closing a deal with "God bless you," or for that matter, showing any interest in our family welfare.

The conclusion of Violet Jessop's convent days marked a major turning point in her life. She so obviously relished not only its enlightened atmosphere but also the very real possibilities study there offered. "I had a goal," she recalls proudly, setting her sights on an examination that, had she sat for it, might have led to either higher education or a well-paid job. But unquestionably, Katherine Jessop's failing health mattered most. So Violet abandoned her academic career forever, stepping into her mother's role at sea.

At 21, Violet was obviously an extremely attractive young woman, so much so that she was almost refused employment with Royal Mail. Then too, with the prospect of passenger tips, a stewardess position offered financial reward. As the family breadwinner, Violet's life as a seaman was about to begin.

# 10

# To Sea at Last

A T LONG LAST came word for me to present myself at the shipping office in Southampton; the longed-for vacancy had occurred. All became excitement at home in preparation for my departure on what we felt was to be a great adventure as well as a necessity.

The boys needed no urging to enter wholeheartedly into the spirit of it all and it was a very animated party that scrambled up the smelly wooden stairs of Waterloo Station to see me off, laden with little parting gifts. There was much waving of handkerchiefs and good advice shouted as the train pulled out of the station. But everything suddenly became dim and blurred, and I was not so sure it was a great adventure I was setting out on after all.

A new world opened for me when the train came to a stop in Southampton, after what seemed an interminably long journey. The docks station was surely guaranteed to tone down my rising anticipation and any exuberance of spirits I might have indulged in. Dark, sooty and evil-smelling, it looked stagnant; age had not mellowed or beautified it. Its soul-killing atmosphere appeared to have transferred itself to the porter who emerged from the mist to help me, flat-footed and tired.

His long, drooping moustache, from which drops of moisture hung, accentuated his cast-down appearance. He regarded me with a hurt, accusing look when I asked if I could have my luggage brought out "as soon as possible." He neither consented nor refused but wearily remarked "It's a nice day, Miss," which I could hardly agree to, as the mist outside had turned into a drizzle.

Leaving the station as fast as the porter would move, I proceeded to look for the lodgings I had been recommended before introducing myself to the shipping office. The address I sought was one of many gray-fronted, slate-roofed dwellings, whose exteriors were devoid of cheerfulness. I was received kindly, however, by the good woman of the house, a quiet, pleasant person, well past middle age.

Her welcome lifted the cloud the station had set on me. She showed me into a dim hall, papered with a depressing, shiny brown wallpaper; the floor was generously covered with little skin rugs that had the appearance of squashed animals, which one instinctively tried to avoid treading on. The whole place exuded the odor of innumerable meals, blended with the fumes of what I was to learn later to be "Faithful Lover" shag tobacco, cherished by sailors. But above all, that indefinable smell of the sea, tar and whatnot prevailed.

I was so hungry, so cold, and so pleased with my reception that my first meal, eaten in a room packed with heavy furniture and surrounded by stuffed birds, wax flowers and shell-encrusted photograph frames, tasted perfectly delicious. People, mostly men, came and went, gentle, unobtrusive fellows, leaving behind them the faint oily smell peculiar to small vessels.

Feeling very refreshed, I made my way to the Board of Trade, to sign the "Ship's Articles" for the first time as a "seaman," for the princely wage of two pounds per month! My first impression was of a sea of faces, of all hues, whose owners, quick to notice I was a novice, subjected me to a keen scrutiny. Today, a woman could enter that same office and not even be noticed.

The clerks seemed to sense my discomfiture and courteously gave me instructions where to go in order to obtain a health certificate from the company's doctor, a necessity before I would be allowed to sign. I found him a kindly bluff man who made no examination but asked if I ever had been seriously ill in my life, to which I unhesitatingly replied that I had not, which satisfied him. There were several other women in the waiting room who adopted a simpering, coy manner with him, which ill-became them and seemed at variance with my employer's remarks when he interviewed me.

As I came out, I found the escort thoughtfully sent by the clerk in charge of our "Articles" to conduct me back to the Board of Trade, a consideration that would not be thought of in these days. When the shipping master appeared, there was a surge of anxious faces, each group of men clustering around the representative of the company they hoped to get taken on by. Then, employers could choose their men; today the "pool" formed during the war years sends a man to the employer; not so good!

Each discharge book—a seaman's passport—was examined and many questions asked. When the final sorting was done, and the rejected ones stood aside to make room for their more fortunate brethren, the shipping master called for silence, in order to read aloud the "Articles of Agreement." The deafening babble of tongues died down and attention, not unmixed with awe, was accorded him.

The "Articles," which are very long and befittingly complicated, would seem to be an endeavor on the part of a benevolent Board of Trade to curtail the rapaciousness of owners and embody all the things a seaman is required to do, eat and wear. Of course, there are many loopholes through which the employer could retreat.

Some seamen make it a hobby of acquainting themselves with their rights as laid down by the "Articles" but these are very few; most trust to luck when they sign, feeling instinctively that whatever happens, the employer has the upper hand. The "Articles" are rarely read out nowadays, men having become apathetic as to their contents.

In that seething mass there was an impulse to stick together, although loyalty played no part in it. This was the herding instinct of creatures up against things; some found themselves befriending people they would not associate with on better acquaintance.

Though aware of the many efforts being made to help me, I did not realize at the time that youth, feminine youth, is almost a fetish to seafaring men and has a tremendous power over them, exacting willing service from uncouth and often uncivil men. I was not to know till years later that the adulation I had accepted as chivalry was largely a demonstration of sexual attraction.

A gray, foggy morning saw me, shivers of apprehension running up and down my spine, sitting hemmed in by my luggage behind a portly, asthmatic cabby, driving a particularly lean horse on whom he used the whip lavishly without producing the slightest effect. We went at a jog trot down to the docks in search of my ship. I had acquired, on that day, the seaman's habit of designating the ship I had been appointed to as "my ship." My heart seemed long ago to have ceased beating regularly, and my pride alone kept my teeth from chattering.

At last amongst the medley of shapes, looming out of the mist, "my ship" emerged, smaller than the rest but quite big enough for me. I could just faintly see the yacht-shaped hull and her figurehead of a woman, which much impressed me; why, I cannot say. The cabby, his eye anxiously watching the cable and tackle lying around, the nearness of the water and the erratic movements of his horse, was glad to deposit me at the gangway, though not so pleased with my tip, which was a generous proportion of my fast diminishing purse.

First impressions are said to be lasting ones, and I suppose there is some truth in the saying or else why should that first gray morning have fixed itself so clearly in my memory? I learned for the first time to find my way about a ship, not as a restricted traveler but as a member of the staff.

Although Violet does not give us the name of her first ship, her Seaman's Discharge Book, reproduced in the illustrations, does. It was the *Orinoco*, one of Royal Mail Line's single-screw sailing steamers built in 1886, sailing in the West Indian service, Jessop's destination.

I encountered the indulgent consideration accorded a passenger, who refers to his alleyway as a "corridor," or the bulkhead of his cabin as a "wall"; and the superior scorn when some quaking novice in the crew made a similar slip. I finally found the cabin I was to share with another woman who had arrived before me. Introducing myself, I noticed that she had already spread herself and her belongings almost entirely over the restricted space allotted by the Board of Trade as "certified to accommodate two seamen."

I felt at once that my method of approach must have been wrong. Perhaps I should have made myself known without a smile and taken my cue from her, exchanging introductions in a frigid manner, for my room companion compressed her lips into a crinkled slit and looked at me with hard eyes as if disapproving of anyone who had dared choose the same work as she did. She coldly informed me that we must change at once into uniform and hurry up to our places for the all important Board of Trade "muster."

I was longing to ask what the formalities of "mustering" consisted of but dared not display my ignorance; besides, my whole attention was needed just then to assemble the dozen and one unfamiliar items that the uniform consisted of, and which were absolutely necessary before I could present myself as a member of the victualing department.

Perhaps it was just as well that I had the freezing personality of my roommate to balance the little attentions I started to receive from all sides as soon as we sailed. But if I did enjoy those attentions, I soon learnt not to encourage them; for I had enough intuition to realize that her behavior towards me was more or less regulated by them.

In strange contrast to her sour personality and stern parchment-like face was that of the first bedroom steward I worked with when we set sail for New York via the West Indies. He was a big West Indian, with a perpetual smile and willing manner, who as the weather went from bad to worse, got more cheerful. He was very concerned when I felt the dread pangs of seasickness, which exactly coincided with the first bell that summoned my services for a formidable lady, whose husband was something in the Government of Barbados, and who gave me the impression she considered that fact sufficiently impressive to keep me from being seasick.

The weather became terrifying as we left England's shores behind. The little ship twisted, pitched and rolled by turns, and the seas she took poured through chinks in the hatches, onto the one passenger deck below, flooding every cabin. I was told it was unusually bad and reflected it would be so, because it was my first trip and I disliked the sea into the bargain; how I longed for the beautiful Kentish Downs!

It did not appear to worry my black steward, for he continued to hum a tuneful ditty as he waded barefoot about the cabins, tucking up his passengers on the settees and wedging them in with their baggage, trying to reconcile me with being wet up to the knees and always answering politely every time someone asked him when the weather would improve. I did notice though that each time this question was put to him, his eyes would roll with greater intensity, which I took as an indication that his endurance was reaching its limit.

I found out very quickly that sea life was going to be fierce on feet and temper, and that my first concern was to get my sea legs. This I learnt was entirely a question of willpower and was neither easy nor pleasant. The days were unthinkably tiring, each with its new problem, probably made more difficult by my over-anxiety to do the right thing.

I could see that I would need to cultivate all the tact possible, to be resourceful and calm in adverse circumstances, though it might be a calmness I was far from feeling. But above all, I would have to be self-dependent in order to avoid obligations.

My one dread during these first weeks was the possibility of getting discharged for incompetence, intensified by somebody's surmise that I would not be able to endure the life for more than one trip. The nights did not compensate for the day's fatigue, as I could not get used to the narrow, short bunk in my tiny cabin perched above the ship's propeller, where I tossed and bumped myself and felt every vibration of the screw.

The one luxury on fine days was a porthole near the head of my bunk, and the pure air, free from ship smells, that soothed my aching nerves. I learnt soon to distinguish in that air the land smell from the smell of the sea, so much so that in a deep sleep as we neared some island, the smell of land would wake me up.

I was homesick and yearned for the affection and sympathy that I had left at home and spent many hours wondering how things were going with the family, and if I'd soon be able to send them some funds.

Even with my short experience I could not help noticing the subtle change that takes place in people, according to the changes of climate. As we drew near the tropics, a great wave of friendliness seemed to spring up among the passengers. Aloofness was dropped, they became gayer, more expansive and often less circumspect.

It was amusing to see stodgy businessmen at the age of retirement or severe Army officers blossom into ardent admirers of some attractive—and sometimes not so attractive—woman, casting a glamor around them that was unfortunately often dropped as the gangway was lowered. Had the same goodwill and conviviality existed in cooler climes, life would have been less drab and deadly on board.

My troubles of adjustment were by no means over. A poisoned thumb turned my life into a nightmare. About this time I also had my first experience of a really long and violent tropical storm, which laid low nearly the whole ship's company with seasickness, including the doctor, a well-known barrister-doctor whose health in advancing years made it necessary for him to escape English winters. When he recovered, he redoubled his energies to cure my infected thumb, which by then resembled a German sausage.

He was a charming person, kindly and with courtly manners, while his outlook on life was a constant source of interest to me. We became great friends. He would explain with enthusiasm the research

work he was engaged in to combat tuberculosis in England, on which
he had written an exhaustive treatise.

Small wonder that on a succession of ships, Violet always established a firm
rapport with the doctors, a predilection stemming from the hospital stays of
her childhood.

The doctor's interest in me had an added advantage. It kept away one
rather persistent man, whose work on board placed him in a favorable
position and whose overtures rather inclined to nocturnal ramblings
and a disregard for other people's feelings.

It was about this time I had my first experience of the selfishness
of passengers. When, after a week of agony and sleeplessness, I had
my thumb lanced for the third time and was returning to my cabin
with as much composure as possible, I had to go through the saloon
where a sing-song was in progress. A woman stopped me and said:
"Oh, have you had your thumb lanced again?" I replied that I had,
and she went on: "You might just get me a glass of brandy, as I feel a
bit faint with the heat in here!"

I was tired and listless from the effects of my indisposition and
during the trip had not been well enough to go ashore at any of the
ports, which was a great disappointment.

When we reached Colón (at the entrance to what was later to be
the Panama Canal), Doctor O'Connor obtained the captain's permis-
sion for me to accompany him across the Isthmus of Panama, as he
wanted to avail himself of an invitation he had received to inspect the
American Hospital on Ancon, on the Pacific side.

I was tremendously excited: My first view of the territory that
was already becoming famous because of this great engineering feat
produced in me mixed feelings.

The Panama Canal was as yet in its infancy. Strewn about its
mouth was the discarded machinery left after de Lesseps' pathetic failure. Though little progress had been made on the new attempt, it had
already cost thousands of lives because of the ravages of the deadly
mosquitoes which the Americans were fighting, with all their science,
to exterminate.

On later trips I saw the endless stream of victims, both white and
black, fill the hospitals, and every ship that steamed to the West Indies carried home the wrecks of what were once strong men; those

who would never recover numbered thousands. Sadder still was the vast number who had lost their minds.

On this my first visit, however, I saw only the beauty of the tropical vegetation on the Isthmus and enjoyed the thrill of exploring obscure corners of the old city of Panama, where the ravages of Morgan, that dauntless British pirate, were still visible, and the natives pointed out with pride some priceless treasure effectively hidden from his depredations. We poked into little shops, Chinese or native, where you could buy anything from a gorgeously embroidered mandarin coat to a shrunken human head, as the fancy took.

The long day ended with a real Spanish meal, a treat I had not had since leaving South America, not the least attractive part of which was the excellent wine that went with it.

Later we returned to Colón to rejoin the ship, feeling tired, dusty and hot after a train journey that had few equals for discomfort, yet with the satisfied feeling of great adventurers. We were met on arrival by a frigid front from all but the captain, who was eager to hear about our discoveries. I saw then for the first time how easily a perfectly innocent action could be misconstrued on board ship by those whose minds are inclined that way. Unfortunately they are legion in number and their insidious influence often made ship life narrow and unhappy.

# 11

# Enter Ned

LIFE ON BOARD was a sequence of jars, which at times hurt deeply, yet it was teeming with interest and, because I was built that way, with limitless hope. Every new place and different character was fresh ground to explore so the racking weariness of limb and feet was often forgotten; there was little time for self-pity if I wanted to absorb everything.

Yet, about it all was a note of sadness. Youth is supposed to be a happy time and personal beauty a wonderful blessing; the combination of both should prove a supreme and enviable asset. I never found this so at sea.

I noticed that youth was usually apportioned the heaviest labor, often so monotonous, so soul-grinding as to overcast any young dreams. Moreover, there never lacked old hands to pry on, criticize and harass youthful beginners. Indeed, I found that sea life up to now fostered all the petty instincts of human nature, without developing any of the finer ones. Isolation overtook me very often. There was an air of insecurity which bewildered me, for at every turn, I might be on the wrong path and every friend might turn out a traitor. It took me years to find out the cause of all this.

Compensations were not lacking, though. I found one in the owner of a pair of roguish blue eyes. Ned Tracy was junior fifth engineer on board, and his introduction to me was an impudent approach on deck one evening, where I had gone to a quiet corner for fresh air and an opportunity to subdue a growing feeling of dislike for much that surrounded me.

His intelligent eyes regarded me quizzically. Without flattery, he started chatting casually about sea life from his point of view, and I sensed at once that in his generalizations about everything to do with the work I had chosen, he was warning me against possible pitfalls and the corrupting atmosphere.

I found he hated stewards unreasonably. There was something vital about him that rebelled against their passivity. He despised their cupidity, their lack of manliness, their submissiveness, and that they mostly subsisted on tips brought forth his bitterest scorn. He refused to attribute these characteristics to their restricted life since boyhood or to the cringing fear of sudden dismissal without opportunity for redress.

In an excess of indignation and loyalty, I tried to find a reason. I argued that employers were to blame, since they only paid a starvation wage for intolerably long hours, saddling the traveling public to look after their employees with tips. I used myself as an example: I was being paid two pounds ten shillings per month as wages, out of which I bought my uniform and paid for its laundering; the only additional money I received was ten shillings a month towards its upkeep. To balance this, however, was a deduction at the end of every trip for breakages.

Nothing that I said succeeded in shaking Ned's convictions. We would end up the argument on a strained note, as he muttered something about throwing a flower on the dung heap. For a while we would be studiously polite and distant with each other, then suddenly his sense of humor would see the futility of it and he'd break the ice with an uproarious laugh.

As for himself, he had a rigid code of morals and was intolerant of anything that deviated from it. His over-emphasis of this was at times embarrassing. After he found out that a cup of early morning tea was brought to me by a steward, he showed disapproval by avoiding coming even near the alleyway where my cabin was situated, if he wished to see me.

Towards me he often adopted a somewhat mocking manner, picking on certain traits of mine in order to distort them for the sake of his own amusement. This made me shy and ill at ease though I strove to appear indifferent. I dreaded his ability to make me care what he said, also his puckishness as when he smilingly greeted me with a remark such as: "Ah, here comes the little girl to be admired," when he knew full well I would do anything rather than place myself in a conspicuous position.

On such occasions I felt I hated him for deliberately misunderstanding my character; but at other times I felt he was only acting, in order to ward off a more serious vein. When he chose to put aside his clowning, a charming warm side of his nature was revealed. We'd get talking about all manner of people and places he knew, about his own folks and home in Australia, the country of his adoption. But above all, he liked to talk of his dreams and ambitions. It would be difficult then to find a more companionable and lovable man.

His colleagues often remarked that he was a genius at his work, and they never expected to reach his standard, yet his insatiable desire to argue, to have the last word and his impish sense of humor infuriated his seniors and made it appear as if he were likely to remain junior fifth for the rest of his life unless he learnt to eat humble pie. Often he remarked with pride that humility was a virtue they did not cultivate in Australia.

Ned had one special pal on board outside his own department. Douglas Black was a purser's assistant. In disposition, he was Ned's complete opposite, studious yet entertaining and never mocking. Debonair in manner, he always seemed to do and say the right thing at the right time, never "put his foot in it," as Ned remarked. His poise was attributed to an early upbringing in France, where he had learnt to speak French like a native.

For two such contrasting natures they had much in common, including me. Each knew the other sought my company whenever possible, but neither commented on the fact. Ned, after a while, became more subdued and I glimpsed occasionally a far-away rather forlorn look in his usually merry eyes, as if some thought troubled him. His assertive personality suddenly seemed changed, leaving in its place a submission to inferiority. It made me feel very sad to see him thus; I preferred his puckishness.

I longed for him to say something that would give me the opportunity to assure him how, in spite of his mocking ways and occasional aloofness, he had become very dear to me, so much so that I wanted his company above all other. But my pride would not allow me to take the lead in such a delicate matter, because I felt as many others did about Ned, that few knew his real self.

Far from giving me an opening, he retreated more into his shell, and seemed deliberately to encourage Douglas to take first place in

my friendship. I thought of a ruse, to surprise an expression of pleasure from him that would give me an opening.

At a convenient moment and when I was certain he was not on
watch below, I made to go to the third class and took the wrong
alleyway, and so passed the engineers' quarters. I knew I ran the risk
of his censure if he thought I went that way on purpose, but I took a
chance and feigned innocence. He was on deck smoking his pipe
thoughtfully and, though I shrunk inwardly from so much expression
of feeling, I openly showed how pleased I was at the unexpected
meeting.

He returned my greeting coldly at first, then said: "Was thinking
of you, little girl, and thought of the promise you made to come for
a jaunt with me when we get to Kingston." Then, before I had time
to reply, he continued in a musing tone: "But I suppose old Douglas
will be escorting you?"

I felt as if I had been slapped in the face, because I had never
shown any preference for Douglas. Of course I remembered the
promise. I had lived for the day, but as it had never been mentioned
again by him, I hated to be so bold as to remind him. He was being
deliberately cruel and unfair, I felt, and I had a sudden overwhelming
desire to hurt back, although I realized that by hurting him, I would
only be punishing myself.

I saw less of him after that. For one thing my duties doubled, as
the number of passengers increased at frequent ports of call. The ship
was a babble of voices and every sort of noise. Large Spanish families
from the Central American ports came with their pots, pans and bun-
dles and bore down on me. In every family there seemed to be an ailing baby who needed special food prepared, and because I spoke
Spanish, my bell never stopped ringing.

Amid all the excitement of embarkation and tearful farewells to
relatives, varied and exacting instructions would be screamed at me in
the strident Spanish peculiar to Central America. I carefully passed
these instructions on to old Jock the pantryman who, through years
of standing in a steaming, squelchy pantry, had developed varicose
veins and an immovable face but had retained a heart of gold.

Although Jock loved babies, he did not attach as much importance to the preparation of their food as the mothers did. With a disapproving grunt against "fads," he dumped whatever I gave him into
his favorite "Banbury"—the old *bain-marie* that was his most impor-

tant utensil—and with complete disregard of orders proceeded with its preparation. Later he would serve it up with a wink for his ingenuity, a flourish in the grand manner, and an air of complete satisfaction with his culinary skill.

Ned met me once surrounded by one of these excited crowds, and unable to refrain from a little sarcasm remarked: "Ha! Your own country's people!" but was nonplused when I quizzed his geography and indulgently reminded him of the thousands of miles that separated these from my country's people.

When we reached Cartagena, which we were calling at for the first time, I was surprised and disappointed that he failed to show up, for I knew him to be off duty in port. We had so often talked of that historical place. He knew I had looked forward with impatience to see it and have places pointed out to me in this old port where the British once fought and suffered defeat long ago.

It all looked so peaceful now, bathed in sunshine, with the bluest sky imaginable above and crystal clear water below in whose blue depths could be seen every sort of dazzling marine life. It was a primitive scene of unique charm and I wished Ned had been there to share its loveliness with me. I marveled at the colorful life of the jetty, where solemn-faced little boys with spitting, chattering marmosets crawling all over them, offered their pets for sale; impassive men sat by their hampers of tropical fruit and exquisite orchids, patiently waiting for a customer, not deigning to notice the looks of suspicion cast at them by some of the ship's very European passengers.

# 12

# Insufferable Passengers

ON A GLORIOUS tropical morning we steamed into Kingston, Jamaica, over that mysterious sunken town of Port Royal, with its tree tops and landmarks still visible above water.

Long before daybreak I had awakened with soft air from the open port gently blowing in my face, bringing with it the faint but unforgettable aroma of growing coffee. Poor Jamaica was only beginning to recover, like some wounded animal, from the ravages of a recent earthquake.

The pungent smell of sugarcane and rum, mingled with ripening pineapples and bananas, hung heavy on the air and the lazy, graceful movements and the lilting laughter of her black population produced a peaceful calm for my nerves; it seemed just the spot to spend my first promised visit ashore with Ned, to have that long talk he had so often hinted at.

Romance put aside for a while, I set off to interview one out of the dozens of smiling, happy-faced laundry ladies who invaded the ship one half minute after she had tied up. They bore down on us like ships in full sail with their ballooning, colorful print dresses. They were laden with bags of pineapples, various other delicacies, baskets filled with bottles of "hot sauce" (the hottest thing on God's green earth, composed of dozens of ingredients). All were offerings for prospective customers.

I was duly presented with my share, in return for the privilege of doing my washing. After being assured that it would be returned next day, I went to get ready for my visit ashore.

One interesting facet of Caribbean ports of call in those days was that local laundresses enjoyed such a brisk trade, washing both passenger and crew clothing. Kingston dockings involved a wholesale influx of Jamaicans on board without any of the security problems that plague contemporary cruise ship arrivals. Here was a useful means by which the island populace could profit from a ship's visit. In today's Caribbean, vessels not only have their own laundries (indeed, it is a valued source of revenue) but they almost never stay overnight in port. As a result, very few ordinary islanders derive benefit from tourists. Though thousands of passengers swarm ashore at St. Thomas year-round, for example, only taxi drivers, restaurateurs, tour operators and shopkeepers derive direct income from them. Of course, one could argue that the island's economy at large benefits; nevertheless, yesterday's picturesque and useful interface between indigenes and passengers is no more.

I dressed carefully, that is, as carefully as one can, when perspiration exudes from every pore, in a cabin so small that to move suddenly meant disaster to some part of one's anatomy. The sun shone in relentlessly through the tightly screwed down porthole and all the bedlam that coaling a ship entailed was concentrated overhead, to the accompaniment of the devastating racket of the ship's winches working cargo, the monotony relieved now and then by the purple language of the stevedores.

I wanted to look as attractive as possible. At last I was ready and we landed. I soon discovered that a lot of the glamor one feels for a new port viewed over the ship's side vanished when one got ashore. Kingston was just then at a disadvantage, and I had overlooked the fact that I would need to negotiate heaps of rubbish, and mounds of broken masonry lying everywhere because of the earthquake. As Ned and I made our way from the ship, I got hotter and hotter and my white shoes, so carefully preserved for the occasion, got dirtier and dirtier.

Getting out of the town and up to Constant Springs was like leaving a furnace for the cool of a garden at evening time. The famous hotel was crowded with our passengers, who seemed to be able to do nothing more original than sit around sipping drinks. They appeared somewhat surprised to see us. I learnt from later experience that passengers generally are surprised if you use the same public buildings they do.

The issue of co-mingling passengers and crew while ashore remains a sensitive one, far more complex in those class-conscious days than today. In general, only a ship's officer, as Ned Tracy was, even though he was escorting a junior stewardess, would have patronized a restaurant frequented by passengers. In truth, most contemporary crew have no wish to spend precious shore time anywhere near passengers but certainly not for reasons of discretion; they see excursions away from the ship as a means of distancing themselves from the often overbearing clients they must serve all day at sea.

Two decades ago, I was on a Caribbean cruise aboard *QE2*. An older barman befriended a single lady passenger and the two of them became inseparable, not only on board—where the woman became a perpetual bar fly—but also ashore. Once away from the ship, the two of them would dress down in bathing suits, mingling openly either on the beach or in hotel pools. But the barman's forearms, alas, were a giveaway, covered as they were with a luxuriant flourish of seaman's tattoos!

However, we did not tarry longer than was necessary to have a delicious and welcome cup of tea before we set forth to explore the island. Ned remembered a spot which had been recommended to him as worth visiting. It was a long way off, near a lovely inlet; we decided to make for it: we might never have the opportunity again. We hired a driver with a buggy, then much used on the island, and sitting behind the energetic, high-stepping horse, Ned's spirits rose. He related in his own inimitable way many amusing experiences of his sea life, stories that seemed very far-fetched to my inexperience.

The magnificent scenery became denser, until finally leaving our driver to have a smoke, we decided to explore on foot. It was interesting but very exhausting.

Dusk was approaching. It comes quickly in the tropics once the sun has set, and arriving at the beautiful inlet we discovered an old log amongst the luxuriant ferns, where we decided to rest for a while before returning. As I was about to sit down, Ned took me in his arms and, looking at me intently with eyes for once serious, shyly asked me to allow him to kiss me. That kiss has always remained my most sacred and wonderful memory.

I was just recovering from its spell and the particular piece of heaven it had opened for me, while Ned regarded me as if I were something too precious to even touch, when, with a little embarrassed laugh, he suggested we sit down on the log for a few minutes to chat. We touched lightly on many things, as people do who don't know each other very well, then he suddenly said with forced casualness: "I promised my mother I would return to Australia unattached, as soon as I took my chief's ticket."

I was so taken aback that for the moment I did not notice a slight movement of the log we were sitting on; suddenly however with a grunting, squelching sound it began to move under us. Ned looked down and I remember his horrified face as he dragged me away by one arm and I saw the tail of a huge old crocodile that seemed to be wakening from a deep slumber.

For the moment our one idea was to find our driver, and we did not stop running and jumping over obstacles till we reached him, very out of breath. His amazement at our sudden agitated return was nothing compared to his anxiety to get away from the place after we had related our encounter. As we sped away, he told us that he had lost a young and dearly loved brother to a crocodile, and since then they were the one terror in his life.

Crocodile or no crocodile, I felt cheated. I suddenly felt like crying. I wanted Ned to take me in his arms and reassure me. Yet I dared not even appear as if such a thought had entered my head, for he had not really expressed his real feelings for me. How deeply I regretted the broken spell of our magic moment!

I tried to fathom if he felt about it as I did. Suddenly he laughed loudly, and said: "I'm an unlucky fellow!" but did not qualify his ill luck, then continued: "You looked incredulous this afternoon when I told you one or two things, and you mocked me with your eyes when you remarked that evidently when unusual things happened I always seemed to be on the scene; what about this for an experience, girlie?"

A surge of anger crept over me. I felt it was the wrong thing to say just at that moment, and I marveled he did not feel more deeply about ourselves. That night I dreamed of loving arms that never quite reached me, blue eyes that faded as I looked, and a world full of crocodiles as I tossed in a temperature of ninety degrees in my narrow bunk.

At sea I soon discovered you can erase things from your mind with greater facility than is possible ashore. The scene is constantly changing and if you are working, the duties which are legion are very often wholly absorbing; this was partly so with me. Besides, New York was drawing near and my curiosity was growing apace. Remembering the many times I had listened enchanted to the talks of my North American school directresses in Argentina, it was a place I had always longed for but never thought I would see.

Various Americans we had taken on at Colón for New York were no doubt so happy to get away for a spell from the inferno of the Canal Zone, that they could not speak of their hometown without exaggeration.

They were interesting, natural, warm-hearted people, kindly disposed and so eager to make friends. They made in three days as much headway as the average English person makes in the same number of months. For example, to my astonishment, I received two perfectly serious proposals of marriage within ten minutes of one another after a few days' acquaintance.

We steamed past the Statue of Liberty dimly looming out of a fog, which the Americans on board resented our noticing, so proud are they of their climate and so much have they maligned ours. On up towards Battery Park just in time to take on board the complement of two small ships that had collided and been badly damaged in the dense fog!

Looking back, I find I have never changed my first impressions of New York: A city of such amazing contrasts, savagely insolent and amazingly kind, rackety and refined, gay and sinister with boiling summer and devastatingly cold winter, but withal a place of pulsating humanity.

My first visit was a real joy, after I had managed to overcome a feeling that its amazing buildings shooting upwards into dim heights would not topple down, and when I had got used to the violent winds that roar round the corners of its skyscrapers with but one apparent aim, that of relieving one of all clothing; I had never witnessed so many public displays of varied human limbs. I found much happiness in wandering from one beautiful store to another, finding great temptation to spend some of my hard-earned money on small gifts for those at home which would give Mother endless pleasure, things indeed that were not to be seen on sale in England for a number of years.

New York should be the average woman's paradise. Its shops are centers of well thought-out schemes to inveigle the hardest-headed, strongest-willed, closest-fisted female into handing over every cent she comes in with. Its salesladies, from the regally turned-out beauties on Fifth Avenue to the little East Side counter girl in the basement of an outlet shop, are intelligent, trained advisers and very style-conscious. Not the least of their assets was their natural kindliness. If they wanted to park their chewing-gum somewhere when addressed, they did so under the counter as a matter of course, quite naturally; and if they thought you had used a misnomer, one would not be surprised or hurt to be corrected by: "Oh, you mean a brazzeer!" when you had asked for a brassiere. It was all done to give you what you wanted in the way you wanted it, and because they were anxious you should have what you asked for.

This art of salesmanship has been quite naturally perfected. Who could, for instance, take exception to a saleslady announcing during the ticklish job of selecting a face powder of the right texture and shade: "Why, Miss, I have just your shading, although I have not got your beautiful English complexion, and I have used this powder ever since it came on the market, see how grand my skin is!" and so on. Or at the stocking counter during a hesitating moment while wondering if it's going to be one pair for a dollar ten cents, or three pairs for three dollars, she remarks admiringly : "My, how I love that necklace you're wearing, Miss! Why, it is just beautiful! Did you get it abroad?" In face of such wholehearted praise of your good taste, you fall headlong into the trap, leaving the shop with three pairs for three dollars and well satisfied into the bargain.

Intermixed with Americans' subtle ingenuity and good nature is a streak of selfishness. They want the best that life has to offer, and they get it in their stride, leaving one panting and exhausted in the process. In later years and on larger ships, how often I have trudged on aching feet and nerve-racked back up and down stairs (we were not allowed to use lifts), to and fro, sweltering in unbelievable heat, to satisfy the gastronomic exactitude of some noted woman. The daily papers may have classified her as an angel of benevolence, but she never hesitated to demand of me what she wanted, no matter how her request upset my daily routine, and in spite of the fact that she liked me, openly declaring to all and sundry that she "simply adored" me, or that I "was so sweet."

In the midst of a turbulent, impatient crowd, all needing some service "at once," she would not hesitate to say smilingly: "My dear, I don't want to bother coming in off the deck just now, it is so much cooler than inside, so I know you will not mind giving dear Fifi (her Pekinese) her lamb cutlet and green peas (be sure they are fresh peas, won't you?), well mashed up."

A little frown would knit her carefully tended brows if she noticed I hesitated, while I remembered those dozen beds I had still to make, or perhaps the latest cocktail party to clear up after, and she would reiterate with emphasis: "I know you will do this."

Or it might be the woman who met me with the remark: "My dear, I cannot possibly take my lunch in the saloon today, it's much too noisy. Besides, I don't like the people near me, so I know you will bring it to my cabin," and with the most winsome smile she would add: "Not before two o'clock, though, because I shall have no appetite before then."

Faintly I'd murmur that lunch was presumed to be over by 2 p.m. She would wave her hand, a heavily jeweled hand, with the remark: "I know you will do it, you all spoil me so, you are all so good, and I always get what I want."

At the end of a typical day at sea, when my shoes felt full of feet and life seemed one big ache, with just enough animation left in me to fetch a bottle of ice water for myself before retiring for the night, I'd meet her sailing towards me, and with a pained expression she would say: "My dear, you do look so very tired, are you going off-duty now?" With what I felt to be a wan smile of doubt in my luck, I would reply that that was my sincere hope, whereupon she'd sweetly say: "Before you go, I know you will leave me some cracked ice and some sandwiches in my room, and, oh yes, some oranges too, or anything that looks good to you."

What use would it have been to tell her that nothing looked good to me at that hour except bed, or that the fruit keeper, long off-duty, would have to be called and would probably rant and rave? The one thing I had to keep reminding myself of was the fact that I should not be needed in my job if she and her kind did not travel. I did get some moral courage from the fact that almost all Americans, however exacting, do consider you a person first, rather than a servant, and that makes a world of difference.

Contrasting that attitude of hers—which is by no means restricted to a particular class but applies to all when humans travel by sea—would be her warm farewell and expression of deep regard and admiration, accentuated by her asking me to call on her, take lunch with her, or come up for a chat whenever I want to get away from "those tiresome people!"

A certain very beautiful lady clung to me during the entire voyage while she recovered from a private calamity, glad of my sympathy and understanding. At the end of the trip I felt a friendship had been cemented and was not surprised by her repeated invitation to visit her at the first opportunity.

She could never, she said, do enough for me in return for the long hours of my off-duty time which I had spent at her side, or for the moral support I had given her. It was difficult to believe as I watched her ready to leave the ship, full of poise and superbly gowned, while she chatted with some equally elegant women of her set who had come to welcome her home, that those intimate and soul-revealing talks had taken place at all between us. Her last words, however, were a reminder to visit her, as she gave me a warm hand-shake.

Months later, on another visit to New York, after ascertaining that she was still at the same hotel and would be "at home," I called on her. I was announced from the desk below, and when the dainty maid admitted me, I heard voices and gay laughter as I was shown in-to the drawing room, where she came forward to meet me with a gracious smile and a puzzled expression.

In a flash, I saw that she had completely forgotten me, but the fact that I appeared to know her made her make a violent effort at recognition. I managed, unobserved, to whisper my name, but omitted to mention our last meeting place and, though she caught the name and gaily turned, still with my hand in hers, to introduce me to her guests, I knew she had not the faintest idea who I was.

New York, therefore, opened to me many vistas, but I knew it would never hold me. Its noise, its incessant movement and restless excitement were very stimulating for the moment, but its materialism rose as a wall that barred affection for it, and repose was as separated from it as the poles.

So I left its shores, homeward bound, laden with good things and many conflicting impressions, glad to let my mind wander to the less exotic thoughts of homeland and the lovely welcome Mother invariably met me with.

I remember the intense joy and peace of my first evening at home with Mother after a voyage, as we sat in the warm kitchen, so quiet now the young ones were all in bed, while I was making little stacks of golden sovereigns to pay the various outstanding bills and wishing rather ruefully that sovereigns were more elastic.

Violet Jessop's evaluation of New York is typical of most out-of-town visitors to the present: Moving at a frenetic pace, they judge the city frenetic. But her loving testimonial to the city's shops and shopping typifies all steamship crews' attitude to a port that remains to this day a haven of inexpensive presents for their families back home. Ship turnarounds were longer then, enabling seamen not only to get ashore but also to become familiar with the city. Generations of foreign-flag crews from all the lines knew—and loved—Manhattan well.

The chapter also bears witness to Violet's particular affection for Americans, regardless how tiresome or demanding some of those accommodated in her section could be. We can date that predilection from her first exposure to Americans in Argentina where young Violet marveled at the two directresses of her school. I sense their independence and initiative served as inspiration for Violet throughout her life. Margaret Meehan surprised me when she described her aunt's accent as a blend of Irish lilt with a distinctly American overlay; apparently, Violet had absorbed some American speech patterns from her years on the North Atlantic run to New York.

# Troubled Voyage

IN OUR YOUNG YEARS, events assume immense proportions and life's changes well might break our heart. As happens on a new voyage, many of the crew had been changed and some of the changes were not happy ones.

We had a new captain. He was a philanderer, as everybody knew, and casting about for some new diversion, his attention had fallen on me. Many were the stories of his behavior towards young girls going home to finish their studies and put under his charge by confiding parents, so I was prepared. Unfortunately, because of his position, much that he did was ignored. Besides, his wife was a shareholder in the company!

When he chose to favor me with his unwelcome overtures, I decided the wisest course was to play dumb and ignore the notes dropped through my door and boxes of chocolates that found their way into my cabin. I could always assume they were intended for another cabin.

But the situation did not fizzle out, as some do when they are ignored. The captain may have guessed my ruse for he began to show displeasure by becoming critical of everything I did, and found many excuses to victimize me, as he was free to do; so life became a little harder than it had been hitherto.

With the captain's vigilant eye looking for cause to find fault, I saw little of Ned or Douglas Black. But as it sometimes happened, when I was free and my duties finished in port, or when passengers were ashore, we met openly.

These visits were my only recreation. Ned's elusiveness and unsettled state of mind, however, seemed to transfer itself to me. He had never attempted to clarify our relationship since the crocodile episode, and whenever we met, rarely missed an opportunity of jokingly saying that a fellow like himself was not good enough for an angel girl like me, and so on.

I took it all with an outward show of fun but was inwardly disappointed and troubled. We were deeply attracted to each other but there was a barrier: I never felt I could really open my heart to him about the things that bothered me most, without incurring some mocking comment. And if it happened to be something relating to some member of the crew, his naturally intolerant mind would prompt him to say things that only distressed without helping.

I could well understand his antagonism towards stewards but they were by no means the only transgressors. I have in mind one steaming hot night in the West Indies, when I was slowly recovering from my first bout of malaria. I had been transferred to a large, very sumptuous stateroom at the purser's suggestion, which I appreciated, though the airiness of the cabin had not helped me to find rest in sleep for many days and nights. At long last, overcome with utter fatigue, I must have dropped into a slumbering stupor, my mind floating into fantastic dream-shapes, when I suddenly awoke with a start in the dark.

At first it seemed part of my dream, then I gradually became conscious of a strange odor, tobacco but not that alone, the smell of a man. Then I heard a sound, surely the intake of somebody's breath, while predatory hands groped over the bed and a voice, scarcely raised above a whisper, spoke my name.

I recognized the voice, with amazement and anger, as that of the purser. Indeed my wrath flared up so furiously, no doubt deepened by the ravages of fever, that I could have grasped that throat in my hands, could I but reach it, and digging my fingers into the flesh, taken pleasure in hearing the breath leave it. Such was the maddening fury that frightened me by its intensity, I, who ordinarily hated killing even a housefly.

It all became clear to me then, the luxurious cabin, the little attentions I had thought quite disinterested. What I could not understand was the man, the very man responsible for our discipline, with a position to uphold. I had always felt rather sorry for him with his foppish ways and the brainless flirtations he often indulged in, but he was regarded by us all as quite a gentlemanly, albeit stupid-headed fellow.

I had barely uttered half a dozen words of reproach in an undertone, when there was a knock on the cabin door, which was not shut, but fastened on a hook for air, as is the custom at sea in hot weather. In those few seconds my mind flew to the possibility of the captain having set a watch on the cabin, and my heart seemed to pound through my side as, controlling my voice, I called: "Come in."

I had not put on the light but was conscious of a rustling hurried movement as the door opened, letting in the light from the alleyway. It was the night watchman who came in to screw up all ports in anticipation of dirty weather ahead.

The intruder seemed to have vanished. I wondered if the watchman noticed the odor as I had done, and I prayed not. Certainly not that of a woman's room, for this was in the days before women smoked in their bedrooms. I consoled myself that night watchmen, during their lonely night-time vigils, are often soothed by their reeking pipes as well as a few spots of "something" to keep their spirits up, to the exclusion of other smells. I trusted it would be so in this instance, as the door closed on his cheerful "Good night, Miss."

As I turned on the light, a white, frightened face with bulging eyes emerged from under the opposite bed, hair disheveled, bits of fluff and dust from the deck adhering to his person. He stood up and, with an effort to regain some of his lost dignity, was about to make a joking, conciliatory remark when he caught my eye.

He must have realized then some of the concentrated fury which my quivering lips seemed unable to utter at the moment, for he bounded for the door, his dressing gown flapping against his hairy legs as he made his exit, uttering some inane remark.

I lay awhile marveling at these men. The effrontery of them! The captain, the purser, many others who had positions to maintain, groveling and sniveling like dogs. Yet they would be my judges, should I or the likes of me make one false step on board; in their power lay our very existence. I was revolted.

I needed someone to talk to, yet there was nobody I could open my heart to who would understand, for I felt that sea life was not the setting for a normal woman, however it might afford her a living. Assuming she was normal, it would be a terrible strain on her to remain so, and keep her personality. She would be surrounded by those whose thoughts seem to be harnessed to a very strong and unalterable herd instinct. Repression was forced, and freedom of speech, idealism or attempts at outside interests were put down.

Those who made up the victualing staff of a ship constantly came and went. There was nothing stable about their employment, since they could on the slightest pretext be thrown out of work which they probably started as youths, sometimes mere lads; blown hither and thither at the beck and call of all and sundry on board, they had no guidance, either moral or physical, only the incessant talk around them of money.

They were handicapped by the scantiest education, and the training a ship afforded lacked co-ordination. No two chief stewards, who themselves had been often promoted from this class, trained alike or had the same sense of values; so there was no enthusiasm, nothing to bind loyalties or foster higher motives, just an acceptance of the scant interest in their welfare and comfort shown by most shipping companies and a docile endurance of primitive living conditions.

They had learnt long ago that words of encouragement seldom came their way; yet in many instances, a kind recognition or compliment produced in their starved lives a spontaneous reaction quite out of proportion to the word of encouragement. They had come to accept the limitations of their life, the struggle for existence, the everlasting uncertainty, the lack of humanity and minimum of consideration most companies afforded them. Both employers and passengers exploited them, though the latter, having paid exorbitant fares, no doubt felt entitled to willing slaves, making demands they would not dare make on their own servants ashore.

Many days passed before I was strong enough to be allowed up after my bout of malaria. How I missed the ministrations of my kind friend, Doctor O'Connor, now back in London! He would have given me the strength and courage I badly needed.

One thing I knew, the "old man," as the captain is called (sometimes in affectionate tolerance but in this case in no such term) would not have hoodwinked him as he did the young doctor who had replaced him. He came to me beaming one day, soon after I was allowed up, to say that the captain had very considerately suggested I should have my chair placed on the top deck near his quarters, where it would be quiet. I thought, was there ever such a farce!

I felt life on board was beating me gradually, and I could not even have the pleasure of bandying words with Ned. I longed to see him. The nearest approach I got to that had been a little sketch of himself, screwed into a matchbox and brought up by a bellboy, and depicting himself as a cadaverous individual wasting away for love of a lady and surrounded by bursting pipes and ruined boilers.

It was so good a likeness and yet so outlandish that it provided my first laugh for weeks, for I could well imagine him as he ripped into things in his characteristic manner, having all kinds of unexpected mishaps and generally finding himself in a fearful mess. Yet in my experience, the more the calamity, the better he seemed to enjoy himself.

He had always wanted to take me down to his beloved engine-room, though I found out afterwards that this was against the rules. Apparently, when a convenient time occurred and things looked shining and nice, some part of the machinery would choose that moment to go bust.

A day came, however, when all was set for my visit. To ensure that no breath of scandal would result from it, Ned had deputized a colleague to escort me down. He appeared to have chosen one whose bearing seemed most correct. My escort was making his first trip to sea and had not yet had the polish worn off manners that had been bred in his father's country vicarage; from his reference to his people and the look that lighted his face as he spoke of them, I could well picture his lady mother in her beautiful and peaceful home and his serene, gray-haired father.

He told me how he looked forward to becoming something in the engineering world later on. He loved his work and hoped to compensate his father for the disappointment he caused him when he put aside the idea of the church as a vocation. He added, rather shyly, that he thought he would succeed, going on to eulogize what he considered Ned's genius. Altogether a most inspiring chat with an unusually nice man.

When we reached the engine room, an oily rag was thrust into my hands, to make me a proper engineer, Ned remarked, and I had my first experience of negotiating the slippery iron ladder of a ship's engine room where the roar of the machinery and the terrific heat nearly made me lose my nerve. My companions got impish amusement from my disadvantage, but Ned dropped that attitude when he went on to explain things. Then his face lighted up remarkably and he went into technicalities, quite oblivious of the fact that I was "only a girl," a phrase he was fond of using.

He pointed out with pride minute steel parts, touching them lovingly, explaining their uses, regarding them with those penetrating blue eyes of his, as if they were children of whom he was especially proud, yet felt a little anxious about.

I screamed questions at him, in the din, asking how it was possible to keep one's head amid such noise, hear anything or even think, to which he laughingly replied: "Why, bless you, I don't notice the noise. What I do notice at once is when one of these gadgets ceases to function, or slows down, then the sound it makes alters a little and I notice that particular one from among all the other familiar ones." I reflected that engineers must be born, not made.

The firemen regarded me with curiosity, their blackened faces and red-rimmed eyes peering at me as they bent their glistening bodies to the task of shoveling coal into those yawning infernos. I had brought with me a good supply of cigarettes so that Ned's greaser could distribute them among his mates. Ned often spoke with wonderment of this man's flow of language which, as he said, was enough to set any machinery in motion had it stopped.

I had food for reflection as I went to bed that night; I was very happy, yet not happy; if I took Ned's remarks seriously, I should really feel elated, seeing that I loved him in return, yet the joy of being asked the one vital question of my life was missing.

I gained some comfort when I remembered that he never did things as other people did them, and at least it was clear there was no secret motive for the silence and aloofness which had worried me. It was his way.

I soon learnt one of the reasons for his moments of pensive withdrawal, and knowing it did not raise the clouds that were for ever hovering near our horizon. One day, while searching in my apron pocket for something, in his presence, I dropped my rosary. A look of annoyance crossed his face and he remarked peevishly: "Whatever do you use that thing for?" A question I thought in the worst possible taste and calculated to hurt, since he well knew what I used it for. I replied, ignoring his lack of tact, that I considered it a very simple and delightful practice of my religion, to use this means of asking the Mother of God for something, in much the same way, as he himself had often laughingly told me, he used to beg his mother to plead his cause with his father when funds were running low.

The matter was dropped like a hot brick for a time, but cropped up in diverse little ways, pinpricks that wounded and surprised me coming as they did from such a kindly character as his.

I was forced to conclude that while his forebears, who had lived in Cornwall and were Puritans, had bequeathed to him a steadfast, upright mode of life and a beautifully clean mind, they had also handed down a considerable amount of intolerance.

In moments of physical and mental weariness or fear for the future, I would suggest—much as it wrung my heart to do so—that, feeling as he did about my religion, it might be as well, when the voyage was over, that we each went our way, carrying with us, before it was spoilt, the memory of a delightful encounter.

At this suggestion, his attitude would immediately change, and from being a fault-finding critic he would become humbly supplicating, saying with deep feeling that he could not let me go, and no matter how he disapproved of my form of worship, if it made me what he knew me to be, then it must be wonderful. A staggering admission that left me without defense.

# 14

# The South American Run

WITH ONE OF those strokes of fate—the unexpectedness of which made sea life so uncertain—I was able to return to South America and was wending my way back to Buenos Aires.

The ship's victualing department consisted of a fairly amiable lot, on the whole, when they were not shaken to the core by the erratic and explosive temperament of the chief steward. His meteoric appearances or vituperative, sometimes childish outbursts were likely to occur at any moment from 5 a.m. till 11 p.m., for the most unforeseen reasons.

It was very early brought home to me that anyone who took it "lying down" would have to do so for the rest of their life on board. The only way to avoid that and retain a little dignity, was to put one's "foot down."

I remember my second meal at his table in the saloon on sailing day, after the passengers had finished. I was tired, for I always found the business of getting acquainted with new passengers difficult. Every sailing day was a bugbear for me.

He was still complaining about some unfortunate delinquent when he sat down to his evening meal. The other three at the table remained silent as he repeated an old saying of his that went the round of the fleet: "If he makes six trips with me, he can make a trip with the devil." His moustache was bristling and his chest expanding as he cast a sideways glance at me, the new recruit, to see what impression he was making and evidently expecting some suitable comment.

With all the weariness rising in me and before I could stop myself, I said: "For a man of your years and position, you say the silliest things." I was stopped from finishing by the sudden snap of his jaw and the friendliest sort of grin as he started on his meal. Had I been older, no doubt my lack of respect would have met with a suitable reprimand; as it was, from that day on, he was one of my most loyal supporters.

I had mixed feelings about the trip. I knew that returning to places after time and separation have changed one's perspective, is sometimes joyful but more often sad. Besides, I was lonely; I missed a pair of laughing eyes. Yet I felt a thrill to be revisiting my childhood home, though I must confess that on closer examination this elation sobered down when I realized for the first time that a place is everything or nothing if it holds or lacks the presence of those who give home a meaning.

I was looking forward to much, however. For one thing, I had never been to Brazil. The little ship that took us to England had not touched at any of its ports; so when I had argued on the merits of Rio de Janeiro harbor with Ned, who naturally held that Sydney was superior for beauty, I did so purely on hearsay and loyalty. Neither of us was sensible enough to allow that there can be no comparison between too vastly different types of beauty.

I am always glad I saw Rio then, when its natural beauty predominated over everything and was unmarred by latter efforts at modernization. From the moment at daybreak when we steamed past Sugarloaf Mountain into that magnificent harbor, my attention was riveted on the careless luxury of its vegetation, with such tender shades of green, the plume-like palms standing sentinel on streets so ornate with black and white paving that I felt I had stepped into a tropical Hans Christian Andersen city.

We already had on board a fair sample of its inhabitants, quiet-voiced people, courteously grateful for services rendered, who contrived to look amazingly prosperous without being at all overbearing; one felt that their breeding had been handed from Portuguese ancestors down the centuries. Aladdin's caves must surely be somewhere in Brazil, judging by the gorgeous diamonds with which its people adorned themselves.

There were a number of interesting people on board, whom you would expect to read about, but never to meet in the ordinary way. I noticed with some surprise that my shipmates were more or less indifferent to the notoriety of their passengers. These had to prove their worth on board in pounds, shillings and pence before a lasting impression was made!

I was very pleased to have Anatole France in my section. This famous French writer was traveling with a lady of flaming red hair but such plainness of features that would have rendered anyone but a Frenchwoman utterly uninteresting. Yet she was most attractive, an effect achieved by fastidious taste in dress and personal charm. He told me he was having a brain holiday: His magnetism and two-edged humor made it always a pleasure to pass the time of day with him; he would remind me that it was good for my French to talk with him!

One day as I hurried along the alleyway, I noticed a lady with two little girls coming towards me. They did not live in my part of the ship and I had not seen them before. There had been some rough seas and people were only now beginning to emerge. As they drew near, the lady's face seemed strangely familiar—bright brown eyes and the rather swarthy skin tinged with a natural warm color on the cheeks. Yet I could not place her. Not wanting to stare, I paused, and appeared to be interested in something near me, until she should pass and I could get a better view of her. As she came up, she too looked very hard at me, seemed about to speak, thought better of it and passed on. I was puzzled.

That evening as I was sitting in the ladies' saloon, very interested in a piece of embroidery—one of the few links with my convent days—she came quietly over the threshold, so gently in fact that I was quite startled to find her there looking at me intently, and said: "You look so like a little girl patient in the British Hospital in Buenos Aires my last year there; she was dying of consumption, and used to sit by the hour sewing, just as you are sitting now. You look very like her but she must be dead many years now."

I replied: "You look very like a nurse a young doctor was courting in the British Hospital in Buenos Aires, and who used to put her love letters under my pillow for him to collect."

We both laughed heartily for the recognition was mutual. She kept repeating: "But you were dying, dying I tell you. How did you come to survive?"

"Just the will to live, I suppose, combined with the wonderful Andes air of Mendoza and, last but not least, a huge chunk of faith in divine intervention," I told her. Then she went on to tell how often she and her husband had spoken of me and the part I played in their romance.

On arrival at our destination I found the charm of Buenos Aires still there, but it had lost its hold on me, a beautiful jewel case without the jewels. There were many changes in public places that pleased me and some improvements that left me cold, but what I looked forward to most was revisiting treasured or familiar spots, streets and houses that I had loved. Old trees in the old plazas, where we children played in the cool of the evening; quaint little shops in narrow streets, that modest little one in fact where Papa had bought me a tiny pair of earrings I had long coveted, to commemorate our *paseo* together on my first day out after a long convalescence.

Government House looking as much as ever like an iced cake with too much pink coloring; Retiro Station, the scene of my gory departure for Mendoza in pursuit of life and health: all these were still in existence—a little faded but having the power to bring back faces and memories of long ago. In spite of Buenos Aires' very blue sky, I felt homesick for foggy London.

I made another change of ship, where I had the misfortune to sail again under the same amorous captain, who now found I could do nothing right. I was much too young for sea life, he said, and, lacking all sense of honesty, reported me to the authorities ashore for "flirting with his officers," for which I was duly dismissed from the company. As there was no union in those days which I could appeal to, I had to accept his verdict.

The reason given for this dismissal did not, however, come under the category of those offenses which would prejudice the report for "ability and good conduct," so very important in the Seaman's Discharge Book issued by the Board of Trade and signed by the captain at the conclusion of every voyage.

The captain found nothing odd in signing my book for both conduct and ability as "very good." I suppose it was proof of my youth that I felt so keenly the injustice of so unfair a dismissal. I was deeply humiliated. I knew that from now on life at sea, if I could cope with it, was going to be a hard challenge, one I must face.

# 15

# The White Star Line

I SUPPOSE THAT ALL of us have had, at some time in our lives, to weigh up the merits or drawbacks of different prospective employers, choosing for various reasons those we would care to work for and discarding the others. So it was in my case.

When, week after week, I had applied to different companies for employment, with unsatisfactory results, I came almost to the end of my list, having exhausted all those companies that attracted me. Now I had to apply to those "not so attractive," among them the White Star Line plying the North Atlantic, an ocean whose tempestuous vagaries I had little desire to sample.

I had heard nothing but good of this company, sailing between England and America. But I also knew the work there to be very arduous and the hours very long. Moreover, the type of passenger who patronized it expected all the service the company could give, and got it.

Needless to say, in the giving of that service, sometimes poor old human nature rebelled, with the result that another berth had to be sought; in this way, we in other lines heard much.

It seemed an unaccountable thing to apply for work, almost hoping for a refusal, but the application was made to salve my conscience, as it were; I felt I had exhausted all other sources. It was dismaying, therefore, to receive a telegram summoning me to sign Articles for a certain popular ship, without having the customary interview before employment.

Violet Jessop's methodology in applying for work at rival shipping lines was quixotic, to say the least, and I wish she had elaborated more fully about some of her other choices. Did she, for example, apply to Cunard, or was any North Atlantic company ruled out because of that ocean's rough weather? But, whatever her options, after receiving no encouragement from her A-list, she then settled for her "not so attractive" B-list, among which she counted White Star.

From the standpoint of marine historians like myself, White Star was one of the foremost transatlantic lines of its day, the envy of many continental rivals and boasting a reputation for luxurious service second to none. But Violet, of course, was a hard-working company stewardess; from her pragmatic vantage point, the prospect of a demanding ship booked by a notoriously demanding clientele was daunting.

"We in other lines," she suggests darkly, "heard much." Jessop and her victualing department shipmates obviously spent hours yarning about and evaluating work conditions aboard ships of every line. And the word-of-mouth about White Star was, she tells us, formidable.

Two final observations about this pivotal re-employment period for Violet Jessop. First, demanding though her new company may have been and despite all her premonitions, she made a great hit with her new employers. Assigned initially to the second class, she rose within months to the first; and that she was chosen to serve on the maiden voyages of both *Olympic* and *Titanic* indicates clearly that she was the right stuff for the White Star Line; apparently, she more than measured up to the company's demanding standards. Second, thank heaven she *did* sign on with White Star; had she not, this volume might never have seen the light of day!

Incidentally, though Jessop never says so, her first White Star vessel was the first *Majestic* of 1890 which she joined on September 28th, 1910.

It was not until I had already been installed as a member of the crew that I met my new victualing superintendent. He did appear a trifle surprised at my youthful appearance but tactfully refrained from comment, for which I was deeply grateful. I understood what his feelings must have been later, when I saw the rest of the staff, all much older, very staid and, from their appearance, surely very sorely tried-out servants of the company. I came to have a great respect for many of them, perhaps more for their powers of endurance than their personalities.

What I was totally unprepared for were the terrific batterings the North Atlantic weather could administer after my comparatively calm trips in southern waters. It needed a certain amount of will power to remain at my post in the second class of a New York-bound liner, learning to assimilate the intricacies of service under trying conditions.

I found at once a warmth and vitality, among both crew and passengers of every age, that made everything go with a swing. This made life seem less of a burden and engendered a fellow-feeling.

The passengers, mostly Americans, required the best they could get. They were friendly, understanding and appreciative. Even those I learnt on better acquaintance to dub "holy terrors" were somehow approachable and human. They acknowledged you as an individual, invariably gave you your name, even went to the trouble of demanding to know it at the first moment of meeting. You felt at once that you were not a cog in a wheel, as you would so often on the South American run. Americans seemed to recognize that you were there to make their trip more comfortable and pleasant and often observed that the work could not always be easy to accomplish. You were faced with the paradox of being considerably overworked and yet much happier and free because of their attitude.

Of course, at times, their idiosyncrasies were difficult to bear. Most Americans want to absorb every new fad and idea as soon as it appears; as a result, they are often left in a state of hectic unrest which naturally transfers itself to those about them. But their generous natures seem to feel this and they try to compensate in a thousand ways.

When the trip is ended, they invariably ring for you to "tell you goodbye," to remunerate you, accompanied by a hearty handshake, and often, no matter who may be within earshot, a few encouraging words, such as "What a difference you have made to my trip."

The majority of North Atlantic passengers in both the first and second class were American, a proportion that would increase dramatically when tourist third cabin replaced third class immigrant space immediately after the First World War. Similarly, in the present-day cruise industry, eighty percent of the passengers are American as well. And the Europeans who build today's cruise ships, no less than the European and third-world crewmen who serve as present-day stewards, would certainly echo Violet Jessop's sentiments about the gratitude of their preponderantly American clientele.

Throughout the world, Americans abroad are perceived as gregarious and, by and large, generous to a fault. Of course, they can be tight-fisted, boorish, demanding and insufferable as well; but, in general, once disembarkation looms and tips are disbursed, stewards' tips from Americans tend to be handsomer than those from any other nationality.

By the same token, Violet apparently took to Americans at once, not only for their generosity but for their genuine warmth and consideration, patently preferable to the British and South Americans she was used to on the Royal Mail Line. We must not forget the fondness she felt as a child for the two American women who ran her school in Argentina. Additionally, she and her shipmates got to know not only Americans but America—for which read New York—as well. Today's cruise ships spend as little time in port as possible, in at dawn and out by dusk. Crewmen seldom get further east than 12th Avenue. But during long turnarounds at the North River piers in the old days, when ships had to be coaled, provisioned and loaded with fresh linen, there was ample time for stewards and stewardesses alike to explore the city and also, as Jessop did on several occasions, to extend shipboard passenger liaisons ashore.

Conversely, Americans in turn felt a special fondness for both Cunard and White Star stewards. Those dedicated company servants not only spoke English but also made it their business to be as congenial, sympathetic and efficient as possible. The traditional love affair between British crew and their American passengers was a strong one, symbiosis based for the most part on a combination of gratitude and respect.

In contrast, passengers of other nationalities expected you to hang about like beggars outside a church, waiting for alms. If they did see you, they eventually gave you a cold tip.

As long as stewards toiled uncomplainingly, very little was done by employers to alleviate difficulties. Even if a protest was made, it was ignored. It was not then surprising that conditions of work and living of the ordinary steward had undergone no improvement in years. Nothing had been done to make labor easy. Men worked sixteen hours a day, every day of the week, scrubbed and cleaned from morn till night, moved mountains of baggage, carved and served food, cleaned a host of apparently useless metalwork till their very souls seemed permeated with metal polish, and kept long watches into the night, all for hasty meals standing up in a steamy pantry where decks were awash with the droppings of the last meal. This filled me at times with discouragement.

But if companies ignored their responsibilities towards their employees, there were those among the staff who did compensate in a measure for their superiors' faults. Such a one was the head of our department. Our chief was an Irishman, a grand man. Most of us held him in awe but all and sundry were united in admiration of him. Deep down I think we all loved him. But there were days—yes, there were days—when he had his funny ways, and there were times when his usually genial self burst forth like a devastating tornado, scattering innocent and guilty alike with the force of his wrath. Nothing roused the chief to the fury of a demon quicker than stupidity.

I can see him now, standing over near the hot press in the pantry. Dinner is finished and he is about to give the order: "Clear away." He looks around, well pleased with everything, when a young stewardess comes up, and in a timid voice tells him that one of her passengers slept through the dinner hour and demands some "now."

The chief prides himself on his dinners, on their being done justice to, being eaten as they should be, freshly cooked. His gaze quickly takes in what remains in the press, and his experienced mind makes a quick calculation as he turns to the girl and says, "Well, I can get the clear soup heated, and the sole too, then there is the capon, that will stand heating too. Yes, I think we can give Mrs. Dennison a nice dinner. Please tell her what I recommend, will you?" with a benign smile.

Less than five minutes elapses and the girl, looking scared, returns to say that Mrs. Dennison indignantly refuses to have a "reheated dinner," whereupon the chief lets out one of his rare yells, which never failed to attract an admiring and awestruck audience. Throwing up his arms, he cries: "My God, my God, woman, did you tell her I was having this food reheated?" "Yes, I did, sir," quakingly admits the stewardess.

Another bellow is forthcoming, jingling all the cups and toast-racks hanging above his head. He turns to her denouncingly and, pointing an accusing finger, eyes blazing, he commands her: "Go away, go out of my sight! Reheated food indeed, what a woman! Go, never let me see you again, pack your box and go at once."

Crushed, the girl escapes from the pantry. If she has any reasoning power left by then, she is wondering how she can obey orders and get out of the ship in mid-ocean.

The chief often sacked a man in the middle of a trip, told him to be gone and never, under any circumstances, to show himself again. But on docking day, the man emerged from the place where he had hidden during the remainder of the voyage. When he presented himself to draw his pay and pass by the "signing on" table, a voice would ring out: "Jones, where are you going? Why aren't you signing, can't you see we are all in a hurry to get home?"

The man meekly reminded him: "Not signing, sir."

"Not *signing*, Jones?" shouted the chief. "What in hell do you mean, not *signing*? Who told you you were not to sign?"

Jones, by then utterly bewildered, believing his own mind had played him false, would reply: "You did, sir." To which an incredulous query would come: "I did, Jones? How dare you say I said such a thing! You sign in your proper place at once, and don't hold up the whole ship's crew."

No one was more tender-hearted or charitable to those in need than he was; all the lame dogs came to him. The Little Sisters of the Poor knew their visit would be well rewarded as they came hurrying on board with their big baskets; they made straight for his office on docking day, leaving some time later with smiling faces and full hampers, carried proudly for them by ship's pageboys, to feed many old men and women for a few more days of their sad old age.

The chief was clever—a cleverness that detects without cunning—as well as bluff and hearty without being coarse; his spontaneous kindness contained not one iota of hypocrisy. He had weaknesses too—he was married no less than three times and reared three families. A pretty face or trim ankle never escaped his eye and yet his admiration was so restrained that it never caused offense. He just could not help being attracted by feminine charms.

He had a big, good-natured laugh, a grand manner and a magnificent approach. When you came under his jurisdiction, he was both interested in you and concerned about you so everyone felt absolutely natural and at ease in his presence. There was nothing mean or petty about his nature; no matter in what part of the ship you unexpectedly met that huge striding figure, with coat flapping as he walked and feet that were planted as if they were meant to stay down, you felt you were never suspected of being "out of bounds." You went unchallenged by him, in striking contrast to some of his subordinates. When the light went out of those fine, honest eyes, many a steward on the North Atlantic lost a staunch friend.

When the day's tasks were over, I sought out Ma Maine in the second class. She always provided me with fresh courage and a good deal of fun.

I can see her now, her portly figure wheezingly making its way to do somebody's bidding. Her face was blotched with years of strain and toil, through sleepless nights tossed on stormy seas in creaking, leaking, rolling ships where she had put up the good fight for many years.

No sign of beauty left, though there were those on board who knew her in her youth and who never tired of describing the spirited girl with the lovely dark curls who was the gayest in the district until the day the ocean claimed her young husband and left her to be the breadwinner for their two children.

Here she was, doing her work to the best of her ability, not smart, only considered good enough for the second class, her dark curls gone now, replaced by a wig that was forever crooked, and which she was either too tired or too hurried to comb. Her poor old feet, always so full of aches, could just barely carry that ample form; and she wore a red flannel petticoat.

Yet, beneath that unattractive exterior beat the simplest, kindest, truest heart on the ocean. Ma never tolerated scandal and there was no looking around corners to investigate other people's business when she was about, for she was just too busy all day long minding her business of keeping others satisfied. If she did sometimes make the chief mad because she dried the babies' napkins on the egg-boiler at breakfast time, who cared? When queried about it, she would retort with a grin that he should not have had his newfangled egg-boiler placed just where she had always dried her babies' napkins, and anyway, babies' napkins were more important than eggs for breakfast!

She was one of those people who could laugh at themselves heartily and her eye had a twinkle as if she saw the humor of life a minute before anyone else. To the door of Ma's cabin would come a stream of people needing something—advice perhaps, or to pour out into a motherly ear a tale of woe or sin. They all got what they wanted and nobody but felt better afterwards.

We all knew her likes—they were few—but a bottle of stout was her "standby." You would often see a youth, grateful for some kindness, slip into Ma's cabin and quietly pop a bottle under her pillow, for her pillow was her safe "against the time she'll need it," he would shyly explain, if he happened to know you had noticed. But you could not get Ma to drink that stout until her regular time.

At night, when her work was done, her small charges safely tucked up in their bunks and the chief's inspection over, she would sink gratefully onto a stool in her favorite corner and enjoy her simple meal of bread, cheese and stout. "No frills about my supper," she used to remark if you tried to tempt her with some dainty dish from the first class saloon.

I used to love to drop in on her, knowing I was welcome, and hear from her some of the incidents that had colored her early life at sea. One night I have in mind, it was very rough. The wind was lash-ing the sea into a boiling cauldron and pounding on the ship's beam, making her list badly.

"This reminds me of the night old man Robinson died; did you ever hear what happened to me that night?" Ma asked.

"No, Ma, but I'd love to hear it now, if you are not too tired to tell me," I replied.

"Well, it was terrible weather for days, just like this, and old man Robinson, poor soul, got worse and worse. His poor wife got so worried that she nearly drove herself and us crazy too. The doctor did his best, but gave little hope, as his was an old complaint and he was too far gone. They had one of the good cabins, but were traveling without servants and had no help but what we could give.

"I did all I could to help the doctor and comfort the wife till Sunday morning. When we were about mid-Atlantic, in the worst weather I'd ever experienced, he died. His wife was broken-hearted and could do nothing but sob and carry on, so it fell to me to lay the body out. I've always been good at laying bodies out, you know.

"Old Mrs. Tims was my mate then, but bless you, she was as scared as could be. The doctor was going to embalm and fix the corpse when the weather eased down a bit, for Mrs. Robinson wanted it taken home. In the meantime, she insisted on him being laid out in his own cabin, she having been put in another. But she would not allow him to be left alone. She wanted a sort of wake but would not remain with him herself.

"To satisfy the poor woman so that she could get a little rest, I promised I would stay there all night. Mind you, I don't want you to think I liked a job like that, because I didn't. I just plain hated it. However, I fixed myself up for the night, put my hair in curlers—I had my own hair then—and was about to go along to the other cabin, when Mrs. Tims, sort of kind-hearted like, came in and said she didn't mind sitting with me for an hour or so, but she thought we ought to have a drop of gin to keep the chill out and our spirits up a bit.

"I've never cared for gin. It's a bit too strong for me. But my bottle of stout went west in the mess the ship made when she lurched, so I took a drop of her gin, hot and sweet, and we went along to keep watch.

"The corpse looked real lovely, it did, all fixed nicely on the bunk. He had been a big, heavy man, so we had taken away the leeboard from the side of the bunk to give him more room when he was ill.

"Old Ma Tims and I got stools and fixed ourselves as comfortable as you can be so near a corpse and all. There was not much room for the both of us, as the trunks had been arranged in the free space so they would not go falling over when the ship rolled, and we were obliged to sit nearer the corpse than I liked. The conversation naturally turned to dead folks and ghosts and such like, which made us feel a bit creepy, so I was quite willing when Ma Tims suggested another drop of gin.

"She was just replacing the bottle in the top of her stocking when there was a fearful groan from the corpse. Ma Tims jumped up and made for the door with her eyes popping, and the ship gave a terrific roll and I overbalanced. As I did so, the corpse, with another awful groan, rolled off the bunk on top of me.

"I yelled with terror but could not move in the small space I was wedged into. That heavy weight was keeping me down. I could just see Ma Tims from where I lay; she must have fainted right away as she tried to open the door.

"Well, I screamed and screamed, and suddenly I started laughing and screaming. That brought the night-watchman, and you should have seen his face when he saw us: Me with my hair in curlers, the poor corpse lying on top of me, and Ma Tims like another corpse by the door! He looked more scared than ever when I started laughing.

"It took three of them to get old man Robinson back in the bunk and lashed down but I didn't finish the night with him, I can tell you. I'd had enough wake for one night. Ah! that was a night, big guns were nowhere in it. And they tell you sea life is a grand life," said Ma Maine with a thoughtful grin.

This is vintage Violet. The whole chapter gives us an incomparable flavor of backstage life aboard *Majestic*. Anent the heart-of-gold chief steward who could not tolerate ineptitude: I wonder whether she was, in fact, the "timid young stewardess." Her use of the present tense makes me think she might have been.

And Ma Maine's comforting yarns over her nightly stout are pure gold. The hilarious account of old man Robinson's corpse hurled from the bunk onto the hapless women keeping their gin-soaked vigil is too extraordinary a saga to have been invented.

# CHAPTER

# 16

# Cabin Drama

THEY BOARDED THE ship at Cherbourg, appearing simultaneously at the door of cabin 59 to claim their respective bunks. They looked at each other with that searching curiosity that people betray who are going to be thrown together in very close proximity for a time, an intimacy that may reveal their most obscure characteristics.

Somber brown eyes in a studious young face weighed up a blue-eyed, good-natured, whisky-soda face of a middle-aged American, and evidently found it to his satisfaction. A cordial exchange of names took place while luggage, the traveler's bugbear, was being deposited in the cabin. Each explained at some length and in unison to the harassed bedroom steward details and markings by which their particular possessions might be distinguished among the conglomerate mountain of baggage on deck, where a multitude of perspiring and agitated stewards, each striving to follow similar minute particulars, were trying to retrieve some piece that appeared for the moment to be at the bottom of the pile.

He of the solemn face was not so worried about his belongings as his companion. In fact, he did not seem to mind much when they were delivered, thereby endearing himself to the over-burdened steward. He further showed his indifference to his comfort by omitting to go down to dinner and was acclaimed by the steward as "some blood" when he handed him a substantial tip, failed to blame him for the imperfections of the ship and courteously declined the steward's suggestion that he take a "bite" in his cabin.

"No, thanks, I was going to turn in," he replied with a longing look at his top bunk, "and be a nuisance to no one." Meanwhile, his companion was away on a voyage of exploration.

They won at once the sobriquet of "Gay Dog" and "Sobersides." Evidently Gay Dog found life decidedly good after a couple of doubles, a full-course dinner, the clinging company of a charming, diminutive *midinette* from the Rue St. Honoré "going for sea business to New York" and, most important of all, complete absence of the usual card sharps in the smoking room.

He missed Sobersides, however, and being a thoroughly matey person, liked to share pleasant things, with the possible exception of the little *midinette*. He tunefully hummed his way down to the cabin in search of him.

There he was, not asleep it is true, but strangely unwilling to enter into conversation, in spite of his room-companion's overtures and cheerful commentary on the good and bad points of the ship. Sobersides was just not interested, silent, lying there immobile with the bedclothes drawn up to his mouth in a most unsociable way.

Feeling slightly rebuffed "and at the start of the trip, by a fellow sharing the same cabin, dammit!" Gay Dog dashed off to refresh his subdued spirits with another double; then, two doubles being still more satisfactory, he downed them too.

Lights began to waver for him, then go out. Having failed to amuse the *midinette* and being conscious of the staring, patient eyes of the exhausted smoke-room steward waiting to close for the night, Gay Dog decided that bed was the place.

Being really a kindly fellow, he decided in his hazy state not to disturb Sobersides and so refrained from switching on the light. After all, undressing in the dark was an easy matter, when he only needed to deposit his clothes on the deck, for a willing steward to pick up in the morning. And so to bed, well satisfied.

Tossing a bit in the narrow space—for sleep, that elusive jade, did not come easily—he ruminated on the perversity of stewards who seldom make a bed guaranteed to keep a man's body from freezing on one side, when suddenly he was conscious that his nose was wet and somewhat sticky; why and how, he wondered.

He ignored it, however, and started counting sheep and his wife's hats, when he felt more moisture dripping on him. Alarmed lest this satisfactory ship had sprung a leak on sailing day, he had no alternative but to switch on the light. He discovered he was covered in blood.

Agitatedly calling out to his companion to help him solve the mystery, and getting no response, he saw that Sobersides was staring at the ceiling, rigidly impassive with a look of almost aloof indifference, having unobtrusively bled to death by his own hand.

More *Grand Guignol* humor from the dark side of shipboard. Jessop spins an engaging yarn and one that might well have occurred, either aboard *Majestic* or indeed on any ship on any ocean in the world.

A memorial pendant that was among Violet's most prized possessions. This pendant appears to be unique, presumably a gift from the White Star Line to crew members. *(Marilyn Skopal)*

RMS *Titanic* outbound from Southampton on the afternoon of April 10th, 1912. Somewhere below decks, Stewardess Jessop is busy within her section of first class cabins. *(Beken of Cowes)*

CERTIFICATE 17 : 18 OF DISCHARGE.

| No. | Name of ship and official number, Port of registry, and tonnage. | Date and place of engagement. | Rating; and R.N.R. No. (if any). | Date and place of discharge. | Description of voyage. | Signature of Master. |
|---|---|---|---|---|---|---|
| 25 | Titanic 131428 Liverpool - 21831 Southampton | 10 Apr 1912 Southampton | Stewardess | 15 Apr 1912 At Sea | Intended New York | Extracted from Agreement 15th inst New York. Registrar General 15th May 1912. |
| 26 | OLYMPIC Official No. 131346 LIVERPOOL Tonnage 20894:20. | 5 JUN 1912 SOUTHAMPTON. | STEWARDESS | 22 JUN 1912 SOUTHAMPTON. | NEW YORK. | |
| 27 | OLYMPIC Official No. 131346 LIVERPOOL Tonnage 20894:20. | 26 JUN 1912 SOUTHAMPTON. | STEWARDESS | 13 JUL 1912 SOUTHAMPTON. | NEW YORK. | |
| 28 | OLYMPIC Official No. 131346 LIVERPOOL Tonnage 20894:20. | 17 JUL 1912 SOUTHAMPTON. | STEWARDESS | 3 AUG 1912 SOUTHAMPTON. | NEW YORK. | |
| 29 | OLYMPIC Official No. 131346 LIVERPOOL Tonnage 20894:20. | 7 AUG 1912 SOUTHAMPTON. | STEWARDESS | 24 AUG 1912 PLYMOUTH NEW YORK | NEW YORK. | |
| 30 | OLYMPIC Official No. 131346 LIVERPOOL Tonnage 20894:20. | 29.8.12 | STEWARDESS | 14 SEP 1912 SOUTHAMPTON. | NEW YORK | |

* These columns are to be filled in at time of engagement.

† In Engineers' Books insert Horse Power.

680439

Voyage 25 from Violet's Certificate of Discharge memorializes *Titanic*'s only voyage, "Intended New York." Note how the date of discharge is written "15 Apr, 1912, At Sea," clipped bureaucratese for that fearful disaster. *(Marilyn Skopal)*

HMS *Audacious*, her port decks awash, sinking off the Irish coast. Lifeboats from nearby RMS *Olympic* are taking off Royal Naval personnel. *(John Maxtone-Graham collection)*

Hospital ship *Britannic* seen from astern at Southampton. *(Imperial War Museum)*

| No. | Name of ship and official number, Port of registry, and tonnage. | Date and place of engagement. | Rating; and R.N.R. No. (if any). | CERTIFICATE OF DISCHARGE from Eng. I. and O.L. | | | |
|---|---|---|---|---|---|---|---|
| | | | | Date and place of discharge. | Description of voyage. | Signature of Master. | CONTRACT FROM AGREEMENT. |
| 1 | Britannic 1874190 Soton 24592. | 13/11/16 Soton | Stewardess | 6/1/17 Soton | Hospital Ship. | (signed) Chas. A. Bartlett MASTER. | |
| 2 | OLYMPIC 131346 LIVERPOOL 22850. | SOUTHAMPTON 15 JUN 1920 | Stewardess | 15 JUL 1920 SOUTHAMPTON NEW YORK | NEW YORK | R.H. Hayes | |
| 3 | OLYMPIC 131346 LIVERPOOL 22850. | SOUTHAMPTON 21 JUL 1920 STEWARDESS | | SOUTHAMPTON. 11 AUG 20 | NEW YORK | R.H. Hayes | |
| 4 | OLYMPIC 181346 LIVERPOOL 22850 | 18 AUG 1920 SOUTHAMPTON Stewardess | | 4 - SEP 1920 NEW YORK SOUTHAMPTON. | NEW YORK | R.H. Hayes | |
| 5 | OLYMPIC 181846 LIVERPOOL 22850 | 8 - SEP 1920 SOUTHAMPTON. STEWARDESS | | 2 5 SEP 1920 NEW YORK SOUTHAMPTON | NEW YORK | R.H. Hayes | |
| 6 | OLYMPIC 131346 LIVERPOOL 22350. | 29 SEP 1920 SOUTHAMPTON Stewardess | | 16 OCT 1920 NEW YORK SOUTHAMPTON. | NEW YORK | R.H. Hayes | |

*These columns are to be filled in at time of engagement.

† In Engineers' Books insert Horse Power.

909I17

Violet's Certificate of Discharge records her sole voyage aboard *Britannic*. Note that her discharge entry is dated January 6th, 1917, the day Distressed British Seaman Jessop finally landed in the United Kingdom. *(Marilyn Skopal)*

On her final voyage to Moúdros, *Britannic* passes battleship HMS *Lord Nelson* and Admiral's yacht *Triad*. *(Imperial War Museum)*

A crowd of *Britannic* survivors—wounded Violet *not*, alas, among them—poses on the foc's'le head of an unnamed Royal Navy cruiser. *(Imperial War Museum)*

## AUTHORITY TO WEAR
## WAR MEDALS FOR THE MERCANTILE MARINE,
### Awarded by H.M. The King
through the Board of Trade

*Violet Constance Jessop*

(Dis. A No. *90911* ) R.S. 2 No. .....................) is authorised to wear the undermentioned medals and ribbons against which the signature of a Board of Trade officer and an official stamp have been affixed.

Marine Dept.,
Board of Trade.

C. HIPWOOD,
*Assistant Secretary.*

| | Authorised. | Signature of Superintendent of issuing M.M.O. with office stamp | |
|---|---|---|---|
| British War Medal ribbon | 4·12·19 | Smith | |
| Mercantile Marine Medal ribbon | 4·12·19 | Smith | 4 DEC 1919 |
| British War Medal (and clasp) | 30·10·23 | | |
| Mercantile Marine Medal | 30·10·23 | Mulhollaston | 30 OCT 1923 |

545ys) (63122) Wt. G512 100,000 1·19 W B & L

*Signature of holder:* *Violet C. Jessop*

Official authorization for Violet Jessop to wear wartime decorations.
*(Marilyn Skopal)*

*Olympic* outbound from New York on a winter crossing in the twenties.
*(John Maxtone-Graham collection)*

An aerial view of the Southampton docks in August 1923. *Olympic* and *Homeric* share the ocean dock while Cunard's *Aquitania* is confined within the floating dock behind them. When this photograph was taken, Violet was in mid-ocean aboard *Majestic*. (*John Maxtone-Graham collection*)

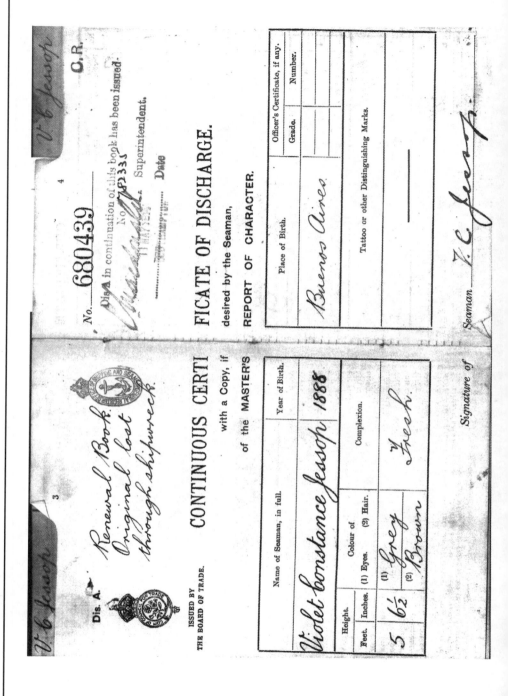

Title page of Violet's renewal book for her Certificate of Discharge, the original having been lost. Note that Violet has advanced the date of her birth by one year! *(Marilyn Skopal)*

CHAPTER

# 17

## *Olympic*

ALTHOUGH I HAD always had uncommon energy and endurance, I alternated between hope that I might be able to stand up to the heavy work and despair that in the end it would overcome me. I could not help wondering why anyone chose such a means to gain a living, and was then faced with the hard truth— money!

But hope plays a tremendous part in the life of the average seaman and I was no exception: Some day, some time, things would be better, something good would come my way. However, when tempting posts were offered me, as they often were by impetuous or appreciative people, I hesitated to accept, on the principle that "the devil you know is better than the devil you don't." Besides, I had often seen how colorless, cramped and slavish the life was of people who traveled with their employers in what the world would term enviable positions.

I never felt sure that promises, however seemingly sincere when made, would materialize eventually. For people, I soon discovered, forget, after they have got over the stress of a voyage, the gratitude and the urge to compensate for services rendered. It is only human, I suppose, but nevertheless often leaves a heartache where hope was once raised. Money cannot repay for certain services, whereas remembering them would.

On the last day of a recent *QE2* crossing, my wife and I were chatting with one of the jam boys, as the most junior commis waiters in the Queen's Grill are called. We asked the young man (in his late teens) how long he had been with Cunard.

"Only a year," he confessed, "and I'm signing off at the end of this voyage." A passenger couple from Palm Beach had taken a shine to him and asked him to come and work for them at home.

I have often wondered since how that arrangement worked out. Apparently, impulsive American passengers are still adopting British stewards who please them. Similar offers were made to Violet Jessop, according to the paragraphs above, and I also wonder, had she accepted, whether "the devil you don't know" would have appealed.

I sense it would not for a very sound reason. When seamen swallow the anchor—as going ashore is called—they must adjust to life without the close shipboard family that obtains aboard all passenger vessels. However scant their privacy, however long the hours, however onerous the chores and however demanding the passengers, once their shipboard duties are finished, crewmen and women are sustained by an irreplaceable, below-stairs camaraderie in compensation.

Though seamen crave leave at home, that steel beehive—as someone once described *Aquitania*—is their other home. Inside it, they are linked to their shipmates by profound bonds, inhabitants of a coherent, shipwide community into which no passenger, however esteemed or frequently booked, is ever admitted. And it is precisely that network of support and companionship that I expect that exiled jam boy will miss in the solitary gloom of his Palm Beach servants' wing.

By the same token, had Jessop accepted one of the many passenger proposals, either for marriage or indenture, I think she would have experienced the same keen deprivation. Additionally, one great advantage of her cyclical, seaborne peregrinations were that they periodically brought her back to her family.

For us just then, the mecca of better times was the prospect of a "new ship." As is always the case at sea, rumors and exaggerations about her were rife, but no one denied she would be a paragon. The great day came when *Olympic* finally became a fact, the "largest and finest" to fly the British flag. [The date was June of 1911.] A crew, hand-picked from every ship in the line, was assembled for muster on sailing day, feeling proud of the honor of being chosen but trying to hide it under a nonchalance that was only too obvious.

She came up to all our expectations and I sensed at once she was going to be a kindly ship, for all ships have a character of their own which some people, more sensitive than others, are quick to realize. That is why there are happy ships, while others have a definitely depressing atmosphere.

The *Olympic* had been designed by one of the finest and kindliest of men it has been my privilege to meet: Tommy Andrews, designer for Harland and Wolff, the Belfast shipbuilder, was loved and respected throughout the fleet by everyone from the lowliest scullion to the "old man" as a real gentleman.

I sometimes think that maybe he imparted some of his generous personality into the ship he had lovingly designed. During the maiden voyage, the staff—especially the victualing department—took the opportunity to thank him personally. We presented him with a magnificent walking stick—he suffered martyrdom from varicose veins, brought on by years of standing about and walking on miles of ships' decks. We wanted to show our appreciation of his persistent efforts to get the men better accommodations, a consideration that was customarily of secondary importance. For instance, *Olympic* was the first ship to have proper bathrooms installed for stewards. The fact that they were soon afterwards taken over by the second steward as storerooms, forcing the men to revert to the inevitable bucket for a washdown, is neither here nor there!

When a new ship is "finding" herself, especially a big one, the process is somewhat of an education. It often causes a few heartaches and, though all have the knowledge that they are not alone in their ignorance or bewilderment in getting acquainted with new surroundings, 98% of the passengers expect the same prompt service they would get on an old ship.

I felt this as I answered the impatient summonses and encountered the haughty, gimlet eyes of a certain well-known society woman, ten minutes after the boat train arrived. Having looked me over while she minutely detailed her orders for the entire week—to commence at that very moment—she proceeded to enumerate her various ailments and their treatment. She was not the least bit reserved concerning the irregularities of her natural functions, for which I was expected to show a deep concern.

There was no word of praise or sympathy for any of us who had put in long hours getting the ship ready to sail, and I knew instinctively that no quarter would be given me if, during the recital of these boring details (which I had alas, heard often before), she caught my wandering eye stray disapprovingly through the studied gloom of shaded lights she always affected, to the beautiful bed with its real lace spread on which reposed, with contemptuous air, her favorite Pekinese, her precious "teeny weeny."

She anticipated any gentle reproving suggestion I might have had the temerity to make by reminding me, "I am a friend of the president of this line," which seemed to say, "look out." The few years I had been in the service of the White Star Line, I could look back on thousands of "friends of the president of the line." An unfortunate man with so many friends and relations.

These were almost outdone by the legion that claimed kinship with the Pilgrims. It was sufficient to have an English accent, which appealed to them, to be told with pride that their ancestors had come over on the *Mayflower*, necessitating a complete revision regarding the capacity of that modest barque. Perhaps it was pardonable, showing by its very simplicity how proud of their English forebears Americans are.

I got a fresh thrill every time I went through *Olympic*'s beautiful staterooms, the Adams room, the Regency room, the Dutch, Georgian and so on, with their exquisite woodwork and sumptuous silk furnishings. I have always maintained that never before or since have such materials of so perfect a quality been used to fit out any ship. The names of all the "best families" appeared on the passenger list, eager as all Americans are "to be there."

Hardly had we got our bearings about the ship, when we had to brace ourselves for arrival in New York. Any docking day is nerve-racking apart from the work, with the sheer enthusiasm expended everywhere. We knew the excitement would be unprecedented and that our early morning arrival off quarantine would be more hectic than usual.

We were not mistaken. Bells rang from a very early hour. Strident and excited voices demanded food, for everybody aimed to be ready to greet their friends with an air of complete assurance as if to impress them that this successful maiden crossing was partly their personal achievement; we mere slaves obeyed instantly to assist them in the illusion. I've so often watched travelers assume that attitude.

It did not help the nervous tension to hear bells impatiently ringing while we stood at attention in a row, mustering for the quarantine doctor's inspection, which was unduly protracted owing to the size of the crew. Passengers may make a hundred trips and know this inspection takes place regularly, in fact see the crew mustering, yet they will go straight to their rooms and ring their bells.

At last the ship got her clean bill of health and proceeded majestically up the Hudson, flag bedecked and gay, fussily escorted by all manner of official and unofficial small craft, up past the huge buildings on Battery Park, the wharves and ships, all of which appeared to shimmer with the moving, cheering mass of people gathered together. Not a window, however small, but had a little flag or handkerchief waving from it, as we slowly passed on to the accompaniment of shrill tootings of greetings from everything afloat that had a whistle to blow.

As we neared the dock, many haughty-looking tugs (for tugs always have impressed me with that appearance, carrying their heads in the air) came to meet us, thrusting their noses into the side of the great hulk, puffing frantically as they pushed her into her berth. Her bows came to rest within a few inches of the dock wall and so the proud ship came successfully to port.

Then pandemonium took possession for two whole days. Panting visitors rubber-necked everywhere. It was futile trying to keep them within certain limits and to cut short their innumerable and sometimes ridiculous questions, to which we were quite at a loss for answers. (All Americans are refreshingly eager for information of any kind, which explains why they are generally much better informed on general subjects than we are.)

On the second night, a dinner was given to 600 White Star agents from all over the United States. Men of every size and age appeared, prepared to enjoy wholeheartedly the lavish hospitality White Star was offering them. All that evening and well into the night, they were being conducted around (between drinks) to inspect various parts of the ship. As the hours wore on, both they and their steward escorts—by now more or less on a brotherly footing—began to show signs of wear.

At 3 a.m., there was a lull in the convivial din, after which men were found sprawling asleep in the most out of the way places: Inside baths and half under beds, where they seemingly had dropped in their tracks, giving the impression it was not an unfamiliar place for them. Others wandered aimlessly about, apparently lost and muttering for some guiding soul to rescue them.

It took many hours to reunite coats, hats and shoes with their rightful owners but everyone voted the *Olympic* and its crew "swell." The surprise was she was not burnt to the water's edge, seeing the masses of cigarette and cigar ends swept up next day, and the burnt patches that could not be swept up.

If arrival day was devastating, sailing day was a nightmare. Any sailing day conjures up in the mind of the average steward a special type of purgatory, quite unimagined by anyone who has not taken part, and which explains the reason so many have to reinforce themselves with Dutch courage at the bar, from an early hour.

All was spic-and-span now for the return voyage, from the huge pantry with the presiding pantryman—who looked like one of the twelve Apostles, and had some of their wisdom—to the "top side" where all was shipshape. But everywhere there was tension.

As the passengers began to arrive, the volume of noise increased to a crescendo that seemed as if it could only end in madness. With us, it was a strange medley of human feelings—tiredness, soul weariness, and expectancy of one knew not what. And from the prospective passengers, devastating leave-takings and unrestrained emotions, voices trying to rise above each other, screaming commonplace injunctions. That babble even blotted out thought, as perspiring masses of smartly dressed, over-scented humanity surged together; yet here and there, a really silent and pathetic farewell was taking place.

Everybody was totally oblivious to the distracted stewards vainly attempting to move enormous pieces of baggage through the crush. Those in charge shouted orders and room bells rang impatiently for drinks, while the stewardesses' additional bugbear—flowers to arrange—arrived with the regularity of snowflakes. Boxes of every size were piled mountain-high. The fact that they were in boxes saved them from utter destruction.

It is puzzling to understand how otherwise considerate and thinking people fail to imagine what can possibly be done with the vast and expensive quantities of flowers they insist on sending departing friends. At times there might be as many as seventeen boxes for one person. In the confined spaces of a ship with always an inadequate supply of receptacles to arrange them in, it is and always has been a sailing day horror for stewardesses. Though most folks love flowers and I myself could not live without them, you need to love them extraordinarily well to survive a day like that. When the quantity assumes alarming proportions, there is a great temptation to give them, as stewards say, "passage" through the open port.

Often you'd meet a soul along an alleyway, looking for a friend at the last moment to say farewell. Failing to find them, they'd leave a message with you: "Tell her goodbye for me, and I've sent her flowers," as if this was really original and wonderful. Once, in desperation, I responded, "Next time send her books. That is the most acceptable gift for a voyage, unless it is one's last voyage," and was rewarded with a stare.

A newcomer to this job has my sincere sympathy when she answers a bell on sailing day and is asked for "eight or ten vases please," and "bring me some very tall ones too." As "eight or ten" was the usual allotment for a stewardess' entire section, severely limited by the company, and as no vase was ever more than twelve inches high, this order never failed to strike dismay into a novice's heart. With Americans, one has to cut the stems of their precious "American Beauty" roses with kid gloves, as it were, for they consider it almost sacrilege for these roses, grown apparently for the length of their stems, to be reduced.

My roommate came from the north of Ireland, and was new in the company. Most people referred to her as a girl though in reality she was seventeen years my senior. I think this was because of her attitude to life, her irresponsible—at times helpless—but often charming ways. She had suffered some kind of private sorrow which apparently left her absent-minded and forgetful. It was sufficient to address her suddenly for her to completely forget what she had been thinking of. She'd walk with a mincing sort of step, half-running along the alleyways as close to the bulkhead as possible, which earned her the nickname "Go-by-the-wall-and-tickle-the-bricks."

The men were not long in discovering her little peculiarities, especially if accosted suddenly. Some would deliberately pop out and wish her "good morning" briskly. She'd stop dead, put her hand to her head and exclaim: "Ah, indeed, indeed, you've made me forget the order I've just taken. I don't know whether Number 18 ordered a chop or a steak. I'll give her a steak." Most of us would have been reported for incompetence.

It was her look of complete childish innocence that was so disarming. She would use it on me whenever I reproved her for waking me in the night by dropping almonds and raisins on my face from the top bunk. She preferred to eat in bed and always after midnight. When reminded of this next morning she would answer softly, fluttering her eyelids and exclaiming in a consoling tone, "Poor, poor dear, did I wake you now? When could that have been?"

A man came to me once, looking for her months after she had left, and said, rather tactlessly I thought: "Where is that very young stewardess who roomed with you once?" As I was the youngest in the ship for quite some time, and had several changes of roommate, I was momentarily puzzled, and asked for a description. He could not give one (she was difficult to describe) except that he repeated: "Oh, she was years younger than you." Then I suddenly knew.

With all her irresponsibility, untidiness, and youngish looks, she managed to get to the United States during the war and land herself a job in a good family, as a trained nurse at a large salary. She then got herself an elderly and wealthy husband. She was rather reticent about admitting this to me years later, probably because she felt that I was one of the very few people who knew she was a fraud.

Neither scenes of splendor nor stress of work will let your forget your problems; my own just then loomed very large. A mute reminder was on my settee—a large box of red roses, whose donor I was never to see again.

While in New York, I had received an urgent summons to the sickbed of a man who I thought was well and happy in Cuba. A charming person, old enough to be my father, with a genial, reliable personality, he managed a shipping company and had his own private estate in Cuba. Once while I was convalescing from malaria during my first months at sea, he had given me some reading matter. Later he wrote me some friendly letters, via the company, to which I had replied in a newsy way.

I was therefore surprised and embarrassed when I visited him in a beautiful private room, filled with flowers—"only business tokens," he told me—in a New York hospital, and received a proposal of marriage. He explained simply that he had felt unable to ask so intimate a question by letter and had therefore waited two long years to ask it personally.

His chivalrous modesty touched me deeply, for I could see he was very much in earnest and was counting on my acceptance. In neither his nor my letters had there ever been the vaguest suggestion of anything beyond mere friendly gossip. He had even built a new house, which he had with great consideration decided I should choose the furniture for.

Two things I had never contemplated doing: Either marrying a man as old as my father or marrying for money. Today, it seems novel that anyone could ever have had such scruples. It was very difficult to refuse so nice a person, for whom I had the greatest respect and admiration. But even had I cared sufficiently, it would have been difficult to accept immediately, since I had very great responsibilities to shoulder at home. I could neither see myself relinquishing them at a moment's notice nor discussing with anyone outside the family the affairs of my home life.

I found it extremely difficult then to talk about anything of a private or personal nature with a living soul except my mother, and I still am dumbfounded today at the readiness of people to detail the most intimate affairs of their lives to strangers. I returned to the ship feeling very depressed.

Sometimes, however, when passengers became particularly obnoxious or some member of the staff more objectionable than usual, I would think of the easy way out, the alluring temptation of a stately home in Cuba where a cool porch overlooked a sun-drenched garden by the sea. But then I remembered a greasy overalled figure and a pair of mischievous blue eyes, crinkling as they looked across the distance, from the deck of a battered, red-rusted tramp steamer.

It was only after completing this chapter that I realized the significance of something Violet told me years ago. She was apparently famous on board her later ships for her love of tramp steamers, the rustier and more derelict the better. Fellow crewmen, she recalled, used to summon her to the railing whenever one came over the horizon.

Suddenly, that curious predilection makes sense: For tramp steamer read Ned. He would leave passenger liners for bulk carriers and, for Violet, I sense that the wistful apparition of a "battered, red-rusted tramp steamer" simply evoked Ned.

CHAPTER

# 19

# Polemic and Lament

THIS CHAPTER, COMING on the heels of the missing chapter 18, is a rambling diatribe about several of Violet's *bêtes noires*—the victimization, hopelessness and greed of her fellow stewards, the despotism of their immediate superiors, the benign neglect of the owners, the indifference of passenger tippers, the evils of beer, and the unsuitability of sea life for women.

Tilting at too many windmills, Violet Jessop undertakes an almost impossible task, trying to sort out the cross-currents, perceived injustices and options of her shipmates in the victualing department. The emotional thrusts of her arguments embrace a fine confusion of attitudes, from pity to scorn, condemning them here and excusing them there, suggesting they cannot be helped yet hoping someone will. This is clearly a subject about which Violet felt strongly.

We must keep in mind that this chapter was written in the early 1930's, long after the earlier events and colored by a dour recapitulation of her career thus far at sea. I find it hard to equate the middle-aged voice of chapter 19 with the contemporary excitement she must have felt as a young girl having just completed her first and obviously very successful year aboard brand-new *Olympic*.

Margaret Meehan, one of Jessop's nieces, concurs, characterizing chapter 19 succinctly and accurately as "one long moan." She goes on to suggest that her mother remembers that, as a young woman, Violet was extremely "sweet-natured. One can only assume that her hard life at sea, with no prospect of change, had a souring effect on her good nature. We remember her as demanding, with very high standards, which could make her critical. But with all that, a loving and generous personality with a great zest for life. She was fun to be with, as I think you'll agree . . ."

I found Margaret's evaluation reassuring for the impression left by much of the material that follows eclipses her aunt's customarily sunny disposition.

I have taken the liberty of extracting and assembling within some final paragraphs all the scattered references to the disadvantages of sea life for a woman.

Years of propinquity convinced me that stewards are extroverts; this was specially borne in on me during my first year in a large liner. This was why they lacked equanimity when confronted with difficult mental situations that might affect their jobs adversely; as a result, they completely lost self-confidence.

The nice ones joined a ship, abided a while, loathed it and tried to leave. But if their financial obligations were so pressing that they had to remain on board, they stayed and the disintegration of their character began slowly but surely.

Had employers consciously set themselves out to kill the spirit of their men, they could not have succeeded more effectively. I have always felt there could never be real joy in a ship's job, apart from senior or executive positions, because there was too much regimentation and too little consideration for the dignity of the individual. Any initiative was usually quashed and the presumptuous ones viewed with distrust or suspicion.

In material things, these shipmates of mine were very honest. Few were thieves, though there was ample opportunity. Among so many lost ambitions and sunken pride, I felt the utter loneliness of sea life.

When stewards, before ambition is quite killed, apply for jobs ashore, they are treated like pariahs, considered unsuitable for any work except in their own line. Yet they have had to be hard-working on board, enduring, patient and adaptable to people of varying temperament and circumstances. Finding the way barred when they try to work ashore gives them an inferiority complex, invariably hidden by bravado. It produces the kind of man who, on the slightest provocation, gets up and shouts, "Rule Britannia, Britannia rules the waves!" and then flops back into apathy.

On board ship, members of other departments—officers and engineers alike, often mediocre themselves with no particular claim to distinction—regard them with undisguised contempt.

I have seen stewards' values fluctuate according to their gains. Real unselfishness is never very noticeable in them. Those promoted to a superior position leave the sordid uphill struggle behind and forget their less fortunate brethren, whose lives they often make hell in order to maintain their own precarious place. In a case of "trouble," where strength of character is needed, they strike out at anyone threatening their position so that they might retain their post, often at the expense of a newfound victim.

Unfortunately, the jingling of coins plays too big a part in the life of the steward and he develops an uncanny gift for sizing folk up. Passengers could not put up pretense as a cloak for they were pigeon-holed from their arrival, and we were seldom mistaken.

For long stretches of time, we stewards were almost forgotten; only during long voyages were we acknowledged. For our part, we would have liked to think that the niceness of those we served was not patronage, that the memory of generous service would live long after the trip was over. But that was hardly ever so: We were the ones who went on remembering long after they had forgotten; they considered they had paid for all with a coin. With indignation I have witnessed my shipmates snarl and snap without provocation at someone who wanted to help them, simply because they dared not do so to the one who really hurt them, those who held out the almighty tip.

I can remember no steward actually lamenting that he could not improve his mind or wanting to make the effort to do so; their only ambition is to get richer. A desire for self-expression is unheard of because, throughout long years, individual initiative has been quashed, leaving hopelessness and futility behind. One rarely heard them complain that they found their work—years of bell-answering, slop-emptying, floor-washing, bed-making, tea-carrying or the trundling of baggage—monotonous or distasteful. They never realized that the very monotony had eaten like a canker into their souls, killing ambition and leaving them content to get along without exerting their minds, their bodies racked with fatigue which they assuaged with numerous beers.

Remember that the very food stewards eat was always taken standing in any available corner of a greasy pantry, amid steamy smells and nauseating, grease-strewn decks, eaten in the quickest possible time in order to get away. No wonder they were dulled to the refinements of life and never escaped the fact that they were everybody's prey.

An insult that would provoke a punch in the jaw ashore is swallowed aboard ships without retaliation, because redress is beyond reach. Any attempt would incur victimization; moreover, there is no moral courage to back it up. A case in point: A certain chief steward, who hated the even tenor of his days to be disturbed, had occasion to take to task some of his staff. In a disgruntled frame of mind, he started his lecture: "You illegitimate bastards . . ." Nobody protested. Nevertheless, such things fester in men's minds and make themselves felt in furtive little acts of meanness.

On those rare occasions when social harmony is achieved, as I later knew it on the good ship *Belgenland*, it is because of a mixed nationality crew. Under those conditions, there seems much more balance, each nationality wanting to uphold a national pride. There is more give and take, more understanding which promotes harmony. But for the most part, ship life is built up of hypocritical veneers, unrecognized on board though obvious to outsiders.

Stewards endure long stretches of either arduous work or inactivity, their existence on board composed of either too much or too little time for the job. There is no time to relieve sore, tired feet, nor daring to absent themselves to relax; they must always await somebody's pleasure. This encourages desultory, idle talk that becomes more habit than accomplishment. Though stewards seem like an agreeable fraternity, circumstances make them utterly indifferent to one another, unless they need something.

Yet however exasperating stewards' shortcomings are, perhaps they cannot be blamed for trying to circumvent the harrowing restrictions that encompass their lives.

Herewith, extracted and reassembled from the original text, Jessop's reflections on a woman's lot at sea:

I knew I would have to fight my battles alone, and without resorting to "reporting," which has always seemed to me defeatist. To maintain balance, I would have to live deep below the surface, because sea life is full of surface gestures and quite joyless mirth.

For a woman, dignity is essential to keeping one's feeling with men, however one might long to relax from it. It entails many sacrifices of simple pleasantries, sometimes a jolly companion or proffered gifts from sincere admirers. All because of possible misunderstandings which are often the cause of many injustices. Men are just as addicted to shipboard gossip as women and the distortion of the most innocent actions.

On a woman, the effect of sea life was not good. It quickly killed the real warmth of heart and the essential womanliness. As for romance, it had no chance whatsoever. One saw only its birth and dis-integration. Marriage was the greatest victim. It was no small wonder that I looked upon my homecoming with its cozy welcome as an oasis in my sea desert.

The "sea desert": those final words convey, to me, a hint of Jessop's abiding sense of loss—loss of her unsuccessful marriage, loss of her innate femininity and, always, loss of her beloved and elusive Ned.

# 20

## *Titanic*

I N THIS CHAPTER, the names of Violet Jessop's *Titanic* shipmates should arouse our keenest interest. But save for a few famous passengers, as well as the shipyard's managing director and one musician, she chose to disguise almost all other names. Perhaps her reticence is understandable for, while she was fashioning this manuscript in the early thirties, she was employed as a stewardess with the Red Star Line and obviously felt the need for discretion.

Thus, in the pages that follow, we encounter Mr. and Mrs. Isidor Straus as well as Colonel and Mrs. John Jacob Astor. But five other passengers—Marcia Spatz, the redoubtable Mrs. Cyrus Klapton, the insufferable Miss Townsend and two gamblers—have either been given pseudonyms or no name at all; neither Klapton, Spatz nor Townsend appear among *Titanic's* list of passengers. As for the gamblers, or "boat men" as they were called, Jessop chose not to identify them. As it was, boat men regularly traveled under different aliases so she might well have been unaware of their *Titanic* maiden voyage monikers.

I suspect that Klapton, Spatz and Townsend were composites of passenger types from past voyages. Insufferable *grandes dames* with Pekineses, an overabundance of luggage and too many flowers recur throughout Jessop's memoir.

Among the crew, Tommy Andrews, her great favorite, is fully identified by name, as is Jock Hume, the Scottish violinist. (A fuller treatment of *Titanic's* gallant musicians will be found at the end of chapter 22.) But the real names of the remaining mentioned crew are lost to us, with only a few tantalizing exceptions.

Crew names occurring in this and the next chapter include: Bearded Chief Pantryman Matthews; Jack Stevens, second class barman; pantry boys Tim and Peter; Jackson and Trole, bedroom stewards; the scullion identified only as Jim; her fellow steward Stanley; the library steward; the (unnamed) second steward; the good old Irish doctor, *Titanic's* senior surgeon; a deck officer she calls Mason and, new to me, Jenny, the fecund ship's cat.

The great advantage we have in deciphering crew as opposed to passenger names is that we are occasionally given a title from which we can deduce the original. To whit, *Titanic* boasted two chief pantrymen on her manifest: Wilfred Seward looked after the second class while J. Walpole was assigned to the first; so for Matthews, read Walpole. Since there is no listing for a second class bartender, Jack Stevens retains his incognito. This is a shame, really, for he was clearly an old and close friend of Jessop's.

We fare no better with tippling Trole and Jackson, scullion Jim, pantry boys Tim and Peter, flannel-foot Jones, and fellow stewardess and cabinmate Ann Turnbull. As for Mason, the officer embarking passengers in her lifeboat number 16, I suspect it was Sixth Officer James Moody, who lost his life; of the two Masons among *Titanic*'s crew, both were simple firemen.

But among the remaining quartet, we strike pay dirt. The ship's library steward was Kelland and the "yellow-faced" second steward surfaces in actuality as Hughes. And there can be no confusion whatsoever about "the good old Irish doctor"; he is clearly Surgeon William O'Laughlin (Jessop's admiration for yet another ship's surgeon is revealed). And thanks to the testimony of Seaman Archer during the American Enquiry, we learn that stewardess Mrs. Elizabeth Leather was in lifeboat #16; perhaps that was the true identity of Ann Turnbull.

Among other endearing touches I relished in this chapter is the sense of *Titanic*'s crew exploring, approving and settling into their new home: Jessop touches on the decoration of her quarters, appraises the amenities on board and with her shipmates, exhibits a genuine sense of pride about their stunning new ship. I found it interesting that *Olympic*'s maiden voyage was far more stressful than *Titanic*'s; second ships of a class invariably enter service more smoothly.

It surprised me that the *Olympic*-class's newly-installed rubberoid interior decking found little favor among the habitually foot-sore victualing staff. Another piece of information new to me was that in those days, bedroom stewards were dragooned to carve poultry at the galley hot presses (steam tables) in addition to looking after the cabins, an overlap unthinkable aboard today's cruise ships where cabin stewards and galley personnel never intrude into one another's domains.


Time flies when you are busy. Certainly the first year of *Olympic*'s life was gone before I was aware it was over, spent in the hectic rush which is typical of a new ship, until the novelty wears off and the fickle traveling public takes its fancy elsewhere.

We had not quite got our wind, nor given our poor feet a chance to recover from longer hours and the long stretch of alleyways with their unfamiliar rubber decks. Used for the first time, they played the deuce with tender feet. Then we were preparing to move again to yet another ship. Once the germ of change gets into you, there is a spirit of expectancy, unrest and uncertainty, not unpleasant but destructive to the nervous system.

Everything struck us as wonderful about this second new ship, *Titanic*. Familiar in many respects because she was to be on similar lines to our present home, but decidedly grander and improved in every way.

Perhaps we felt proprietary about this last ship because, in our small way, we were responsible for many changes and improvements. These were things of seemingly small importance to the disinterested but of tremendous help to us, improvements that would make our life aboard less arduous and make her more of a home than we had hitherto known at sea.

It was quite unusual for members of the catering department to be consulted about changes that would benefit their comforts or ease their toil. So when the designer [Thomas Andrews, naval architect and managing director of Harland and Wolff, the shipyard that designed and built the *Titanic*] paid us this thoughtful compliment, we realized it was a great privilege; our esteem for him, already high, knew no bounds.

It was therefore like a big expectant family that we joined her, each looking for his or her pet innovation. The staff, composed of men from the *Olympic* and other ships in the company—all picked crew—were delighted to find that their welfare in the matter of glory holes [traditional shipboard name for stewards' quarters] had not been overlooked. No place can be so utterly devoid of "glory," of comfort and privacy and so wretched a human habitation as the usual ship's glory hole. It was a foul place, often—nay, nearly always!—infested with bugs; a place where all that was low in men seemed to gain the upper hand.

But in this instance, they found themselves of some importance in the scheme of things. They no longer needed to be aggressive to get a hearing, and consideration was being offered them. So they responded by a spontaneous vote of thanks and a personal gift to their champion, "Tommy" Andrews of Harland and Wolff, a very humane gentleman.

Rather diffidently, they asked this always approachable man to honor them by a visit to the glory hole, which he did to receive their warm-hearted thanks. His gentle face lit up with real pleasure, for he alone understood—nobody else had bothered to understand—how deeply these men must feel to show any sentiment at all; he knew only too well their usual uncouth acceptance of most things, good or bad.

Life aboard started off smoothly. Even Jenny, the ship's cat and part of the crew, had immediately picked herself a comfortable corner;

she varied her usual Christmas routine on previous ships by present-ing *Titanic* with a litter of kittens in April.

She laid her family near Jim, the scullion, whose approval she always sought on these occasions and who gave her a warm devotion. This big, patient, overworked fellow, whose eyes did not match and whose good humor was contagious—often irritatingly so when you were not in the mood—seemed always to need something to be kind to.

But Jim was quieter than usual and somewhat distracted that trip. He had left behind a slip of a wife, generally as cheerful as himself but on this occasion annoyingly anxious that he should not join the new ship's crew. There was a reason of course: The first and most impor-tant baby in the world was due to arrive soon. He did so want to give in to her wish for she demanded so little of him, but there was the one-roomed home to keep going, so Jim sailed on *Titanic*, with a promise to bring a beautiful baby set from New York.

Eagerly we joined the new ship—hundreds of curious eyes, each looking for what interested them most. Yes, there was my bunk placed the way I had suggested for privacy and there was the separate, though small, wardrobe for my companion and myself, one of the im-measurable blessings when two people of absolutely different tastes have to live together in a confined space. No longer would there be anxiety as to whether a companion's clothes bore testimony of her de-votion to whisky and smoke.

Ann Turnbull, my present companion, was the last person in the world I would accuse of that. She was a staid, placid good soul, most restful and of a certain dry wit, a wit that bore not a trace of malice. We went aboard, she and I, in plenty of time to go on a hunt of dis-covery. We enthused over the then-quite-novel idea of small private decks for the best suites, the superb lace bedspreads we each had in our sections. We marveled at the masterpieces of woodcarver's art from Ireland and Holland. Surely there was nothing missing to satis-fy the long list of distinguished names on the first class passenger list. Well-known names they were, both in Europe and America.

We felt the thrill that the unknown always gives, when we scanned that list and found world-famous names but, as yet to us, merely names. We speculated if their owners would tally with our con-ception of them; but what concerned us even more was what their idiosyncrasies might be. No doubt we would find them all very dif-ferent to what we pictured, for people nearly always are. The romance one cannot help weaving around certain personalities, due mostly to the press, is often shattered on contact.

So it was not surprising when John Jacob Astor brought his bride of a year on board, about whom there had been so much publicity. Instead of the radiant woman of my imagination, one who had succeeded in overcoming much opposition and marrying the man she wanted, I saw a quiet, pale, sad-faced, in fact dull young woman arrive listlessly on the arm of her husband, apparently indifferent to everything about her. It struck me for the first time that all the wealth in the world did not make for inward contentment. Privately, I was satisfied I had withstood the allure of a beautiful home in Cuba for the love of a pair of quizzical eyes.

My daydreaming ended with the further arrival of passengers. My heart sank as Mrs. Cyrus Klapton, clutching her pet pekinese, bore down towards my section followed by a downcast maid. She had invariably reduced each successive maid to submission ere she boarded the ship. Their spirits would finally be broken by a combination of Mrs. Klapton and the rough sea voyage. I reflected that although in many ways my job was not that prestigious, I could consider myself lucky when I looked at that maid and saw what her position had done to her.

Two affable and well-groomed men passed by. Every busy trip seemed to find their sort traveling. With their suave manners and cold eyes, they would go to the smoke room and all the victims therein. I felt sure that if one could but look through our late purser's album— his hobby and kept safely under lock and key—those faces would stare coldly from the pages of his rogues' gallery.

Next appeared a delightful old couple—old in years and young in character—whom we were always happy to see join us: Mr. and Mrs. Straus had grown old so gracefully and so together. They were, as usual, charmed to see us and with all the arrangements made for their comfort. They gave each of us an individual word of greeting as they made their way to the deck above to wave farewell to friends.

Suddenly, like the meteoric person she was, Miss Marcia Spatz arrived, all packages, hat boxes and flowers galore. Neverending boxes of flowers from innumerable sources, presumably thank offerings to mark her departure. She came with her habitually determined look, meaning to get service from the start. On these occasions, I pulled out the register of my patience to its fullest capacity, knowing I would need all my reserve before the day was over.

I went forward to greet her. She appeared surprised to see me, registering both pleasure and annoyance: Probably pleased because she would have someone who understood her many and strange needs, and yet regretting it was not a stranger she could bully and vent her spleen on to her heart's content.

In the distance I could see old Miss Townsend arrive. She had been blacklisted by another famous shipping line because of her utterly unreasonable behavior and her demoralizing effect on other passengers. She began by demanding mirrors everywhere and that the furniture in her luxurious stateroom should be changed "at once." Probably her happiest moments were spent watching the agonized struggles of a couple of perspiring stewards tackling the job, their red faces, however, not all due to their exertions on her behalf.

They took the precaution, when detailed for Miss Townsend's cabin, to step down to the pantry bar and refresh themselves with a couple of quick doubles, which whipped up their flagging spirits and sent them back to her presence with the determined purpose of "telling her off, good and proper." But one glance at those chilly eyes only redoubled their efforts with the furniture. The one hope uppermost in their minds was getting her "bedded down and quiet" as soon as possible.

Some uncanny instinct attracted the second steward to them, drawing him from a crowd of stewards vainly sorting baggage minus labels. He whispered a warning anent the further use of whisky, which was received with an innocent look of surprise by those two "old soaks." The mere sight of the second steward always had the effect of sobering them as if by magic—although they never admitted it—for he was the object of respect, wonderment and fear all round.

He had the power to detect the many transgressors among us. I had known him to be down on E-deck, busily engaged in an absorbing job, when suddenly and without reason he would dart up to B-deck and walk straight into the cubby hole where poor old flannel-feet Jones, the bedroom steward, prior to taking his place behind the pantry press to carve poultry at dinner time, was secretly enjoying a surreptitious cigarette, an offense regarded at that time as a most heinous crime in passenger accommodations!

On this particular day, he looked satisfied, for the day so far had gone well. The baggage, the bane of a second steward's life, had been satisfactorily distributed in spite of some passengers' eccentricities about labeling it. However, this would not prevent him later on from having Trole and Jackson on the carpet over the "spot of whisky" incident, a fact they were equally sure of in their bones as they sweated and puffed old Miss Townsend and her belongings into order.

Gently, *Titanic* disengaged herself from the side of the dock and we were off on a soft April day. Slipping gracefully away, full of high hope, over the din of send off—goodbyes, fluttering flags and handkerchiefs. We were proudly escorted by the tugs, tooting their farewells and Godspeed, while from the dock the sounds grew fainter.

Few members of the staff had the time or opportunity to witness a departure. I had often wished to see the ship I sailed on from some other vantage point at sea, to know just how she moved on her way. I'd have liked to have been a watcher instead of a worker, and on that sailing day my desire was very strong. But however beautiful I pictured our new ship, I realized only too well, it would have to be a wish only for a long time, until the day, in fact, when rent and coalman's bills and little pairs of boots did not loom so startlingly on the horizon.

Jessop makes no mention whatsoever of *Titanic*'s near collision with the *New York* as she steamed southward past Southampton's dock peninsular. Although she dwells at length on her inability to witness *Titanic*'s departure on deck, surely the drama of that near mishap would have been the talk of the ship for several days to follow, in France, Ireland or out at sea. So many ex-*Olympic* crewmen and women—including Jessop—were on board that many would have remarked on the eerie parallel with the *Hawke/Olympic* imbroglio the year previous.

Ah well, a new scene had opened for us on that bright spring day; who could foretell whether it would be farce, sweet comedy, or tragedy?

Getting acquainted either with people or a ship is not an easy matter in bad weather. Both show to the worst advantage under unflattering conditions, but in this case, nothing prevented the spread of harmonious peace and good fellowship. The sky was blue and the sea a lazy calm as far as the eye could see every day. Contentment and restfulness, following the recent strain of departure, spread over *Titanic* as she cut her way proudly across the Atlantic.

Even the "old soaks" had their beer in peace. The second steward was taking things easy after his feverish activities of the last few weeks in Belfast. In fact, the well-known cranks among the passengers appeared to have become a little more human. We took full advantage of this lull in their demands to get settled down, hard to do on any ship but infinitely more difficult on a new one.

Ann and I started on our cabin, putting in place all the knick-knacks from our former cabin, like the family pictures and the calendars of restful country scenes, given us at New Year in anticipation of "the new ship." Also, the "tidies," [receptacles for odd scraps] made by well-meaning but not always practical friends, had all to be placed to the best advantage under some extra light fittings; these had been procured, with much ingenuity and tact, without the chief electrician's knowledge and fixed up on the Q.T. ["on the quiet"] by willing juniors.

All these things had to be done in spare moments and the constant tap-tapping of busy hammers came from many a staff cabin. The work was helped along by the jests of curious colleagues who had dropped in to help a bit, but in reality for a drink and a smoke which the privacy of our cabin afforded.

It seemed too good to be true to have a breather during duty hours to pay social calls. I took the opportunity to run up to the second class bar for a friendly call on Jack Stevens, to hear all about his new home, his wedding and, most important, his bride. We had been friends for a long while, Jack and I, the kind that don't mind giving each other a bit of frank opinion when the occasion arose, without fear of forfeiting comradeship. We had always got much enjoyment exchanging experiences, for Jack had a strong sense for seeing the ridiculous in sea life. Besides, we could always use each other's company as a shield and safeguard against social dangers, trusting each other as people do who know exactly the footing on which their friendship is based.

We had ended these delightful days of palship in the grand manner and by mutual agreement, the week before his wedding.

It was not strange, therefore, that I should seek him out to exchange opinions about our new venture. He alone knew I did not like big ships, that I was secretly afraid; however, we drank a toast to his happiness and *Titanic*. Then he proudly showed me all his new improvements to make his bar work easier and chaffingly added that we women were not the only ones with something to show off about.

I find it interesting that Violet Jessop recalls here, for the first time, that she is uneasy on big ships, mention never made in connection with almost identical *Olympic*. My feeling is that this self-observation might well be hindsight inserted long after the fact, the kind of Monday-morning-quarterbacking exhibited by so many connected with the doomed vessel. Throughout my shipboard travels, many fellow passengers frequently suggest that they had grandparents, great uncles or friends who, on arrival at Southampton in April of 1912, had felt uneasy about the vessel and refused to embark. Was that reluctance, I wonder, a genuine premonition or merely a post-disaster fabrication?

One night after dinner, I ran down to hear old Matthews, the chief pantryman, tell of his experiences in Belfast while "they got her ready," beaming proudly as he surveyed his extensive pantry. He strutted about like a benevolent Father Christmas, dispensing hospitality in the shape of double helpings of "plum duff" to the boys, "the boys" being all stewards from the age of fourteen to sixty.

On our round of visits we did not forget the good old Irish doctor, whose ever-open door was always a temptation to bandy words with one who regarded life with a twinkle in his eye but kept clear of the whirlpools. To peep into his magnificently appointed cabin and hear his sometimes extravagant description of how he spent his holidays, was always a joy to me. We often teasingly asked him how anyone so charming, so kind and so gay had remained a bachelor, and counseled him to take a good wife to keep him from frivolling, to which he would reply:

"Sure, haven't I worn all the knees out of me pants proposing to ladies and sure they won't have anything to do with me at all."

Meanwhile our eyes wandered round his room adorned with silver framed photographs of some of the most beautiful and talented women of both hemispheres. He was our dear "deluderer."

Often during our rounds we came upon our beloved designer going about unobtrusively with a tired face but a satisfied air. He never failed to stop for a cheerful word, his only regret that we were "getting further from home." We all knew the love he had for that Irish home of his and suspected that he longed to get back to the peace of its atmosphere for a much needed rest and to forget ship designing for awhile.

It was all so happy and peaceful. If the sun did fail to shine so brightly on the fourth day out, and if a little cold nip crept into the

air as evening set in, it only served to emphasize the warmth and lux-
uriousness within. On that Sunday evening, the music was at its
gayest, led by young Jock the first violin; when I ran into him during
the interval, he laughingly called out to me in his rich Scottish accent,
that he was about to give them a "real tune, a Scottish tune, to finish
up with." Always so eager and full of life was Jock.

Would, in fact, any "music have been the gayest" that Sunday evening? Just
what time and why would this supposed encounter with Jock have taken
place? In the next paragraph, Jessop talks of sunshine being replaced by
grayness, presumably before dusk. She suggests, by use of the time frame
"during the interval" that the musicians were involved in some sort of formal, staged performance given in two parts. If this were the case—and I
think it unlikely on a vessel where reserved Sabbath decorum was the rule—
how and why would Jessop have "run into him during the interval?" Is it
likely that Hume would have returned to crew country between gigs rather
than wait adjacent to the orchestra's performing venue, either the reception
room outside the dining saloon or up in the drawing room? Again, I suspect
authorial hindsight was at work here or, perhaps, the exchange with Jock
Hume, if it occurred at all, took place on any day but that Sabbath.

Grayish skies replaced sunshine but the calm sea continued, a calmness that only the ocean knows: Perfect serenity for miles, broken by
the rhythm of the water lazily lapping against the ship's side, as her
great hulk clove through it.

   Colder and yet a little colder, gray sky deepening into haziness as
evening fell, making the water look like molten silver as it caught the
soft beams of a misty moon.

Jessop's recreation of that Sunday evening is flawed; there was no moon, only brilliant starlight.

A soothing peace and an ever increasing chill set in that drove one indoors, an excuse for bed and a good book.

   I slipped out on deck, my nightly custom before retiring, for a
few moments alone with my thoughts. It was all so quiet, but how
penetratingly cold it had become! Little wisps of mist like tiny fairies
wafted gently inboard from the sea and left my face clammy. I shivered. It was indeed a night for bed, warmth and cozy thoughts of
home and firesides. I thought of the man in the crow's nest as I came
indoors, surely an unenviable job on such a night.

The alleyways were mostly deserted except for a few stewards on late watch, yawning with one eye on the companion clock. A few people here and there, some returning from the smoke room with friends to finish their conversation in their sumptuous staterooms over a last drink. Others were just slipping up for a blow before turning in.

I passed the honeymoon couple we were all so interested in, a charming pair who had not yet found themselves. They averaged one big quarrel per day which, though nobody witnessed it, was easily recognizable by the tense, determined expression on both young faces; later, there would be radiant smiles after the clouds had rolled by. Once again it looked as if a deep disturbance had taken place in their relations; she sat alone, the picture of affronted dignity. Funny youngsters!

How good it was to be in my cozy bunk at last, devouring a batch of English magazines which the library steward had thoughtfully dropped in the cabin as he passed. Good old *Tatler* and *Sketch* could catch my imagination so quickly and transfer me to other scenes with all the latest gossip and the newest clothes. I was back in England for a few moments amid it all . . .

But wait! I remembered that I had an extraordinary prayer translated from the original Hebrew, reputed to have been found near the tomb of Our Lord and composed by nobody knows who. It had been given to me by an old Irishwoman with strict instructions to study its strange wording and say it daily for protection against fire and water. Every day I had meant to look it over but had always found something else to claim my attention. So it was left unread in my prayer book, a prized and loving memory of dear old convent days.

My conscience smote me. The trip was half over and my promise to the giver unfulfilled. I made up my mind there and then to read it. I peeped over at Ann in her bottom bunk and warned her that she had better share the safeguard of this prayer, passing it down as I spoke. She returned it after she had read it, saying it was indeed a beautiful prayer but a strangely worded one.

I then composed myself to read it devotionally rather than as a piece of quaint writing. I pushed my magazines to one side, the better to relax and concentrate on my devotions. At the end, my book closed, I lay lazily reflecting on many things, comfortably drowsy.

Crash! . . . Then a low, rending, crunching, ripping sound, as *Titanic* shivered a trifle and the sound of her engines gently ceased.

Quiet, dead silence for a minute. Then doors opened and voices could be heard in gentle enquiry. Quietly, restrained voices passed our door, answered just as quietly.

I lay still. Not even to myself would I express what was in my mind. I must not show at that moment the ever-present fear that I had so far successfully kept locked in my heart. Only once, in an unguarded moment during a raging storm, had that fear betrayed me, causing my pride pain from the jests and jeers of others afterwards.

I waited for Ann to speak, for I knew she was awake. I looked over the side of my bunk at her, and she returned my look saying in her calm way, for all the world as if she were commenting on eggs and bacon, "Sounds as if something has happened."

I suddenly wanted to roar with laughter at her unconscious placidity. "Something has happened!!" She could hear as well as I could that they had started to draw the ship's fires, though neither of us commented on this ominous fact.

Violet never identified exactly which cabin she and Ann Turnbull occupied. Probably one on E or F Deck but well above the boiler rooms on Orlop Deck. Could those two women, experienced stewardesses though they might be, have actually heard boiler fires being drawn? I have my doubts.

Suddenly, there was movement. Men were returning to duty they had but recently left. I realized that I too, must hasten on duty, for I had quite a number of women in my section.

Ann and I started to dress rapidly and in silence. My teeth chattered a little and I found my fingers were all thumbs.

Good, faithful old Stanley, one of my bedroom stewards, came knocking at the door, his face whiter than usual as he remarked casually, "I'm calling all our people, sister." He always addressed me as sister when we were alone. "Anything you'd like me to do for you on my way? You know the ship is sinking?"

Sinking? The word repeated itself without fully entering my understanding as I finished putting on my uniform and quickly followed Stanley to our section.

Sinking? Of course *Titanic* couldn't be sinking! What nonsense! She so perfect, so new—yet now she was so still, so inanimate; not a sound after that awful grinding crash. She that had so short a time ago been so vital was now the embodiment of immobility.

My mind, usually adjustable to sudden and unforeseen happenings, could not accept the fact that this superperfect creation was to do so futile a thing as sink. Automatically, I untied and readjusted a child's lifebelt, much to the little one's interest and sleepy bewilderment.

I continued through my section trying to reassure, answering questions to which there seemed no answer. Everywhere I found extraordinary calmness. To satisfy my pride, I assumed an indifference to facts all too obvious. People who had been asleep were dressing, fumbling sleepy-eyed with buttons. They were unemotional, probably thinking as I did that it was all too fantastic. Those who had not yet retired for the night were standing in groups on the companion square, chatting in the restrained, well-bred manner of the day.

Suddenly orders came down, striking a deeper chill to the consciousness. Everybody to the boats, but just as a precautionary measure, of course.

We continued to fix lifebelts, reminding people to put on warm clothing, take blankets and valuables. Yes, of course, we reiterated from room to room, just a precautionary measure!

Reluctantly, slowly, people started up the companions, still inclined to chat by the way, some joking and quite unhurried, taking their time about it. From above, officers' anxious faces peered down, loathe to give undue alarm but wishing people would bestir themselves. To those few who showed concern, a reassuring answer was forthcoming: "There are plenty of boats in the vicinity; they'll be with us any moment now." Those dear youngsters in the cabin opposite ours thought it all was a "grand show."

All passengers upstairs at last, I looked around. There was no sound, *Titanic* as steady as a rock; she might have been in dock and all the crew gone home. I returned to my room and found Ann.

What to do next? Absently, I began tidying up, folding my nightgown, putting things in their place, when I saw Stanley at the door again, watching me. Then he almost shouted as he seized my arm: "My God, don't you realize that this ship will sink, that she has struck an iceberg, that you have to follow the rest upstairs as quickly as possible?"

Without replying—there suddenly seemed nothing to say—I started fumbling in my wardrobe for a coat, then remembered I had no warm coat with me. It was spring, beautiful spring a few days before; who had thought of coats to meet icebergs? Fussily, Stanley made to grab what he saw on a hanger in the depths of the wardrobe, while Ann laboriously got into a mackintosh.

"No, Stan, that won't do," I said, as he brought forth my new spring outfit, all trimmings and things. "That's no rig for a shipwreck, all fussed up and gay." Suddenly I was trying to be jocular, afraid if I wasn't I might cry.

"What about a hat?" said Stanley, opening my hat box.

"What, that thing with sweet peas all around it? No, Stan, you would not wish me to go up in that, even for precautionary measures." I twitted him as I tied on a borrowed scarf, locked our door and called out, "So long, Stan, come up soon yourself, won't you?" as I preceded Ann up to the boat deck.

Halfway up, I looked down and waved to Stan. He was standing with his arms clasped behind him in the corner where he usually kept his evening watch. He suddenly looked very tired.

Good old, ugly-faced, big-hearted Stanley!

Jessop's recall of those surreal last moments down in her *Titanic* cabin are haunting as she and Stanley debate about which coat or hat to wear for the lifeboat. So too, her final glimpse of Stanley, patently resigned to his fate. He had come back down below specifically to alert his two delinquent stewardess colleagues, knowing that they would find the lifeboat seat that he, because of his sex, would be denied.

# Into the Lifeboat

YOU COULD ALMOST imagine this a scene of busily curious people with not very much to do. True, there were officers and men briskly getting lifeboats ready to lower, their tense faces strangely in contrast to the well ordered groups wandering about. I felt chilly without a coat, so I went down again for something to cover my shoulders and picked up a silk eiderdown from the first open cabin I came to. How strange it was to pass all those rooms lit up so brilliantly, their doors open and contents lying around in disorder. Jewels sparkled on dressing tables and a pair of silver slippers were lying just where they had been kicked off.

I gathered my eiderdown and went up. On my way I passed a group of officers, still in their mess jackets, hands in pockets, chatting quietly on the companion square as men do who are waiting for something. They smiled at me and I waved back.

Nearly four decades after writing these words, Violet Jessop told me that the four men in question had been the master, Captain Smith, Bruce Ismay, managing director of the line, Purser McElroy and Doctor O'Laughlin. She characterized their nonchalance convincingly: "Nobody, John, was taking the seriousness of anything."

As I turned I ran into Jock, the bandleader and his crowd with their instruments. "Funny, they must be going to play," thought I, and at this late hour! Jock smiled in passing, looking rather pale for him, remarking, "Just going to give them a tune to cheer things up a bit," and passed on. Presently the strains of the band reached me faintly as I stood on deck watching a young woman excitedly remonstrating with an embarrassed young officer. He wanted her to get into the lifeboat he was trying to fill but she refused to go without her father.

"He must wait," responded the officer, "till the decks are cleared of women and children."

Up one of the emergency stairs two young figures struggled, laughing as they nearly dropped their load. It was young Tim and Peter from the pantry with an awkward load of bread, which toppled as they came over the high step out onto the boat deck. One of them stumbled and partly fell over another object lying in their path. Both they and I looked. It was an open gladstone bag, filled with gleaming gold sovereigns. The man who had brought it up came from the purser's office. He was taking a breather, for it was very heavy and he yet had to move it to a lifeboat.

Somebody else passed by hurriedly and kicked the bag in passing. Some of its precious contents scattered, to the mortification of the man in charge. As he tried to rescue the coins from under moving feet, his mate came up with a heavy dispatch box and joined him.

Out on deck, the first arguments started over who would and who wouldn't go into the boats which appeared to be suspended miles above the yawning blackness below.

Nobody was anxious to move; *Titanic* seemed so steady. To justify their reluctance, some pointed to a light on the horizon: another ship's lights! People were reassured, content to bide their time.

One boat was already being lowered with very few people in it. When this was pointed out as a shining example for backward souls by the officer near me, he got a rather alarming response as the crowd surged forward to embark. The boat was lowered very full, almost too full this time; and so on. Always, some held back in need of coaxing while a few were too eager.

A steward stood waiting with his back to the bulkhead, cigarette in mouth and hands in his pockets. It struck me forcibly as the first time I had ever seen a steward stand thus amid a group of distinguished guests.

Jessop suddenly used the word "guests," contemporary cruisespeak among upscale lines to describe passengers but not used aboard Edwardian steamers; the traditional, honest and appropriate word "passengers" always sufficed. Regardless, the image of that smoking steward, hands in pockets, remains as a poignant but understandable glimpse of disciplinary erosion toward the end.

A woman standing near me gave an approving glance as John Jacob Astor handed his wife into a boat, waving encouragingly to her as he stepped back into an ever-increasing crowd of men.

Ann Turnbull, still silent and unmoved, dragged a little behind me. I suggested we keep together and we stood awhile to watch. There was nothing else we could do. Dimly I heard a shot.

Glancing forward I caught my breath as a white rocket shot up, then another. Distress rockets! They went very high with great noise. The lights on the horizon seemed to come nearer. That cheered up the group about us, who had slowly started to fill a boat. Young officers urged them to greater speed, showing unlimited patience, I thought. Another rocket went up into the night.

A few women near me started to cry loudly when they realized a parting had to take place, their husbands standing silently by. They were Poles and could not understand a word of English. Surely a terrible plight, to be among a crowd in such a situation and not be able to understand anything that is being said.

Boats were now being lowered more rapidly and a crowd of foreigners was brought up by a steward from the third class. They dashed eagerly as one man over to a boat, almost more than the officer could control. But he regained order and managed to get the boat away. It descended slowly, uncertainly at first, now one end up and then the other; the falls were new and difficult to handle. Some men nearby were throwing things over the side—deck chairs, rafts or any wooden thing lying nearby. [Two of them were Thomas Andrews and the chief deck steward.]

Suddenly, the crowd of people beside me parted. A man dashed to the ship's side, and before anyone could stop him, hurled himself into the descending boat. There was a murmur of amazement and disapproval.

I turned to say something to Ann. Looking along the length of the ship, I noticed the forward part of her was lower now, much lower! For a fraction of a second, my heart stood still, as is often the case when faith, hitherto unshaken faith, gets its first setback.

One of the mailmen from our sorting office joined us. His work was finished, he remarked unemotionally. "The mail is floating up to F-deck with the water," he told us.

I tried not to hear what he said, not wanting to believe what he accepted so stoically. Instead, I listened to the faint sounds of music from Jock's men. They were playing *Nearer My God to Thee.*

My arm was suddenly jerked and I turned to see young Mason who had been busy filling a boat. His face looked weary and tired, but he gave a bright smile as he ordered my group into the boat, calling out "Good luck!" as we stepped in, helped by his willing, guiding hand. I nearly fell over the tackle and oars as I tried to assist Ann in beside me. She was suffering with her feet, I could see, and found her lifebelt got in the way of moving freely.

Before I could do anything, young Mason hailed me and held up something, calling as he prepared to throw it, "Look after this, will you?" and I reached out to receive somebody's forgotten baby in my arms.

It started to whimper as I pressed it to me, the hard cork surface of the lifebelt being anything but a comfort, poor mite. The boat was full now, full of people with dull, inquiring faces. I spoke to one woman but she shook her head, not understanding a word I said.

Groaning, the boat descended a fearful distance into that inky blackness beneath, intensified as the lights fell on it occasionally.

Jessop remarks, unlike any other passenger or crew account I have ever read, on the effect of descent past successive rows of brilliantly lit portholes, the contrasting flare and blackout as the lifeboat creaks down.

"Surely it is all a dream," I thought as I looked up the side of the ship, beautifully illuminated, each deck alive with lights; the dynamos were on the top deck. I tried to make myself believe it could not be true, all this. I even noticed a few people leaning over the rail, watching in an unconcerned manner; perhaps they too were persuading themselves it was a bad dream!

We touched the water with a terrific thud, a bone-cracking thud which started the baby crying in earnest. Somebody in the forepart ordered oars out and we slowly pulled away from the side of the ship. I noticed one of the few men in the boat rowing; he was a fireman who had evidently just come up from the stokehold, his face still black with coal dust and eyes red-rimmed, wearing only a thin singlet to protect him from the icy cold. Taking a cigarette from his trouser pocket, he offered me half, poor devil!

Fascinated, my eyes never left the ship, as if by looking I could keep her afloat. I reflected that but four days ago I had wished to see her from afar, to be able to admire her under way; now there she was, my *Titanic*, magnificent queen of the ocean, a perfection of man's handiwork, her splendid lines outlined against the night, every light twinkling.

I started unconsciously to count the decks by the rows of lights. One, two, three, four, five, six; then again—one, two, three, four, five. I stopped. Surely I had miscounted. I went over them again more carefully, hushing the whimpering baby meanwhile.

No, I had made no mistake. There were only five decks now; then I started all over again—only four now. She was getting lower in the water, I could not any longer deny it.

As if all could read my mind, the women in the boat started to weep, some silently, some unrestrainedly. I closed my eyes and prayed, prayed for one and all but dared not think of anyone in particular. I dared not visualize those people I had just left, warm and alive as I was. I tried to busy myself with the baby, but could not refrain from looking up again. Only three decks now, and still not a list to one side or the other.

Desperately, I turned to where that other ship's lights shone on the horizon; surely they should be getting nearer by now. It was such a long, long time since we had first seen their comforting glow. They should be with us by now, taking off those patient waiting people over there. But no, she did not seem nearer, in fact, she seemed further away. Strange!

A tiny breeze, the first we had felt on this calm night, blew an icy blast across my face; it felt like a knife in its penetrating coldness. I sat paralyzed with cold and misery, as I watched *Titanic* give a lurch forward. One of the huge funnels toppled off like a cardboard model, falling into the sea with a fearful roar. A few cries came to us across the water, then silence, as the ship seemed to right herself like a hurt animal with a broken back. She settled for a few minutes, but one more deck of lighted ports disappeared. Then she went down by the head with a thundering roar of underwater explosions, our proud ship, our beautiful *Titanic* gone to her doom.

One awful moment of empty, misty blackness enveloped us in its loneliness, then an unforgettable, agonizing cry went up from 1500 despairing throats, a long wail and then silence and our tiny craft tossing about at the mercy of the ice field.

The tantalizing vision of what would later be identified as the Leyland liner *Californian* floated nearby like a cruel wraith that night. Violet Jessop was not alone in her inability to estimate how far off the mystery vessel lay, either from *Titanic*'s boat deck or, even more challenging, down at water level. Early next morning in her lifeboat—as we shall discover at the start of the next chapter—she was persuaded that she was moving further away. In actuality, by the time the sun was up, *Californian*, finally privy to the tragedy once her radio operator had come back on duty, would have been maneuvering towards the rescue ship *Carpathia*.

Others on *Titanic*'s boat deck saw *Californian* that night. And there has arisen, over recent decades, an interminable argument among historians as well as students of the events that night as to just how far away the Leyland liner lay. That debate—nay, furor!—continues to the present. The vexing question of the two vessels' proximity is not only in dispute, it is pivotal in placing blame as well.

Establishing that figure as distant, it is argued by those who favor Captain Stanley Lord, the *Californian*'s master, might expiate the taint of indifference and dereliction that their opponents feel is Lord's due. Depending on one's allegiance—either for the hapless master or against him—that crucial distance varies. The Lordites, as Captain Lord's supporters are described, push the figure up to 20 miles, arguing that drifting *Californian* was on the far side of an impenetrable ice field and hence physically incapable of reaching *Titanic*'s side in time. Lord suggested at one point during the British Inquiry that he was 30 miles from the other liner.

I stand among those who put the two vessels much closer together. My informant in this event was one of the White Star liner's quartermasters, George Rowe, whom I interviewed in 1970. He told me that the lights of the mystery ship lay, without question, "no more than four miles off."

Rowe was intimately involved with the *Californian* riddle that night. He had been instructed by Captain Smith to bring a box of distress rockets— "detonators," he called them at the British Inquiry—up onto the bridge and fire them off. Just prior to *Titanic*'s maiden voyage, Rowe had completed an advanced quartermaster's course; parts of its syllabus had been determining distances between illuminated vessels at night.

The relative position of the two stationary ships would have been a matter of intense interest and speculation to three men, Quartermaster Rowe, Captain Smith and Officer of the Watch Murdoch, all of them waiting in vain on *Titanic*'s increasingly sloping bridge for some acknowledgment of their desperate pyrotechnical plea.

For the record, *Californian* was bound for Boston with a cargo of lumber. She carried no passengers and had, since ten o'clock that chill Sunday evening, been drifting without power in the ice. In other words, Captain

Lord, who had never encountered severe ice conditions before, was doing exactly what Captain Smith, his opposite number aboard *Titanic,* should have done but did not: *Stop his vessel until morning.* How cruelly ironic that in the aftermath of the tragedy, Smith, who ignored multiple ice warnings and lost both his ship and his life, nevertheless retains a halo of maritime sanctity while sensible Lord was to endure a lifelong stigma.

He and all the *Californian's* bridge officers would testify at the British Inquiry headed by Lord Mersey later that year in London. They appeared solely as witnesses; none had been indicted. Their testimony served, to my mind, as the dramatic highlight of the inquiry. Herbert Stone, the vessel's second officer, who was standing the midnight-to-four watch, admitted seeing the liner and all eight rockets. Through a speaking tube, he immediately informed Captain Lord, who was dozing, fully clothed, on the chart room sofa directly below the wheelhouse. Hearing about the rockets, Lord prevaricated, asking what color they were.

On the face of it, his question was legitimate. Lord thought that the signals might have been what were called at the time company signals, variously colored combinations of Roman candles that oncoming vessels on the North Atlantic routinely fired at night, to announce not their identity but that of their owning company. The practice continued long after the 1895 advent of wireless communication.

In fact, had *Titanic* been merely firing White Star signals, she would have sent up two green lights, the company's registered recognition colors. Testifying at the inquiry months later, Lord insisted that some company signals were white. But, in fact, although some company signals may have *incorporated* white Roman candles, they were always displayed simultaneously with other colors: Hamburg Amerika Line vessels, for example, threw up red, white and blue stars, seven of them in quick succession while Anchor Line masters were instructed to put up red and white lights.

But the rockets that both Stone and Apprentice Officer Gibson saw from the *Californian's* bridge that night were not only all white, they also had an additional characteristic, a loud report and shower of illuminated fragments at their apogee of flight; "throwing stars," it is called. Distress rockets were called detonators with reason.

After Stone informed the Captain that the rockets were white, Lord asked to be advised of any further developments, and went back to sleep. It was a sleep so sound that the Captain disremembered when young Gibson woke him with further reports about the rocket-firing liner.

Captain Lord spent the remainder of his life, as did his son, in a dogged attempt to clear his name. After years of petitioning, the Ministry of Transport—successor government agency to the defunct Board of Trade—finally reopened the investigation by appointing a one-man board of inquiry in 1990. Captain Thomas Barnett, retired principal Surveyor of the Transport Department, reconfirmed the *Californian's* 10-mile proximity. But, astonishingly his superiors disagreed with Barnett's findings and dismissed him. He was replaced by another one-man board of inquiry, Captain James de Coverly, who arrived instead at a widely disputed 20-mile figure, a spurious estimate that will only confound the debate for generations to come.

Captain John King, master aboard *Royal Princess* in the early nineties, suggested to me that, regardless of right or wrong in the case, he suspected that Captain Stanley Lord was, more than anything that night, completely exhausted. As a fellow captain's judgment, I feel it deserves respect.

One revealing piece of testimony from Lord Mersey's Inquiry comes from a highly qualified witness aboard *Californian*. He estimated that the ocean liner he saw at 11:30 that night, just ten minutes before *Titanic*'s collision with the iceberg, was no more than five miles distant. The name of that observer/witness? Captain Stanley Lord.

A final observation about George Rowe, totally apart from the *Californian* imbroglio: None of *Titanic*'s quartermasters was lost, a singular and unique record of survival for a single crew component from the lost liner. Only four of *Titanic*'s navigating officers were left alive and every one of the engineering officers was lost. But, assigned as they were to positions of command in the lifeboats, all six quartermasters clambered aboard *Carpathia* the following morning.

# 22

# Rescue

**D**AWN BREAKS SLOWLY when the watch is long and hazardous. It seemed as if it never would come that April morning. After a night of calm sea and floating mists, the wind rose to an icy keenness, cutting through our numbed bodies, paralyzing senses already dulled by shock and cruel disappointment.

The light we had followed with so much hope since 2 a.m. was discovered at last to be retreating from us further and further. It had drawn us for hours off our course into immeasurable wastes. Our boat seemed all too tiny as the sea began to lash itself against its frailty. Huddled into grotesque heaps by the violence of its movement, we prayed sobbingly, staring into space. I tried desperately to overcome the nausea that threatened me and strove vainly to bring my mind back from the lonely stretches where it kept roaming.

A weak cry from the baby in my numbed arms helped me regain control of myself. The hard edge of my lifebelt was not comforting to its ill-clad body and its little face looked old and pinched in the dim light. I tucked the eiderdown tightly round it, for I feared, suddenly, that this stranger's child might die in my arms. After the horrors we had experienced, a child's death seemed disproportionate; nevertheless, it shook me. The baby stopped whimpering at last and slept while my mind drifted back to recent happenings; Ann sat stoically by my side.

As I saw again with my mind's eye those crowds walking the decks aimlessly after our boat had been lowered, a fresh horror was borne home to me: There were no more lifeboats to take them off! The ghastliness of the realization was unbearable. I felt I had no right to comparative safety when so many must have perished; no human being could live long in those frozen waters.

The sea became more violent, tossing our overloaded boat help-lessly about. Only four people in it could row and we were too cold, totally unequipped to resist the unrelenting strength of the waves. We had no light, no water and no food, nothing in that boat to keep body and soul together or help us battle the elements.

My stunned mind seemed to remember that in a dim past there had always been inspections by qualified officials in Southampton for all such as we now lacked, and I was perplexed. It was not doing jus-tice to beautiful *Titanic* to leave her without the barest essentials.

As the faint streaks of dawn lit the horizon, majestic shapes of icebergs like fairy castles crossed our vision, passing in panoramic pro-cession. But what once had been for us objects of interest now ap-peared sinister monsters of destruction; their beauty had changed into revolting dread.

Nothing was in sight, none of our other boats, just water and ice everywhere. We realized how far off our course we had gone by fol-lowing that elusive ship.

I think it doubtful that "overloaded" lifeboat 16 could have made any head-way at all in pursuit of the mysterious vessel. Jessop talks of "being off our course through following that elusive ship," when in fact, a heavily laden lifeboat with only four working oars in rough seas can scarcely sustain any course at all.

Ann never moved her position, remaining silent. The men in charge of the boat tried to cheer us with a few feeble songs but these soon died down; their lips were too frozen to move and they needed all their strength to row. My mind wandered for a few moments from the tragedy, fastening onto something irrelevant. I thought of recent things I had done. I regretted having started to buy a piano before we sailed—I had always longed to have one but could never quite man-age that little extra that represented the first installment; now I might never need it.

Then, suddenly, a flicker of hope revived. Somebody woke from their lethargic state and pointed a trembling finger at a dark speck on the horizon—a ship! Not going away from us this time but getting closer and more distinct every minute.

Sudden joy seems, at times, almost as disastrous to the human makeup as sudden fear. Many among those poor weeping, frozen people, murmuring prayers in a soft monotone, nearly died with emotion when they sighted that ship. They must have been thinking more of their dear ones than of themselves, hoping in their bewildered hearts that there might be a chance yet that those missing loved ones could have been picked up by the approaching vessel.

One poor soul sitting beside me, who had kept her head buried in her arms since we had taken to the boats, thought as she looked up that we were nearing the *Titanic* still afloat and that she would soon regain her husband and two sons; all the women in our boat were immigrants who had left their menfolk on board.

Violet Jessop told me during our interview that she was in lifeboat 16. It is not surprising that she found herself in a boat full of immigrant passengers, simply because of lifeboat 16's geographical placement on *Titanic*'s boat deck. Suspended from the aftermost davits on the port side, it was nearest the most viable approach route for passengers of the third class, clambering up to the boats from their well deck aft.

As the ship loomed nearer, we saw her stop and realized she was doing so in order that all surviving boats might make their way to her and she would avoid the risk of so much floating ice.

We were the last to reach the good ship *Carpathia* which had turned back from her journey towards the Mediterranean to pick us up. As kind hands helped us aboard, our eyes searched for familiar faces, mostly in vain. As we reached the deck, glasses of neat brandy were poured down our throats; it went down like molten fire.

While I stood, still clutching the baby in my frozen arms, a woman rushed up, snatched the child and ran away with it. In the confusion and process of thawing out, the baby's whereabouts slipped from my thoughts; when things became more settled in my mind, I did wonder why, whoever its mother might be, she had not expressed one word of gratitude for her baby's life.

Then started the saddest search it has ever been my lot to witness. Alas, so few were reunited. We also looked without success for so many with whom we had ties of friendship. For our dear Tommy Andrews, for the good doctor, for the boys that made life aboard easier for us, for good friends in all departments. But they were all among the missing when the roll was called. Not one engineer of all that gay crowd answered his name and but two officers whose presence seemed a miracle. [In fact, four officers survived.]

It is only when something is over, when your mind is detached from immediate surroundings, that you visualize actual details. One of these surviving officers had gone down with the ship and then been blown up with the explosion; he somehow managed to get clear and was picked up by one of the boats.

This was, of course, Second Officer Herbert "Lights" Lightoller who, struggling in the water near the sinking ship, had been drawn down and affixed atop an engine room grating as sea water flooded into it. But that same inflow of water proved the instrument of his salvation. It apparently struck a still-hot boiler, fracturing it. The ensuing explosion miraculously blew Lightoller clear of the wreck and he managed to clamber aboard an overturned Englehardt collapsible lifeboat that had been launched inverted when *Titanic* went down. His subsequent leadership throughout the night on that overturned boat with thirty precarious survivors standing atop it remains one of the most heroic sagas of the wreck.

He at once took charge, probably saving many lives by his resourcefulness. The other, quite a young man, had some difficulty with the people in his boat and asserted his position at the point of a revolver. Those were the shots I had heard just before we were lowered.

Another surviving officer was Fourth Officer Joseph Boxhall but it is generally accepted that it was not he who had fired the shots. That was Fifth Officer Lowe.

Tirelessly, the rescuers worked and held out hope to all, reminding us that many ships, even our sister ship *Olympic*, had received the call and might have picked up survivors. *Carpathia*'s crew did everything to relieve suffering and anxiety, attending to the wounded and tenderly caring for mutilated remains that were beyond help. But there was little that could be done to comfort those who had lost and knew it should not have been.

So *Carpathia*, having searched vigilantly, turned back to New York. She seemed weighed down with her extra load of human cargo. There were not enough cabins so we slept on the deck, on benches, watching the stars at night and were thankful.

In the dusk of evening, we crept up the Hudson into New York, where a crowd waited, hoping against hope that messages received had been false and that relatives might be among those on board. Long before we got near the dock, despairing enquiries were shouted across the intervening waters. It was only then that we learned that no other ship had found a soul. The horror was renewed all over again.

Next day, with practical forethought, a group of people had collected clothing of every sort, which was brought down to the dock and spread out on tables, reminding me of a rummage sale. Had it happened when we were in a happier frame of mind, we might have derived much fun from the grotesque figures some of us cut in full array. But for once we were not coquettes.

For the clothes, though good, were used articles covering many seasons of fashion and some had obviously been stored for years. We certainly gave the appearance of a lot of dismal wet hens. The men looked better, there being not so much wild imagination in their clothes.

Of course, complete strangers in New York wanted to be nice to us, to "show us around" or arrange platform lectures, but speaking for myself, publicity just then seemed absolutely abhorrent and all our thoughts were concentrated on getting home, though we secretly dreaded the sea trip. Happily, the *Lapland*'s captain chose a more southerly route for our return and we did not have to pass near the ill-fated spot in the Atlantic where the swells sweep across the edge of the Grand Banks.

Whenever the subject of the disaster came up in the years that followed, I discovered, through insinuations and sometimes tactlessly expressed comments, that an erroneous opinion prevailed that survivors of the crew had "done well" out of the tragedy. This of course was wild exaggeration. I can vouch from my own personal experience that, apart from the gift of twenty-five pounds very generously given by the London newspaper *The Daily Telegraph*, and the full trip's wages given by the Company [normally seamen's wages cease from the moment of a sinking], we received no other emoluments or gifts.

When we eventually reached home, we received a letter from the mayor of Southampton, asking us to present ourselves at his office on a certain date. This we did and received his congratulations and a gift of ten pounds, for which we were very grateful, as we had to renew our lost uniforms, no mean item of expense. We were greatly shocked, however, when later we received a request from the mayor, who had heard of the *The Daily Telegraph*'s gift, that we should return the ten pounds to his office. We did so with bitter feelings.

Ever since that date, one particular service commemorates the 1500 lost in the *Titanic* : Every 14th of April, a United States Coast Guard cutter comes to pay the homage of the Ice Patrol, which owes its inception to the disaster. With engines stilled and church pennant at the masthead, officers and men line the deck in full dress, while the commander reads the burial service. Three volleys of rifle fire can be heard, then the cutter passes on, leaving a lone wreath on the waves above the broken hull.


Violet Jessop's *Titanic* memoir is full of interesting and fresh detail. I wish she had documented more of her time aboard *Carpathia*. My friend and colleague Don Lynch, of the Titanic Historical Society, wondered if she had encountered any resentment among the passengers that as crew, they should have been saved when so many passengers were lost. If Violet did, she does not say it.

I would like to elaborate on the musicians. On her maiden voyage, *Titanic* had aboard a total of eight, carried on company rolls as second class passengers. Regardless of that apparent cachet, their quarters were not in second class country at all but down in the bowels of the ship, port side aft on E Deck. During normal ship's routine, the eight were divided into two separate and autonomous groups. A piano quintet played daily for the first and second class, while a piano trio performed exclusively for patrons of the *A La Carte* Grill, the vessel's extra-tariff restaurant on B Deck. The man in charge of all musicians was orchestra leader and violinist Wallace Hartley; Jock Hume played second violin in Hartley's quintet.

It was around midnight of Sunday, April 14th, the night of the collision, that Purser McElroy, acting on behalf of the master, ordered all musicians mustered. Hartley organized his men into one makeshift orchestra. In fact, only seven actually participated because one of the two pianists—either Percy Taylor of the trio or the quintet's Theodore Brailey—would have to have dropped out as redundant; there was only one piano in the A-deck lounge where they first played that night.

Later on, Hartley was instructed to move his players forward into the boat deck lobby atop the main staircase. The seven could continue playing as before because an upright piano was located permanently there. After having completed several selections, Hartley moved his men once more. Temporarily dismissed, they all trooped below, all the way down to E Deck, to don overcoats and lifejackets before reassembling at their third venue of the night, outdoors on the port side of boat deck, just aft of the first class entrance vestibule.

For this final performance, only a string sextet played, since the remaining pianist would also have to have dropped out without a piano being available outdoors on the deck. Since none of the musicians survived, we shall never know how those two idle pianists filled their last hour. Did they remain with their colleagues or might they have wandered off, investigating their chances of entering a lifeboat? My sense is that they probably stayed within reach, bonded, even *in extremis*, to their fellow professionals. Shipboard musicians to the present tend to stick together.

It has often occurred to me how difficult it must have been for those remaining instrumentalists to play out on deck. Of the six, Roger Bricoux and Jack Woodward were cellists and Fred Clarke a bass player. Whereas Clarke habitually played on his feet, the two cellists would have needed seats. What, if anything, did they sit on? Would Hartley have had them bring chairs outdoors or did they remain standing? Cellists I have discussed this with suggest that playing on their feet would have been difficult even if they only plucked a pizzicato accompaniment. Cellist Timothy Eddy of the Bach Aria Group tried playing for me while standing but announced after a few measures that he did so "only with discomfort." Some present-day jazz cellists have their instruments equipped with extra-long spikes for playing on their feet but it seems unlikely that such a refinement existed in 1912.

For violinists Hartley and Jock Hume as well as George Krins, the ship's only violist, there must have been different problems. One can only guess at the awkwardness of playing while clad in overcoats and lifejackets; keeping the instruments tucked beneath their chins cannot have been easy. Moreover, although there was doubtless ambient light from deck lights as well as spill from the lounge's forward windows, they must have had to play largely from memory, not necessarily difficult for professional palm court or cafe musicians. Moreover, if they had needed sheet music parts, the question of music stands arises—were any brought out on deck? We simply do not know. One necessary adjustment, common to all six string players, was the necessity of retuning their instruments once they emerged into the cold; low temperatures raise havoc with cat gut.

When Wallace Hartley's body was pulled from the sea and brought aboard the *Mackay Bennett*, his music case was still strapped across his chest. Although, in the absence of music stands, it was unlikely that any parts would have been distributed that night, perhaps Hartley took the case with him either out of habit or because it contained sheets that he valued. I wonder what music was in it; might it have told us something, if not of the actual final selections, at least what Hartley had *wished* to play? As it was, the musicians seem to have played popular ragtime airs, familiar tunes to which passengers had danced or listened ever since Southampton.

What did they play at the end? My dear friend and colleague, Walter Lord, doyen of *Titanic* historians, hypothesizes persuasively in his *The Night Lives On* that it was neither *Nearer My God to Thee* (which Jessop and several others claimed to have heard) nor the hymn tune *Autumn* but a waltz. The waltz in question, although written by Englishman Archibald Joyce, had a French name, *Songe d'Automne* (Autumn Dream).

It was *Titanic's* surviving radio operator Harold Bride's offhand response later in New York that created the persistent confusion about that hymn tune. When asked by reporters what the band had played, he merely said "Autumn," titular English shorthand for the longer, more challenging French name.

Two separate, fragmentary accounts of the musicians' final moments remain. At the British Inquiry, Steward Edward Brown testified: "I do not remember hearing them stop." But stop they did and surviving passenger A. H. Barksworth conjures up a final image:

"I do not wish to detract from the bravery of anybody but I might mention that when I first came on deck, the band was playing a waltz. The next time I passed where the band had been stationed, the members had thrown down their instruments, and were not to be seen."

That precious stringed instruments were precipitously abandoned by their owners tells the tale: Hartley's gallant band had played to the very end.

In fact, I have two taped recordings of *Songe d'Automne*, appropriately recorded at sea by subsequent ship's musicians. The first version is played with piano accompaniment, as though in *Titanic*'s lounge, and the second just by strings, so that it sounds just the way it must have sounded out on deck that night. It is a bittersweet composition, with themes that are alternately lilting and pensive.

# CHAPTER

# 23

# Australia and Ned

I KNEW THAT IF I meant to continue my sea life, I would have to return at once. Otherwise I would lose my nerve, for I had no love for it. But I needed the work.

The fortnight after Lord Mersey's *Titanic* inquiry finished saw me back on my job. A weariness seemed to have descended on me since the disaster. I saw people and their aims with extraordinary clarity, not unmixed with resentment; and what I saw did not give me the peace I yearned for.

I wanted the quietness of happy contentment, not the hectic turmoil of riches which sapped simplicity and spontaneous kindness out of people. I wanted desperately to shut out the encroachment of sea life on my inner self, to retain something I feared I was losing, when a kind action is performed for the love of pleasing and not for gain.

I had gained one thing: I learned to look very deeply into people and to value them for what I found. Famous names and possessions no longer moved me. I was more confident when confronted by some powerful woman whose cold eyes, as I served her breakfast, might once have shattered me. But each day it was more difficult to be my simple self, to ignore the pettiness, artificiality and frothy gaiety that encompassed a stewardess' life on board ship.

Violet Jessop's recurring distaste for her chosen profession aboard ship remains a leitmotif throughout the memoir. She particularly resented her fellow stewards' base reliance on tips. It has always been symptomatic of shipboard employment, right up to the present day aboard the world's cruising fleet, that companies rely on the generosity of passengers to supplement the miserly wages they pay their hotel workers. Today, third-world stewards and waiters aboard cruise ships are paid a pittance of a monthly wage. But with the addition of passenger tips, they can realize a weekly take-home pay of several hundred dollars, an amount in Indonesia and the Philippines, for instance, that makes them comparatively rich.

It is scarcely surprising, on board Jessop's vessels near the turn of the century, that her colleagues in the victualing department—overworked, underpaid and away from their families for much of the year—would work the main chance as fervently as possible. And inevitably, that main chance was financial, the prospect of passengers' generosity. These were the inescapable realities of shipboard life and there is not one of us, similarly employed as a steward aboard a steamship back then, who would not have been equally anxious for as many substantial tips as possible.


One day a letter came from Ned, telling of a heart that was torn with shock, full of self-reproach for having left me and anxiety for the future. One sentence in particular, criticizing my faith, brought me to a decision: "If I could only speak with you over this matter of your faith, things would be straightened out, I feel sure. Letters are always unsatisfactory in cases like this."

Poor Ned! When he could have spoken, he was silent. Now he craved a chance to unburden himself, to find reassurance for his doubts. He needed me, so the thing for me to do was to go out to Australia for that heart-to-heart talk to clear up everything. We would both be happier afterwards.

Decisions like that are easier made than put into action. Getting out to Australia was not going to be easy. True, I had the opportunity of leave from my own company, for *Olympic* had been laid up after *Titanic*'s loss, to be reinforced against risk of ice, a matter of six months' work. But there were no vacancies on our boats going to the east without displacing someone already established.

So I tried a new company. I had joined my own company at a younger age than was customary so I knew things might not be easy. But, after much perseverance and scheming, I did manage to get an interview with an autocratic old gentleman, superintendent purser and dispenser of jobs such as I sought. I think the only thing that gained me the interview was a warm letter of introduction from an old colleague of his which he could not well refuse.

He regarded me coldly over his glasses and told me I was much too young. He just didn't want young women in his ships, I could see, insisting that sea life was too full of pitfalls. I felt guilty I was not old and staid. Though his intentions were for the best, my subsequent experience of sea life proved that the older people became, the less staid they were.

With modesty, I tried to tell him how reliable a person I could be in spite of my years, though he did not seem convinced. I left with the promise that he would consider my application and I would come back in a week's time for another talk.

Never had youth been at such a disadvantage. In the outer office, I found a sympathetic senior clerk whose duty it was to submit stewardesses' names to his chief when vacancies occurred. He promised to put mine—if I was engaged—on the Australian and not on the Indian list, where newcomers were generally placed.

He also suggested that for my next encounter with the great man, it might help if I dressed more dowdily. So I arrived one foggy morning in February, very shaky at the knees, dressed in the drabbest things I could collect and with a droop that would have done credit to any of Ealing's professional weekend beggars. I looked ten years older.

I got the job! I went home treading on air and my reaction was that I wanted to buy everyone a present. They all entered into the spirit of my great adventure. Getting about the world then was not just jumping on a plane as it is today, it was an undertaking.

Mother, anxious to be cheerful under all circumstances, combined suggestions for my welfare with encouraging messages to Ned as she smiled me away from Tilbury one gusty March morning. "I'll be watching for the postman to bring all your grand news," was the last thing I heard as the ship slowly pulled out of sight. [It was the Peninsular & Oriental steamer *Malwa*.]

From then on my world was a stage of infinite variety. I will not pretend that it was all pleasant going for me on that P & O boat or that I looked forward to sharing a cabin with two other women already established. But I was lucky for they proved treasures. The joy in my heart helped to smooth over the rough patches. It helped me ignore the cold snobbishness of the memsahibs from India returning from their periodic visits home.

I often reflected that there must be some quality in a sea trip that affects character, or maybe its enforced propinquity that emphasizes how awful normal folk can become: Mean, paltry and selfish to a degree when they are in the position of indiscriminate power.

I mean this of men as well as women, though it is unexpected in the former. For it is generally assumed that men are superior to women in this respect. I have not found it so at sea. But I was magnanimous now, everything showed in a rosy light. When I had the opportunity for a little sightseeing after a particularly heavy day's work in sweltering cabins, when I'd emerge hot and extremely footsore, I could drop it all for the fascination that awaited me around every bend.

I found contentment, for example, when I first walked through the Cinnamon Gardens in Colombo, luxuriating in the tropical scents around me. They lulled me into a perfect restfulness that even aching limbs had not the power to dispel, perfect compensation for the supreme effort of getting ashore from the throes of a coaling ship.

I had always imagined that to take tea in Ceylon would be the acme of tea drinking. I approached my first Colombo cup reverently, but it proved the vilest lukewarm beverage I have ever tasted. I soon forgot it in the spell of the sunset hour, all the colors of the world displayed over the heavens, accentuating those three lonely bending palms at the Galle Face Hotel. All the magic of a tropical evening gathered around me as the Indian Ocean breakers thundered in and the palms nodded and dipped their tall heads understandingly, as if the recipients of many confidences over the years.

Youth and love converted my world into something so high that its shortcomings faded out. That was why, when a steward ran amok with a knife because I would not let him kiss me one sweltering night, I was able next day to forget that yesterday had ever been. And ashore, even a rascally old pirate offering a piece of blue glass as a "number one sapphire," with the additional promise of a ten pound note thrown in as a further guarantee of its authenticity, was in my eyes only a sorry human being. Probably others outside my magic circle felt my optimism.

Only one nagging thing chilled my enthusiasm for my visit to Australia. I recalled all the splendid things Ned had attributed to the girls of that land of open spaces. I had heard of their talents—their prowess at sport, riding, the arts of housewifery and, above all, their adaptability. Yet, some spirit of contrariness silenced my tongue about the things I could do. I wanted him, for instance, to discover for himself that I was my own dressmaker. Knowing that one personality can outshine thousands, I now relied on his infectious charm to envelop me in Australia, so that my shortcomings might pass unnoticed.

After enduring the unmerciful buffeting that the traveler is subjected to in the great Australian Bight, when all good resolutions go by the wall and death would be welcomed as a happy release, I had enough eagerness left to be at the head of the line for the first batch of mail that arrived on board. My heart nearly stood still when I saw my first letter from Australian soil, my welcoming letter from Ned. At first, I wanted to rip it open at once but decided instead to enjoy it when I was absolutely free of duties and company, to assimilate every dear line and the surprised welcome it no doubt contained.

At last, in the toilet—generally the only place a person can be sure of privacy on board ship—I opened my letter. The first sentence was a tiny bit cooling, making my heart first jump, then, sickeningly, contract. Ned's comment was that the cable announcing my journey, or rather the envelope containing it, had given him a shock, coming so soon after news of *Titanic*.

But he seemed overjoyed at the prospect of seeing me, never querying how I had managed it. He would be down to meet me, of course, at Sydney, but I was not to be disappointed if he should be a little late. He had started a little business in partnership, giving me the impression that he did most of the worrying. However much his new venture might interfere with my anticipated reception, it was certainly a cause for rejoicing, the beginning of his getting settled down.

He continued in a somewhat quizzical tone that I must overlook any lack of preparation for my arrival, in view of the fact that his mother had sprained her ankle a few days previously. Besides, as she had remarked, I would probably make allowances since I was coming uninvited.

Suddenly, I needed air. I felt I must think quickly what explanation to give to Mary and Jean, the two kindhearted souls with whom I shared a cabin. Like people without any romance in their own lives, they took a warm interest in mine. They had made plans to ensure me privacy for my meeting with Ned and, more important still, freedom from duties for the rest of the time in Sydney, so that I might remain away from the ship. They were waiting now, I knew, to share in the delight at my first letter. My pride forbade that I should let them see the small shadow overclouding my happiness, for I could not explain. I might be doing Ned an injustice and it was perhaps only his inability to express his feelings in a chaotic state of mind with a new job to face, a mother with a sprained ankle and me into the bargain.

Sydney had shrouded her splendor in deep mists as we entered the harbor I had so longed to see, the harbor my beloved was so proud of. I had the greatest difficulty controlling my excitement when the first batch of officials and visitors arrived; in spite of his warning, I felt sure he would be among them. Had I been in his place, I would have been at all costs.

Suddenly, I wanted to disappear to the most distant part of the ship so that when I got news of his arrival I might have time to subdue my emotions before we met. Minutes dragged into hours and hours wore on, leaving a chill behind them. Though Mary and Jean were very optimistic, still there was no Ned.

Children caught at a disadvantage sometimes assume a forced gaiety to cover inward qualms. Ned appeared like that to me when he finally turned up, when all but my facial expression had been chilled. What he lacked in punctuality he made up for in originality when describing the obstacles that had detained him. His new business, too, had kept him back, he explained. It crossed my mind that if men's business claims first place in their thoughts, surely there is a moment when it might take second; but then I felt disloyal.

The welcome Ned's mother and father gave me compensated somewhat for my disappointing wait of the morning. They were hospitable and charming, but I thought I occasionally caught a commiserating expression in their eyes; later, I learnt to associate this with Ned's erratic ways, still apparently a matter of concern to them. They attributed it to a trace of genius which, instead of proving an asset, only accentuated his idiosyncrasies.

Days have never been long enough for me to accomplish my allotted tasks, but those Sydney days seemed never ending. Ned left very early, long before the family was astir; and since it was a very conventional household, I was not expected to be about either. Quite late at night, he returned in a quizzing mood, invariably denoting fatigue or worry.

We had not yet visited the many places he had conjured up for me in those far-off Jamaica days. When his mother and I went to visit those people she deemed it necessary to present me to, I fear I could only force a frozen smile of thanks in response to their congratulations.

Sometimes, I'd put on my prettiest dress to go into town to see him at his little engineering shop. There I'd find him covered in grease from head to foot, eyes glowing with enthusiasm over some object that looked to me like a scrap of old metal. I would follow him from bench to furnace and back while the whole process was minutely detailed. Meanwhile, I kept a weather eye on my white shoes which generally soaked up the residue on the floor.

One day he appeared in a jubilant frame of mind. He had decided to take a few days off from his business and to take me to the Blue Mountains. There, in Katoomba, he had cousins old enough to chaperone me. Indeed, that appeared his greatest concern, that I should be suitably protected. Apparently he never saw the incongruity of this, after my struggle and success in coming twelve thousand miles to see him, unaided and unchaperoned. But I was too happy to have him all to myself, away from his bits of metal and his furnace, to even comment about it.

All my doubts and unhappiness dropped from me like a chrysalis as we sped up by train towards the incredibly beautiful Blue Mountains, lost in mists that became denser before merging with snow-covered summits. Here and there were gurgling, dashing waterfalls, cascading through magnificent vegetation, while as far as the eye could see was the blue of the gum trees. Katoomba, with its snows and its peace, was like a fairy tale Christmas card. Here, I felt, I could linger quietly and sanely over problems, feeling that any obstacle could be surmounted in the serenity of the place.

There was a little spot, high up on a snow-covered height, where you could look down into impenetrable blue depths; it will always remain fresh in my mind. The only sound to break the silence was a chattering waterfall with just our two selves to admire it. I was returning to duty in a few days, but my mission had still not been accomplished. Not one of the problems Ned had so often written of had been touched upon.

I felt that, if he did not broach the subject, I must for both our sakes. He had been very lovable and happy in his impish way that day and, as we were lazily brooding over the peaceful scene below us, I tentatively suggested that here and now was a good opportunity for that "heart-to-heart" talk about our future.

I shall never forget—for it has shaped my life since—the look of tolerant, mocking, good humor as he teased, "What on earth does the little girl want to talk so seriously about now?"

My heart seemed to miss a beat. I suddenly felt an overwhelming pity that he should be totally unaware of something so obvious to me. And I knew, beyond the shadow of a doubt, that all the anticipated joys, shared hopes and lovely dreams would never be. I had to face the inevitable: All I had cherished, all that which had sustained me to face my lot at sea, must now be locked away in my heart; the key to that treasure chest I would drop into the surging waters below.

Just then, a startled bird in flight dislodged a pebble that fell to the depths with the tinkle of something broken. I shivered; it was so final. And to Ned's anxious question, all I could answer was: "Oh, there's nothing the matter, dearest. Let's go along now, it's getting mighty chilly."

So we bent our steps homewards.

As the streamered *Malwa* pulled away to vociferous Australian farewells, I saw Ned's eager eyes scanning the decks for me. He looked lonely with the face of a small boy who has been chastised twice for the same offense. Dear Ned, fine and clean, one of nature's gentlemen but utterly incapable of finding that road hedged with understanding and paved with faith.

It was characteristic of him to write years later, after my gay and gallant brother Philip's death in the First World War:

"Dearest, I must have missed some of your letters. It is only after diligent searching I ever manage to retrieve my correspondence from the agent's office.

"I suppose they forget us poor devils buried away in places like Canton for endless ages, after long spells in Hong Kong too.

"I left your photo in Sydney but it's no use, I know every line of it by heart. It is not all in Sydney, part of it is on the negative of my brain.

"It may seem strange to be writing like this after such a long interval, but your letters left me wondering whether it would not be kinder of me to disappear from your horizon as I could only be worrying you. At first, I thought you might be married, but when another letter came, I must say I was relieved; although I cannot understand how stupid people must be, not to see how rare and beautiful a jewel that girl is, who used to love me.

"I should have married you long ago. As it is, I work like mad, and I suspect I am just trying to dodge that lonely feeling too. If I had some money I would make a beeline for you, and try to win back some of that love I deserve to have lost. As it is, I rip into things here but don't collect much for it.

"I have a crew that don't care a d . . . They have to be that way, for this old crock of a ship is bound always for goodness knows where, any place we get a cargo for.

"Poor old Phil! It was a terrible shock to me, your news. I often think of Philip. I see him as I last saw him, finely set and manly, and I say: 'Philip, old man! I am not fit to shake you by the hand, and there are tears in my eyes. But I feel proud of having known you. You died a hero, facing fearful odds, knowing the end and keeping your post; fighting for your dear ones at home and your country's honor, slam-banging past the gates of hell, to the reward of a just god's grace.'"

(Philip [a corporal with the King Edward Light Horse] had volunteered with four companions to man a machine gun post covering a crucial retreat road being used by the British. They kept this open for three days and were blown to pieces on the fourth.)

I always half expected to find Ned smiling one day on the doorstep, yet, when he failed to come, I was not surprised.

What better moment to plumb the depths of Violet Jessop's disappointing love life!

Margaret Meehan told me that her aunt had, in fact, married in the late 1920's, so briefly and disastrously that not even her husband's name remains extant within the family. All that is known is that he was a fellow crew member aboard one of her ships—presumably a Red Star Line vessel—but apart from that sketchiest of glimpses, the man's identity, his position on board and even the dates of his flawed marriage to Jessop remain bafflingly blank.

Of the 34 numbered chapters comprising her original manuscript, one—chapter 18—has vanished. Though it is tempting to conclude that those lost pages might have included some mention of her marriage, I think it unlikely. Violet's narrative adheres to a fairly strict chronology and the missing chapter *precedes* her passage down under in hopes of becoming engaged to her "beloved." For her to have accepted another's proposal prior to writing off Ned seems unlikely. For the balance of her days, both Meehan sisters agreed, "companionable and lovable" Ned remained the unrequited love of their Auntie Vi's life.

Ned's letter to Violet on the occasion of Philip's death reveals to perfection the man's lilting, quixotic appeal. He writes prettily and evocatively, with sometimes Conradian resonances. Though he once suggested to Violet that "letters were unsatisfactory," he is clearly more eloquent and comfortable on paper than face to face. Incidentally, since he had apparently met her brother Philip, we must conclude that Ned had been introduced to members of the Jessop family in London, visits to which Violet never once refers.

How her life might have changed had she and Ned married as a result of this Australian episode! The tenor of that visit, incidentally, bore all the hallmarks of, if not a formal engagement, at least a familial understanding. That Violet's potential mother-in-law took Ned's English girl on a round of social calls to her friends implied far more than ultimately emerged; yet, predictably, his parents seemed no closer than Violet to nailing down their quicksilver son.

Had that marriage come about, Violet would inevitably have given up the sea and settled down to married life and presumably children in Australia. The sole argument—apart from Ned's diffidence—against their future had been hinted at earlier by Jessop's refusal of several prior marriage proposals, both from passengers and that mysterious New Yorker with the Cuban plantation: As the Jessop family breadwinner, she had an overriding sense of responsibility towards her mother. Indeed, I see her almost-too-quick realization of Ned's ineligibility as a husband as concern that his precariously financed workshop might never produce sufficient income for her to continue supporting her mother.

Throughout her life, Violet Jessop cherished her independence; whatever the shortcomings she perceived of her sea-going career, it had the advantage of producing regular if modest wages and tips. I think she would have thought long and hard before renouncing it.

There is, I am told, a contemporary publishing abbreviation "O.S.S.," inhouse shorthand for "obligatory sex scene." I am convinced that were Jessop's manuscript to adhere to those tenets—candid autobiography, warts and all—she would doubtless have been obliged to include an exposé of the backstage sexual peccadilloes aboard turn-of-the-century ocean liners.

But she remains firmly discreet, product of Edwardian mores no less than her sound Catholic upbringing. Moreover, she might well have been sexually traumatized by the attempted molestation she had experienced as a child in Argentina and, once again, by her employer when she was a governess in Kent. Then too, there was the upsetting and distasteful behavior of the philandering purser on board one of her earliest ships. Small wonder, then, that reticence and discretion color much of her account of off-duty life on board.

Jessop was 21 when she first went to sea on the *Orinoco*; that she considered herself "too young" for the life she confesses more than once. Most of her fellow stewardesses tended to be mature women and we can only conclude that Jessop, the vivacious, young shipboard novice, must have cut a wide swath among her male shipmates. Photographs of her in her early twenties reveal a vital, intensely attractive young woman with a slim waist—eighteen inches, according to her nieces—good clothes sense, a ready smile and a pair of sparkling gray/blue eyes with lashes so long that they tangled in the veils of her hats. Then too, she was blessed with that irreplaceable Irish gift of the blarney that bewitched everyone with whom she came in contact.

That she spoke her mind frankly did not apparently diminish her appeal; indeed, it may well have enhanced it. I sense that her abbreviated childhood fostered a precocious maturity, imprinting on adult Violet a devil-may-care insouciance; this remained an irrepressible facet of her shipboard persona. If she seemed to flirt, she did so unconsciously. One can be certain that the philandering captain who dismissed her for "flirting with the officers" was only concluding a personal vendetta against the plucky stewardess who chose to reject his clumsy overtures.

For every crew, shipboard life, then as now, is paradoxically hectic yet monotonous, the passage of days blurred by fatigue and routine; crossings blended one into another save those marked by storm or accident. The appearance of a fresh young face would inevitably have created, if not a sensation, at least a frisson of admiration everywhere on board. Violet says it best herself, remembering on the *Orinoco* "all the little attentions I received." Also, how much she disliked one "persistent" colleague whose overtures inclined toward "nocturnal ramblings" and the *Malwa* crewman who went berserk with a knife when refused a kiss.

Indeed, colleagues were not her only admirers: Senior shipboard personnel as well as passengers apparently found Violet Jessop devastatingly attractive. She realized it herself, belatedly: "I was not to know until years later," she confesses rather naively when boarding her first ship, "that the adulations I had accepted as chivalry were largely a demonstration of sexual attraction."

Compounding the difficulties, shipboard dalliance of any kind inevitably became common knowledge. In the matter of liaisons especially, there were no shipboard secrets. Moreover, in a milieu where new conversational topics were scarce, rumor and gossip proliferated within the hothouse confines of every glory hole and wardroom. Early on, Jessop learned to be careful. Even the perfectly innocent attentions of the elderly ship's surgeon on her first excursion to Panama triggered unwarranted sexual innuendo.

Always, the subject of physical attraction brings us back to Ned, inescapable nexus of Violet's abortive love life. Her account of their first outing ashore together in Jamaica is couched in terms that seem lifted intact from the chaste prose of a romance novel: The bliss of their first kiss became "the piece of heaven it opened for me"; en route to Australia, her breathless anticipation of seeing him again, the angst about their meeting and the fluttering disappointment of Ned's every inconsistency is painfully documented; and after that final, bittersweet denouement in the Blue Mountains, Violet vows that she will keep Ned's memory "locked forever in her heart," its key thrown into the depths of that chattering waterfall.

But despite that renunciation, throughout the long life that remained her, it seems clear that for Violet, no-one—least of all the man she briefly

married—ever matched up to the blue-eyed, quizzical and infuriatingly elusive Ned. And perhaps the saddest part of her never marrying successfully
was that she bore no children. Both nieces recall that whenever Violet held
a baby, her face glowed with a special light.

# CHAPTER

# 24

# Shipboard Romance

KATHERINE DUNCAN'S INCLUSION in the passenger list was a godsend to me on the voyage home. At once a warmth of understanding sprang up between myself and this dark-haired girl with the restful voice.

She was so extraordinarily natural and human. Her depth and charm often made me wonder why anyone so gifted should be unattached and even uninterested in her immediate neighbors. She was always ready to talk about books and when drawn out, proved that she had thought deeply about most subjects; on other occasions, she would discuss her admiration for her one remaining brother for whom she kept house in England. Though Katherine Duncan never spoke of her own life, I gathered she had done much traveling.

We soon looked forward to our little chats in her cabin. She invited me when I could relax from my duties in the afternoons. I would find her beautifully dressed, as if to receive afternoon callers, with an aura of hospitality about her. There was always a box of sweets handy and we'd find ourselves deep in enthusiastic discussion about some subject we both had in common. Sometimes it was pewter and old lace, which like all things unobtainable I yearned for, but very often it was the hundred and one things we had seen in some hole-and-corner, perhaps in Petticoat Lane of London's East End or the Thieves' Market in Hong Kong, or perhaps in one of those centuries-old, tumble down shops in a side street of Lisbon; something we wished we had bought.

Like myself, she could not resist that which appealed to her sense of beauty, though it might often leave others wondering what one could see in such "junk." Her face would sparkle with unconcealed delight if I considered she had got what my mother would call a "dead bargain" and a treasure as well.

As we drew nearer her destination I noticed an occasional wist-fulness about her and this puzzled me, for she had told me she was on her way to visit an aunt, of whom she was very fond.

When I asked her one day if she had slept well, a queer fright-ened expression flitted momentarily across her face and her frank eyes regarded me with an inquiring look.

"Because if you don't," I continued, "I'll make you a soothing ti-sane and bring it to you just before I go to bed." She looked really alarmed at that and assured me that she needed nothing to induce sleep.

My cabin was insufferably hot one night. No air seemed to come through the open port and in spite of the fact that it was not yet dawn, I put on a cloak and went up on deck on the weather side.

I was glad Katherine Duncan's cabin happened to be on this side, I mused, as the balmy air revived me; at least she would be spared be-ing parboiled as we poor wretches were on the lee side of the ship. The decks seemed peaceful now and so deserted in contrast to the daytime with its hectic pursuit of energetic games and the incessant buzz of voices. For this peace I would readily forfeit my rest. There was no moon but the stars shone brightly. One big star's rays made a silver path across the waters.

I was dreamily enjoying my isolation in a secluded corner, when I heard a strange scraping sound, then a groan and a splash. I ran to the ship's side but saw nothing. Light here and there came from portholes below me but there was nothing to solve the mystery of that groan.

Suddenly something I was leaning against moved and gave me an uncanny shock. I had been pressing against a piece of rope which I could see, in the dim light, had been loosely tied around the ship's rail and was dangling over the side.

Again, it jerked. Peering over, I saw, faintly, a white hand come out of an unlighted porthole, grope about and, touching the rope, grasp it with nervous urgency, tugging at it in a futile effort to pull it down. For no reason that I can explain, I noiselessly undid the rope and as quietly let it slide into that hand which quickly disappeared.

Only then did I realize that I was standing directly over Kather-ine Duncan's cabin. But what would she be doing pulling in a rope from the upper deck at that unearthly hour? I resolved to keep my counsel and say nothing.

I came on duty after a sleepless morning and was serving the end-less teas and early morning fruit, without which British voyagers cannot start the day. I noticed one of those "Do not disturb" cards so reminiscent of American hotels pinned to Katherine Duncan's door. I was surprised, for only once after a dance had she ever used it, when she laughingly said she'd chance the "old man's" disapproval as he made his inspection of the passenger cabins.

Up in the pantry, men preparing breakfast were discussing the disappearance of the second Marconi operator. He had failed to report for duty at 4 a.m. A likable fellow, particularly popular because he was a good mixer and a sport enthusiast, he was often able to arrange for the men of the victualing department to get a cricket match ashore, making a break in the sameness of their days.

At noon, Katherine Duncan's bell rang and I found her extraordinarily apathetic and wan, with all the color drained from her face. When I insisted on bringing her a cup of broth, I received one of her fleeting, old-time smiles, as if she wanted desperately to appear as usual. Lifting a cushion from her settee to help prop her up, I noticed a length of rope. She must have noticed my start, for she burst into tears as if all the pent-up sorrow of years was let loose. Then she explained, half chokingly, while she clung to me.

She had met Peter Carstairs on a rough Channel crossing when a slight mishap served as introduction. Their meeting had turned quickly from friendship to love. She had never thought it possible to care for anyone as much as she cared for Peter, and only regretted he always seemed to think she would be unwilling to share his life on his rather small salary.

When she learned he was being transferred to this route, she had arranged to return to England on his ship and readily acquiesced to Peter's suggestion that their friendship should be kept secret on board. He dreaded ship's and, particularly, stewards' gossip, he said.

One day, boasting of his athletic prowess, he told her he would in future visit her by way of the porthole by means of a rope, and at a time when nobody was about. She tried hard to dissuade him for safety's sake and because it did not conform to her ideas of propriety, though people on board ship were more lax than ashore. But with Peter she frankly admitted, she would always give in.

The previous day they had been through their first lover's quarrel, so his coming this morning was all the more longed-for. She had been near the port to guide him in as she had done on previous occasions when the rope gave way and all that remained to her was the sound of that groan.

While I vainly tried to comfort her, my mind went back to a day not far distant, when young Peter Carstairs had been toasted on his return from a hurried wedding, so gay, so charming, such a hero of romance that day. It was not for me to speak; nothing could be undone. I felt I wanted her to keep what idealism she had about him. I would have hated to see those gentle eyes shine bitter and hard; I had seen too much of that already at sea.

Nobody on board connected Peter's mysterious disappearance with Katherine's desire for solitude, and she knew it was not necessary to swear me to secrecy, for in my work I had long been used to guarding the secrets of others.

Years later I learnt she had trained and volunteered for nursing service in one of the outposts of the Empire. I hoped she found happiness there.

Elements of this bizarre affair of the lady passenger and a radio operator may well be true. Illicit liaisons between married officers and single passengers are as old as the first passenger vessel and are not unknown aboard many ships to the present day.

But as Violet tells it, the mechanics of this particular tale strain credulity. Understandably, the lovers' clandestine cabin meetings would have to have been surreptitious, for a junior Marconi operator had no business late at night in passenger country; hence his desperate but, to my mind, improbable subterfuge. It is a romantic scenario fraught with problems. Peter's feat—regardless how agile and muscular—of lowering himself over the ship's side and clambering through an open porthole, seems better suited to a Douglas Fairbanks swashbuckler than reality.

Of more interest to me in this chapter is the warmth of the relationship she enjoyed with Katherine Duncan. However spurious the affair with the radio operator, the pleasure the two women—stewardess and passenger—took in each other's company rings true. We discover that not all of Jessop's lady passengers were necessarily imperious Margaret Dumonts. I am reminded that it was Violet Jessop's beguiling concern for another passenger years later—my mother aboard the *Majestic*—that brought her to my attention to begin with.

# A Nurse in the Great War

THE DOGS OF war were unleashed soon after I returned to service on the Western Ocean. August 4th, 1914, found us in mid-Atlantic on our way to New York with passengers of all nationalities. Thankfully, they managed to preserve an equable social intercourse till the completion of the voyage.

Not so below stairs, where the niceties of good form are not always the accepted rule. One or two crew members had long been suspected of using their stewarding as a cloak to international interests. Their tenaciousness in holding their position had often been resented, and they now came in for a good deal of private and unauthorized strafing. On our return, it appeared that a similar view was held by the British authorities.

Those first days, a wave of animation swept over everybody, very likely because the unknown is very exciting. Most of these people had never known war. Everyone seemed revitalized and a new purpose leapt into many hitherto colorless lives. Some of my own department felt this too, and momentarily, money interests were forgotten in the thrill of patriotic fervor. As subsequent years proved, some of their best intentions remained unfulfilled.

When eulogizing the Merchant Service, people's minds nearly always visualize the men in jerseys, sailors with weather-beaten faces fresh from storm-swept decks, or engine room men with blackened faces; rarely do they envision the sallow-faced, white-jacketed stewards of the victualing department, who themselves have learnt not to expect to be considered heroes, and yet . . .

It seemed uncanny, journeying back to England, to goodness knows what, in a huge darkened *Olympic*. The first sight of a large ship with the unmistakable signs of cruiser about her did make our

hearts beat swifter. It was the Cunarder *Aquitania,* already converted
to an armed merchant cruiser, looking very much like a woman showing off a beautiful new dress, which we duly admired, gratefully.

War did not diminish the magnetic charm of homecoming with
all its animation, its gaiety and zestful exchange of experiences. We all
foregathered and needed no outside entertainment. Indeed, it took
many years of wandering and contacts before I realized the heaven-
sent qualities that made our own particular little family reunions so
different. Now I know the keynote was laughter, real heartfelt laughter, that merriment which bubbled up from our innermost being. It
enabled us to soar over sordid cares with a feeling of lighthearted
hope and courage. Perhaps it was due to our persistent habit of seeing our own daily lives comically, of being able to laugh at ourselves.

I was greeted by a bunch of cheery youngsters in khaki. My brothers rejoiced in the pride of their new responsibilities, tall and slender in
their fair, young manliness. Even at that early date they had not escaped
sneering enquiries at work: "When are you young Argentines joining
up?" I pointed out this was probably only an indication of minds themselves torn by indecision and was proved right long afterwards. When
the war was over, and we had already suffered a gap in our beloved
ranks, my remaining brothers were bidding goodbye to their former
chiefs at work before sailing away to a new life in Australia. They found
their solicitous inquirers had not joined up and were now foremen or,
as they sheepishly put it, "indispensable to the Government."

I made several more trips in the early stages of the war. Because
of *Olympic*'s size and inadequate berthing accommodations for very
large liners on the West Coast, we were transferred to the Clyde in
Scotland. Had this not happened I might never have had the good
fortune to get better acquainted with a people I had loved from my
childhood out in the Argentine pampas; it had been a Scots woman
who brought me into the world.

We anchored in Greenock and, after a week of roaming, a week
of mists and hills and heather, to say nothing of some delightful fish
dinners, I could not help wondering why so many Britishers go galli-
vanting to arid corners of the world when there is so much magnificent scenery, kindly good sense and generosity over the border.

During my last trip on *Olympic* we got our first experience of
naval action and I decided to throw in my lot with the British Red
Cross.

For the sake of clarity, I think it makes sense to document the historic events prior to reading Jessop's account. The year-old Royal Navy battleship HMS *Audacious*, under the command of Captain C.R. Dampier, struck a mine during gunnery practice on the morning of 27 October 1914, only two months after the outbreak of war. Ironically, the enemy vessel that had laid the string of 200 mines earlier that week was the converted German liner *Berlin*. *Audacious* and other battleships of the Grand Fleet had been moved to the waters off Northern Ireland because the Admiralty was concerned about the vulnerability of Scapa Flow to German U-boats. Remarkably, no Royal Naval personnel were killed. Try as she might, *Olympic* was unable to tow the vessel into shallower water. *Audacious* turned turtle later that same day and, just before sinking, blew up.

Because of the Admiralty's consternation that a single mine could destroy their latest warship, attempts were made to suppress news of the loss. *Olympic*, under strict orders from Acting Admiral Sir John Jellicoe, was temporarily interned in Lough Swilly. However, it was a futile stratagem; there were too many witnesses aboard the rescuing White Star liner, all of whom would disembark days later in Scotland.

The smell of land on a beautiful autumn morning brought us that satisfying odor of peat-fires as we skirted the coast of northern Ireland on our way to Scotland.

We had noticed at a distance gray shapes that proved to be some cruisers out for target practice, we thought. Suddenly there was a dispersal and change of tactics indicating that something was amiss. Putting on speed, we soon found one of the largest cruisers had been struck. As we hurried to the scene, all our lifeboats, with voluntary crews including a great many stewards, stood ready to lower.

On the swell of enormous waves, the huge battleship rhythmically rose and dipped. Serrated ranks of men in blue lined her decks, watching groups of their comrades being swept over as monster waves washed the decks. The next wave, however, brought them back again and not one man lost his life through drowning.

As our lifeboats laboriously made the crossing, appearing at times to be completely submerged in the trough of the sea, we held our breaths. Then as they came and went, transferring groups of those extraordinarily well-disciplined men with their cheery, grateful faces, the whole ship began to smile as one man. We watched those somewhat embarrassed men being rendered still more tongue-tied by the warmth of welcome they found as willing hands pulled them aboard *Olympic*. Their eyes lit up at the sight of comrades already brought to safety. I was touched by their eager, simple wonder as they made comparisons between the appointments of a luxury liner and their own austere surroundings.

All day we labored frantically to take that huge hulk in tow. Everybody not otherwise engaged, including passengers, helped transfer the large steel hawser from one part of the ship to another, after our first cable had snapped. It seemed a superhuman effort to move its unwieldy end onto the waiting tugs and destroyers standing by, waiting to connect it to the distressed ship.

But it was all hopeless. It snapped again. As evening drew near we left the *Audacious* a wounded and tired giant, heaving herself up every now and then, only to sink lower and lower in the restless sea with the setting sun's rays illuminating her doom. We steamed for Lough Swilly, near those Donegal hills where the lights and shadows of indigo and purple always wove a different picture. Here and there, tiny spirals of smoke from the cottagers' peat-fires curled heavenward like incense at evening prayer, filling the crystal clear air with its unforgettable odor. The only sound was the tinkling church bells echoing faintly through the valleys, calling the faithful to early mass.

A fairy-tale setting discovered by accident, it was a most realistic place in which to be "interned." It was hoped by this internment to avoid the publicity about this latest disaster. The news would doubtless leak out once the passengers—some of them most important— were free to go their different ways; many, moreover, stood to be great losers by the enforced delay.

I am afraid all the precautions to keep the news from leaking were in vain, for while we were still living in that pool of peace, Lough Swilly, the news was already being yelled abroad by newsboys in the capitals of Europe.

With regret, we weighed anchor from that beautiful spot where we had got familiar with jolly Royal Navy men, who had the entire freedom of our ship when duty permitted. I noticed that they never lost an opportunity to take advantage of our hospitality, accepting things that sailors appreciate.

Our commander, Captain Haddock, was himself a Royal Navy man, a lovable character and a true English gentleman of the old school. His unpretentious appearance, quiet manners, old-fashioned side whiskers and a coachman's top coat when ashore, often caused landsmen to mistake his calling. He loved to relate such incidents to the passengers at his table, chuckling softly with one eyebrow whimsically raised.

Once he went in person to a well-known nursery in Southampton to choose a large quantity of stuff for his garden. When the transaction was completed, the salesman, a new employee, said confidentially: "If you can arrange to get us Captain Haddock's regular orders, we will give you a good commission." Whereupon the good captain was forced to admit he was not his own coachman-cum-gardener.

To a stranger, perhaps the attraction of this rather unprepossessing man lay in his charming and restful voice, probably the result of generations of good breeding, and his steadfast eyes. When surprised, they would widen into a questioning, slightly bewildered stare and, without a word, he would turn to whoever was with him and invariably scratch the top of his head with a sort of childish perplexity.

But to us all, the thing that drew our unquestioning loyalty was his naturalness and his intensely human manner of dealing with his fellow men.

Later in the war, when he was in command of Q-boats [armed Royal Naval anti-submarine vessels disguised to look like merchantmen], there was a scramble amongst his old crews to serve with him.

Violet Jessop decided to join the war effort as a junior nurse, enlisting in the V.A.D. or Voluntary Aid Detachment. This was a nursing organization first set up in 1908 by the British Red Cross Society at the invitation of the War Office; it would form a hospital arm for the newly-established Territorial Army. By the end of World War I, there would be 4,083 V.A.D. detachments made up of 126,000 women.

Nursing was a profession for which she was extremely well-suited, as though the long hospital stays of her childhood had somehow heightened her sensitivity to suffering. Violet had, according to Margaret Meehan, wonderfully soothing hands which could effectively banish a headache merely by stroking the sufferer's forehead.

After duly swotting for weeks trying to assimilate all that a V.A.D. should know, I was declared by the examining doctor capable of those entirely unglamorous tasks that are the routine of every hospital junior nurse. I found the training I had acquired in the hard school of the sea invaluable. I loved the nursing profession, though not necessarily the people who chose it as a life's vocation; I often found them antipathetic.

I suppose one of my first shocks soon after joining the staff of an East Coast hospital was the jauntiness with which some of my colleagues expected to run before they could walk. I particularly remember one girl who was furious and sulked for days because she was not allowed to do a gruesome surgical dressing alone. She treated me to a pitying, half-contemptuous stare when, trying to console her, I remarked that for myself I had not yet enough fortitude to bear any of these cases on my conscience.

We were fortunate in having a London Hospital-trained Scots woman as matron. She was helpful to us novices and human in her approach to everything. Yet she failed to understand the psychology of the average "Tommy," why he needed to do all those little childish things which gave his soul so much satisfaction.

She never did see eye to eye with the fellow who bashed in the face of the hall clock with his boot when he heard he was being discharged, because it had ticked away the days too slowly. And she always regarded with a hurt expression, a sort of personal hurt, the delinquents who slipped out at night through the ward windows, while the night nurse was engaged elsewhere, and went carousing with friends down the road to the local pub.

Their peccadilloes were only too evident by the condition of their wounds next day, and the look on Matron's face as she redressed the wounds, must have robbed the adventurers of much of their joy. Eating cordite to send their temperatures up when they felt like a day in bed, was something she just could not understand. The memory of her plaintive, "Why do they do it, nurse?" still makes me smile.

But for downright good-heartedness, there was no one to beat her. She was a wonderful nurse to whom I owe a great debt of gratitude for all she so painstakingly taught me when faced with maimed humans.

I knew that hospital life was not going to be smooth going and shuddered every time Matron said: "Oh, nurse, you're used to discipline, so I'll expect you to look after so-and-so." Once she saw an unfortunate V.A.D. sterilizing instruments; after dropping a probe, she picked it up and replaced it among the clean instruments. Matron nearly expired.

The enforcement of Matron's rules was often the cause of bitter enmity between patients and nurses. For instance, all bed patients had to have their feet washed before the day nurses took over in the morning. Nobody likes their feet washed on a cold gray dawn and Tommies were no exception. But it had never occurred to me to break Matron's rule. It was not till long afterwards, when it no longer mattered, that I learnt the reason for the black looks given me, in spite of my placating them with my quota of sugar. Most of the nurses had not insisted when a man showed a strong disinclination to have his feet washed. Needless to say, I felt that at times my sense of duty was distinctly irksome to my patients.

Yet there were many compensating moments. I remember spending long hours of the night by the bedside of a man whose nights were hell, though by day he was one of the cheeriest souls in the ward. But in the silence of the dark he paid the penalty, twitching in agony as he lay on his face, for his poor back was partly blown away and drugs no longer helped much. He used to say it helped him if he could grip my arm during those racking onslaughts of pain. And who knows, perhaps a little of my vitality did enter his body, for he would gradually sink into sleep while I carefully disengaged my arm from his grasp and shaded the light from his pinched face. Then I would tiptoe out for a cup of hot coffee to keep myself awake. I would have given anything to lie down on the floor and sleep. Yet, when my time came for sleep, I lay wide-eyed.

Perhaps the greatest satisfaction I got was on those days when we received new batches of wounded. We all worked feverishly to attend to their needs and make them feel at home. We always gave an encouraging welcome to each fresh batch as they stumbled dazedly into our midst with wide-open, hurt eyes, like children in a strange land. They always asked the same question as they came anxiously over the threshold: "Where are we, nurse?"

It may have only been coincidence that so many of our patients came from the North, too far away for their relatives to make the journey to see them. I used to hate seeing the look of disappointment on their faces.

By the time I took over night duty, my four brothers were serving in the trenches, so whenever I arrived on duty after a fresh batch of wounded had been admitted during the day, I took over with great trepidation. The fear was ever with me that one among them might be from their regiments, proving they were in action and that I might hear something I was afraid to learn. Nevertheless, when all were set-

tled down and the ward was quiet, I'd go from bed to bed, eagerly
looking at the badges on every new man's cap as it lay, according to
rule, on his locker top.

Sometimes false alarms would render my nights unbearable with
anxiety. Once, finding a badge of the London Irish after the battle of
Loos, I inquired of its owner about my youngest brother, hesitatingly, wanting yet not wanting to hear facts.

"Oh yes, I know him," he said. "He won the high jump in the
battalion sports, he's a fine sport, but I'm afraid he did not return after the do the other day. All the signalers went over before us, but
none returned, I was told." Many days later, however, we heard that
he had returned safely.

Weighed against all the misery of anxiety for my own folk, the
tiredness and the lack of rest, was the stimulation of giving comfort
or alleviating some pain which my particular capabilities made possible. But we were understaffed and undersupplied, and even the satisfaction of being of use at times turned to misfortune.

I had such an experience, which was eventually the cause of my
leaving the hospital. Among the very severely wounded was a boy
with a badly suppurating arm which required dressing every two
hours day and night, consisting of the insertion of many drainage
tubes.

He was in a fearful state of nerves and got the idea that anyone
who dressed his wound, with the exception of myself, hurt him beyond endurance. This was partly imagination perhaps, because I had
to remove the draining tubes from his wounds just as the others did,
but he insisted that I alone never jabbed him. So, after consulting
with Matron, I agreed to do his dressings day and night, which meant
I had very broken rest.

Possibly during one of the nocturnal dressing sessions, overtired
and not so careful, I must have pricked my finger. Soon afterwards, I
suffered the torment of a poisoned hand which, in my rundown condition, took a long time to recover. Weak and listless, I crawled about
my duties until a doctor suggested that if I could get a sea trip and
the air I was used to, I might get back my strength and zest.

I wrote off at once to the White Star Line, explaining everything
and asking to be allowed to make a trip somewhere, to which they
replied most agreeably, promising me the first vacancy in their magnificently fitted hospital ship *Britannic*, *Titanic*'s sister ship.

In the interim, the sudden illness of one of their stewardesses allowed me to make the short trip to New York in the *Cedric*. This enabled me to meet once again my well-loved school directress from South America, who was just then visiting her New England home.

Anxious as I was to get a place on board so that I could recover my health, I don't think the thought ever crossed my mind of the danger thereon. It was not till we were well past the coast of Ireland that we received the first warning of an enemy submarine's approach.

Everybody took the danger signal very serenely, collecting life-belts and handy valuables and trotting quickly up to their stations with a joke and a resigned air. As I made the rounds of my section to see that all were up at the boats, I witnessed an amusing scene. There was a young mother, very deaf she was, who always prepared her baby's bottle at that hour. I went to see if she had been warned, and arrived at her door to find the steward had forestalled me.

A most genial, good tempered fellow ordinarily, the steward was now wearing an expression of bewildered exasperation, as he regarded the little lady who with unconscious calmness went about preparing her baby's food. Quite oblivious that he was trussed up in a lifebelt like a pouter pigeon, she said to him in the gentlest of tones, "Steward, I am now ready for my hot water." He replied as calmly as possible: "Madam, it's not hot water you need but a lifebelt."

I was thankful to reach New York still alive. I was reunited with my school directress, who immediately took me to her aunt's home in New England. Everything about that home had a soul-satisfying charm.

No sooner had I arrived home from that trip one raw November day than I was summoned to present myself the following afternoon to sign Articles for the hospital ship *Britannic*. Almost simultaneously with my orders came news that William, my eldest brother, who had been wounded, was now very ill with malaria in a Malta hospital. I was glad to be going in that direction, for it would be grand to see those cheery gray eyes again and that old ready smile which I somehow felt would never fade out, whatever the odds. He was built that way.

Suddenly our kitchen was transformed into a hive of industry to get my uniforms ready. Piles upon piles of garments lay around in confusing disarray. At last, my trunk was waiting, beautifully packed with all my keepsakes which helped me feel less lonely while on the seas. There were tender goodbyes and I was on my way.

It was like going into a new world, after being used to passenger liners, to board that stately hospital ship. For all the world, she looked like a great white swan. Soon renewed friendships made me feel more at home, for at sea you always meet someone you know.

It was not until I sailed that I learned to my disappointment that the great ship (she was *Titanic*'s sister ship) was bound for Moúdros and not Malta. Her massive size and draft precluded her from Malta's Grand Harbour. However, I did get to Malta, but that is another story.

Red Star's *Belgenland* outbound from New York; Coney Island's Halfmoon Hotel is just beyond the stem. In terms of highest crew morale, she remained Violet's favorite ship. *(Edwin Levick photograph, Everett Viez collection)*

Keepsake from famous Mary Pickford, a grateful passenger, vessel and crossing unknown. *(Marilyn Skopal)*

Among a cheerful trio aboard *Andes* after World War II is Mary Meehan, who worked briefly as one of the vessel's telephonists. *(Margaret and Mary Meehan)*

Looking extremely well turned out, Violet Jessop ashore in Colombo en route to Australia aboard P&O's *Malwa. (Margaret and Mary Meehan)*

An irresistible passenger snapshot from the late forties. Inscribed on the reverse: "Mavis and I during a rehearsal on board the *Andes*." *(John Maxtone-Graham collection)*

The end of an era: Party in the third class dining room on the *United States* in the early 1960's. *(Sheridan House archives)*

Probably the last shipboard photograph for which Violet ever posed, on board *Andes* at a retirement party for the chief engineer. Violet is in the last row on the right. *(Marilyn Skopal)*

The house at 22 Vallis Way, Ealing, that Violet shared with her mother. *(Margaret and Mary Meehan)*

Margaret and her Auntie Vi pose in front of Maythorn in the summer of 1954. *(Margaret and Mary Meehan)*

Maythorn, Jessop's idyllic
retirement cottage in
Suffolk. *(Margaret and Mary
Meehan)*

The Meehan sisters today in their London garden, Mary on the left, Margaret
on the right. *(John Maxtone-Graham collection)*

Far Eastern treasures enrich the Meehan sisters' garden. An inveterate shopper wherever the ship called, Violet purchased these two cachepots; in the background is the giant clamshell she once brought home triumphantly to Ealing in a taxi. *(John Maxtone-Graham collection)*

# 26

## *Britannic*

I N THE FIGURATIVE encyclopedia of lost ships, *Britannic* rates little more than a footnote, compared to the deluge of material still being published about *Titanic* or *Lusitania*. Perhaps the modest loss of life contributes to this neglect as well as the exigencies of wartime censorship and security. Newspaper accounts are vague or incomplete and interviews with survivors are few and far between. What little we can glean about *Britannic* and the disaster that befell her come from disparate sources, among them passages from fellow V.A.D. Vera Brittain's *Testament of Youth*, V.A.D. Sheila Mitchell's admirable memoir *Pages from a Nursing Sister's Diary* and a tantalizingly brief account written by the Reverend John Fleming, the vessel's Protestant chaplain.

The two following chapters provide us with additional detail concerning a wartime loss still shrouded in secrecy.

It was the feast of Our Lady, November 21, 1916. The early sun was shining through the windows of the lounge, across the faces of khaki-clad figures of officers and men as they knelt at early mass, fingering their rosary beads.

The padre was a big man with a face like a rough mountain crag. His eyes were both child-like and humorous, eyes that seemed always to be asking the world to be kinder, though their owner was far too shy to ask anything. Now he addressed his congregation. As he raised that rich Irish brogue, you could see by the unconsciously rapt expressions around him that this man knew just how to reach the side of men's hearts that is very simple and very human. He had spent many months in the trenches and, rumour had it, still longed to be back there.

Mass over, everyone rolled out amid laughter and jollity in the wake of the padre. The men had adopted him as their chum and counselor. He was the most popular man on the ship except for Major

Priestley. The major, a modest, quiet man whom anyone could approach, had escaped and helped others to escape from Ruhleban, that notorious prison. He was a hero to the troops.

Everybody scrambled down to breakfast, talking and joking, for breakfast time was quite the nicest, friendliest time aboard. And on this day the animation of good spirits, coupled with the prospect of hard work ahead—we were to embark wounded that afternoon at Moúdros—was noticeable everywhere. Banter was rife, even at the austere commanding officer's table, I noticed as I passed through the saloon to get breakfast for a sick sister I was looking after.

Suddenly, there was a dull, deafening roar. *Britannic* gave a shiver, a long drawn out shudder from stem to stern, shaking the crockery on the tables, breaking things till it subsided as she slowly continued on her way. We all knew she had been struck.

As one man, the whole saloon rose from their seats. Doctors and nurses vanished to their posts in a trice. The pantry where I stood, holding a teapot in one hand and a pat of butter in the other, was cleared too, as men dropped what they were doing and jumped over presses with the agility of deer. In seconds, not a soul was to be seen and not a sound had been uttered.

This contrasted so forcibly with my recollections, not so far distant, of *Titanic*'s night of doom. The unhurried calmness with which we then confronted the unexpected left an impression that has remained with me vividly ever since. But this was different. War, with all its anticipated horrors and ghastly possibilities, filled the imaginations of those who feared and yet had not foreseen danger.

Fascinated, I watched the movement about me. My own fears, never absent from me for one moment of my sea life, were now, strangely, forgotten. Then I suddenly remembered I must go to the nurse in sick bay, help her to dress and send her to the lifeboats.

There was a hubbub of conversation on the decks below. Doors stood ajar, revealing sisters and nurses hurriedly collecting belongings and little treasures, commenting with relief at the fortunate absence of wounded on board, while they tried hard to smother their feelings of concern at Matron's command for haste.

Two of them thanked me in passing for having made them get up early for mass. But for that they would have gone to breakfast, as they invariably did, wearing pajamas under their uniform because they could never manage to get out of bed till the breakfast bell went.

I found my own special charge trying to dress herself with fingers shaking with weakness from her recent illness, dropping more garments than she put on. We made a pretense of chattering and joking as we completed her toilet and I sent her with a companion to join the others on the boat deck.

The babble was stilled as the last nurse made her way up. The alleyways were almost deserted as I went to my own cabin. There the breakfast my roommate had assembled for us both lay temptingly before me. I was very hungry, for not a bite had passed my lips since the previous evening, as I had taken communion at mass.

My companion had already taken her coat and lifebelt and was gone. I sorted out things to take, the things I treasured most, Ned's ring and my clock, of course. The clock was a precious gift from a friend whose simple philosophy had helped me in many dark moments. Then there was my prayer book and my toothbrush. This latter because there had always been much fun at my expense after the *Titanic*, when I complained of my inability to get a toothbrush on the *Carpathia*. I recalled Patrick's joking advice: "Never undertake another disaster without first making sure of your toothbrush." Additionally, I stuffed all sorts of things into my pockets, even a roll from the breakfast table.

Violet told me in 1970 that after she had put all the above-listed items, including the toothbrush, into the pockets of her uniform apron, she had then folded up the bottom of the apron and tucked it into her waistband, covering the pockets and insuring retention of the objects despite her subsequent immersion in the water.

I donned the new coat for which I had saved so long, brought especially because I wanted to be so smart when I met dear old William. Carelessly, I put my lifebelt over the coat, contradicting my own admonishments to others when assisting at lifeboat drill, to always put on a lifebelt under the coat, so that in moments of emergency the weight of a coat could be easily discarded. I did not bother to change, however, as I felt reassured that this time there would be room in the lifeboats for all and I did not expect to be in the water.

Our comfortable cabin, which, if the ship had been used as a passenger liner, would have been the doctor's cabin, looked very cozy as I put out the lights and went up on deck, a little self-conscious at the incongruous mixture of a smart coat and a uniform cap, though being on board and on duty it never would have occurred to me to remove that cap.

The blaze of sunshine that met me out on the boat deck was both warming and reassuring. But I was taken aback by the look of surprise on an officer's face as I emerged in the midst of a crowd of soldiers and sailors. When I asked, "Where are the others?" I was told they had all gone in the first two boats. Indeed, I could see those boats slowly drawing away clear of the ship. *Britannic* was still steaming ahead, making the lowering of lifeboats a ticklish job. I gave that foolish, nervous laugh, as people sometimes do when faced with an unpleasant discovery and a doubtful alternative.

An officer came up and told me hastily that as all the women had left, I must take my place in the boat assigned to me by the official boat-muster list. Number four happened to be mine. Nicely forward, I reflected, away from that churning water aft, where the propellers were having their little joke with anything in their way. Just at that moment, a lifeboat caught my eye. It had been lowered safely to the water but then drifted with sudden impetus, resisting the efforts of unskilled oarsmen, right into those cruel, swirling blades.

Number four boat filled rapidly, but everybody was focusing fascinatedly on those blades aft. Though hands were lowering boats mechanically, eyes were looking with unexpected horror at the debris and the red streaks all over the water. The falls of the lowered lifeboat, left hanging, could now be seen with human beings clinging to them, like flies on flypaper, holding on for dear life, with a growing fear of the certain death that awaited them if they let go.

The ship started gradually listing to starboard as our boat prepared to lower. The little sea scout near me took a deep breath as he got in; it was a long way down to the water, even in sunshine, and he was only a kid, despite his manly bearing.

He got his first shock when our lifeboat, hooking itself on an open porthole, whose circular, brass-rimmed glass jutted out, tilted us considerably; then, righting itself, started gliding down rapidly, scraping the ship's sides, splintering the glass in our faces from the boxes, which formed, when lighted, the green lighted band around a hospital ship's middle, and making a terrible impact as we landed on the water.

I was fascinated to read that the obligatory green band encircling *Britannic*'s hull was highlighted with illuminated, glass-fronted panels. We can only assume that these were not a continuous equatorial belt but periodic accents.

The boy's eye caught the struggling people in the water, left in the wake of the churning propellers, again reducing the poor little fellow to a frightened child. He had been hanging on for dear life to one of the boat falls and nothing would induce him to let it go. He kept giving me reassuring smiles every now and then, as if to say, "I'm not really afraid, I'm only doing this to keep the boat steady."

After we had touched the water, I looked round to see how my small friend took the impact, only to find him hanging half way up the ship's side now, still attached to the rope! It took the forceful persuasion of a boatload of men to get that youngster to let go and drop back into the boat.

Meanwhile, we were not making much headway getting free from the ship's side; the boats clustered together in a hopeless group, fumbling hands struggling unsuccessfully to get control.

*Britannic* was still proceeding under her own steam. A few minutes after the lifeboat first touched the water, every man jack in the group of surrounding boats took a flying leap into the sea. They came thudding from behind and all around me, taking to the water like a vast army of rats.

Not a word, not a shout was heard, just hundreds of men fleeing into the sea as if from an enemy in pursuit. It was extraordinary to find myself in the space of a few minutes almost the only occupant of the boat; I say almost, for one man, a doctor, was still standing in silence beside me. I turned around to see the reason for this exodus and, to my horror, saw *Britannic*'s huge propellers churning and mincing up everything near them—men, boats and everything were just one ghastly whirl.

I turned in consternation to the man beside me to find he, too, had slipped silently away. In another moment I would be under those glittering, relentless blades, unless . . . I looked at the equally inexorable sea and, for a fraction of a second, hesitated, for I have always been afraid of water. Drowning was my one irrational fear all my life; I had not been able to learn to swim because of the loss of part of one lung in those far-off Argentine days.

Then suddenly I was no longer conscious of fear. I knew I must go into the sea and had to make that decision alone. I just jumped overboard, leaving everything that was solid, not even wondering why I did so, going down and down into what seemed bottomless depths, clutching desperately at my lifebelt which was something tangible, though it had become loose and was bothering my chin.

Why had I put my belt over my coat was my one thought, as I felt its weight drag me down deeper. I kept my eyes tightly closed and held my breath instinctively, though it was the first time in my life I had been under water.

I felt myself rising and my head came into violent contact with something solid, something that prevented me from reaching the surface. Then again, there was another terrific crash above me and something very solid struck the back of my head a resounding blow, but happily on that part where my plentiful hair was thickest.

My brain shook like a solid body in a bottle of liquid. It was a very unpleasant feeling and at the third repetition I imagined the next time would be the last.

Suddenly some twist of fancy made me see even then, under water, the humor of my situation, and I chuckled—that was very nearly my undoing for I swallowed what seemed gallons of water and everything that was in it.

Panic seized me then and I remember making frantic efforts under whatever was keeping me down to catch on to something. Reaching out in despair, I groped blindly in that water that was now a thundering center of noise, every sound magnified a hundredfold.

Suddenly, joy of joys, I touched something—an arm—that moved as mine moved! My fingers gripped it like a vice, but only for a second, until my almost senseless head remembered what is said of the people drowning, that they retain their hold after death, bringing death to another. With that cheering thought, I let go.

Just as life seemed nothing but a whirling, choking ache, I rose to the light of day, my nose barely above the little lapping waves. I opened my eyes on an indescribable scene of slaughter, which made me shut them again to keep it out. In that moment I felt I was sinking; my lifejacket was loose and not sufficient to support me. Just then another went floating by so I grabbed at it and felt a little more confident; at last I had something to hold on to.

The first thing my smarting eyes beheld was a head near me, a head split open, like a sheep's head served by the butcher, the poor brains trickling over on to the khaki shoulders. All around were heart-breaking scenes of agony, poor limbs wrenched out as if some giant had torn them in his rage. The dead floated by so peacefully now, men coming up only to go down again for the last time, a look of fright-ful horror on their faces.

Wreckage of every sort was everywhere and, at a distance, strick-en *Britannic* slowly ploughed her way ahead, the white pride of the ocean's medical world. She dipped her head a little, then a little low-er and still lower. All the deck machinery fell into the sea like a child's toys. Then she took a fearful plunge, her stern rearing hundreds of feet into the air until with a final roar, she disappeared into the depths, the noise of her going resounding through the water with undreamt-of violence.

Jessop paints that horrific scene in the waters alongside stricken *Britannic* so deftly that there is no need for further amplification, just a couple of histor-ical points.

Only 28 lives were lost in the sinking, which happened because of a mine sowed the day previously in the Kea Channel by a mine-laying U-boat; a smaller hospital ship, *Braemar Castle*, struck another mine from the same crop a few days later. It was extraordinarily fortunate that *Britannic* was car-rying no patients. Had she sunk en route home from Moúdros with a full complement of wounded, the death toll could have been appalling, rivaling or very likely surpassing *Titanic's*. The reason for the tragic woundings and fatalities caused by the vessel's propellers was that Captain Bartlett was try-ing desperately to drive his sinking vessel into shallower waters, unaware of the carnage he was inadvertently perpetrating at the stern.

CHAPTER

## 27

# Aftermath

THE WONDER OF finding myself alive will always remain in my memory. Not being able to swim, I scarcely dared breathe or move in the water for fear of sinking again so I just floated along, gripping my extra lifebelt in a vice-like hold. I had not the courage to let my eyes wander around for fear of seeing the awful sights surrounding me.

The sun was shining brilliantly. In the distance, I saw one of the ship's motor boats coming at top speed in our direction, slowing down as she drew near the human wreckage. Her crew was picking up some and leaving others for whom human aid was useless.

I heard a voice quite near me hail the boat and cry: "There's a woman in the water here!" As I turned my head in surprise and gratitude for such an act of generosity, I saw the owner of the voice give a fearful gasp and disappear from view.

I felt then the least I could do was to keep as calm as possible and found myself able to smile when it was my turn to be hauled in. This seemed to occasion surprise, though I could not imagine why I shouldn't smile after such an escape.

When I tried to stand, however, I discovered my leg was badly torn and deeply gashed. I had not felt it happen; all I had been conscious of underwater was my head being battered almost to a pulp. As I crossed to a seat in the launch, I noticed a young lad looking at me with a twinkle in his eye. He had nicknamed me on board "The Queen" and, as my eye followed his, I knew the reason for his humor.

My coat had been ripped from its back yoke and was trailing behind me like a train, while my hair had come loose; attached to the very end of it was the dilapidated remnant of the cap I always took such pride in. As I sat down, the lad murmured with a chuckle: "Queen, you've taken an awful beating." We both crossed our fingers.

On my left was a man with both arms hanging by pieces of skin, but still quite cheerful. He kept telling me how lucky he was not to have been killed. We watched, fascinated, the quick work of rescue, looking anxiously for signs of life as each person was pulled into the launch.

Several did not respond. Here a poor scullion with his apron still on, there an R.A.M.C. orderly [Royal Army Medical Corps, one of the personnel who manned His Majesty's Hospital Ships], now a wee, fair-haired sailor boy; I looked on miserably as the order was given to drop them overboard again and saw them floating away. I remembered the dead bullocks on our crossing from Argentina so long ago. Those floating bullocks had looked, to my youthful imagination, so alone as we left them behind; now it was floating men and how much more alone they seemed.

Just then our commander, who had lately given up a good shore job to take command, was retrieved from the water in his pajamas, his face as unperturbed as ever.

I heard a frantic shout for help as a man begged in agonized tones to be rescued quickly. He was sinking, he moaned, and he held up a torn stump that was once an arm; the weariness of his face seemed to tell that he had waited an eternity.

The commanding officer, never a popular man, replied in a curt tone from the security of the boat: "Wait your turn." I can still see the look of incredulity, of helplessness as that pair of imploring eyes met a pair of cold eyes.

Finally, when the waters were cleared of human flotsam, we made our way to the tiny island of Kea in the Cyclades, where the little barren quayside was strewn with our horribly mutilated wounded; those awful propeller blades had done their work well.

Doctors, themselves cut and torn (many had left the ship via the falls), were working frantically without equipment, trying to save lives that hung by a thread. The inhabitants, open-eyed with horror, offered us, in a language we could not reply to, all the hospitality they had to give. Graciousness needs no language, however, and pretty soon everyone understood each other.

An elderly man, in an R.A.M.C. uniform with a row of ribbons on his breast, lay motionless on the ground. Part of his thigh was gone and one foot missing; the gray-green hue of his face contrasted with his fine physique. I took his hand and looked at him. After what seemed a long time, he opened his eyes and said: "I'm dying." There seemed nothing to disprove him yet I involuntarily replied: "No, you are not going to die, because I've just been praying for you to live." He gave me a beautiful smile and just then a doctor came up to ask my help in cutting lifebelts up for dressings. That man lived and sang jolly songs for us on Christmas Day.

One of the inhabitants, a very friendly woman, took me into her bare whitewashed house and put me to bed while she set about drying my clothes on the small porch. When I slipped out later to get these, expecting they would be dry, I found a crowd of the ship's staff there and had to retrieve my wet corsets from where they had stuck to the fat backside of a colossal doctor, who sat swapping fantastic stories with our popular purser. In any case, the destroyer HMS *Foxhound* arrived to take us away before the drying process could be completed, and we left in a squelchy condition to join the flagship *Duncan* in Fáliron Bay.

A journey on a destroyer must always be a thrilling adventure for a civilian, and certainly my battering did not prevent me realizing this to the full as she flew over the waves, her nose parting the flying spray. But it was the warmth and caring of the welcome we received aboard that revived me; the calm faces of her crew gave me fresh courage.

How perfectly heavenly it was to be asked, in the kindest and the nicest voice imaginable, if "a hot bath would not be a great comfort after such a ducking?" And how thrilling it was to follow a stalwart Jack Tar up and down interminable steel stairways, over high iron doorsteps, round dozens of corners and arrive finally at a wee cabin, the size of a box, where an old-fashioned tin hip bath was ready, full of steaming hot water.

I was left with the instructions to help myself to fresh clothing, and would I like my corsets to be dried in the engine room? I looked at the neat pile of vests and undergarments; socks and handkerchiefs so proudly displayed, offered so generously for my use. Indeed, they seemed to be mutely asking to be made use of, and I wondered where the lady, mother or maybe wife, was who had darned the little hole in an obviously cherished fine wool undershirt so beautifully.

I reveled in the prospect of deep contentment a hot bath always conjures up, and felt that even my injured leg would not minimize its luxury. While I wallowed in its soothing influence, my eyes strayed round the tiny cabin till they caught sight of words scrawled across the top of a door almost behind me: Magazine Room! No more luxurious thoughts or indolent enjoyment for me. I was up, dressed, and hurriedly limping away as far as possible.

My fluttering heart was revived as I reached the deck to find my good friend, the sailor, beaming and waiting for me with a cup of Navy cocoa, so thick that the spoon could stand up in it. Just then, as our beautiful craft skimmed over the sea, raising her nose like a disdainful lady, the wind rushed past us, taking with it the entire contents of my cup and leaving it as if it had never been used. The expression on our faces caused a burst of amusement that broke the ice for several silent, dismal souls sitting about.

My whole body felt one big ache, starting from my head which I felt would burst at any moment. But I was afraid to mention this lest I should once again have people rushing at me with aspirins. It never occurred to anyone, then or later, to investigate the pain I endured. Years afterwards, quite by accident, it was discovered that my skull had been badly fractured.

By the time we had been transferred to the *Duncan*, I had lost interest in everything. But two cheerful faces grinned at me as I came haltingly up the gangway and one said, as he assisted me: "I know what saved you today, young lady!" and I recognized the two doctors beside whom I had knelt at Holy Communion that morning.

Dimly I heard the chatter of reunions and noticed all ranks on board being solicitous for our comfort. Only when I dodged another offer of aspirin did I realize I was fearfully hungry, for nothing had passed my lips since the previous day, barring the salt water and cork dust I had swallowed. I managed to slip into a quiet corner behind a stanchion where I heard a group discussing my demise! As the obituary references became more gruesome, I came out of hiding and said: "Please, won't you stop having me chopped to pieces and get me something to eat?" Since they were all strangers, it took a bit of explaining that I was the person they were referring to.

The reunion with my roommate when I reached the hotel in Piraeus was touching and, at the same time, not without a certain humor. Always a gentle, quiet person, she was now so harrowed by all she had heard about my supposed end, that she looked like a corpse herself, at the point of collapse; indeed, I had to give her assistance till she recovered. She looked so ill that people were constantly mistaking her for me and offering her sympathy!

The memory of my first meal still calls forth a shudder. After we were at long last transferred from the *Duncan* to the hotel in which we were to stay, I managed to get to bed. I was then told that all the available food and wine had already been consumed by those that had arrived earlier in the day. After an interminable wait, I was presented with a cup of lukewarm liquid they said was tea, and bread spread with a white, frothy, vile-smelling substance they told me was butter made from goat's milk. It was the rankest thing I have ever tried to eat.

Afterwards, while I was brushing my teeth, trying to get rid of some of the oil and cork dust, there was a knock on the door. Assistant Matron looked in. She evidently thought it superfluous to congratulate me on being still alive, or to enquire if I were hurt; what she did say, however, was: "Wherever did you get that toothbrush?"

I replied, rather weakly, as I was afraid if I spoke I would retch, "I brought it with me." Her look of astonishment and suspicion led me to wonder if she thought I was in league with the enemy and had prepared a weekend bag before joining the lifeboat.

But her callousness no longer had the power to affect me, nor did it prevent me wakening next morning with a revived interest in life, albeit aching all over. Neither Matron nor anyone else troubled to enquire about my injuries—a fractured skull and a leg pierced to the bone—which took nearly three years to heal.

From my childhood days in Argentina, when dreamy speculation was my constant recreation, Greece stood for perfection of beauty. So my first impression of extreme aridness was quite a shock. The magnificent blue sky did not compensate for the glaring, red, rock-strewn earth. How my eyes ached for the restful sight of a patch of green!

Of course, it was impossible to do justice to what remained of ancient Greece with a badly wounded leg and a head that didn't seem to belong. I confined myself to watching the people who came to watch us, gorgeously dressed women with double chins and ample proportions. I had expected to see a trace, just a trace, of those faces and figures associated with Greece, but the nearest I got to my ideal was one of the hotel maids who was very beautiful.

I don't think we were particularly welcome guests at the hotel, or maybe in Greece, judging by the unconcealed malevolent expressions on the faces of the staff. However, what the locals lacked was made up for by the cheerful attention of the Royal Naval units stationed there, particularly towards our nursing sisters. To my amazement and great relief, they thawed out and became so human that it was difficult to realize they were the same women of a few days previous. Moreover, the good-natured efforts of a few British residents helped us forget our recent tragedy.

Suddenly one day word came that we were to leave as soon as possible. I have the nicest memories of kindly sailor faces, so eager to send messages home, made more poignant by their death during the bombardment of Fáliron Bay a few days after we had sailed.

The hospital ship *Grantully Castle* was already packed with wounded when she called to take us aboard for Malta. One beautiful morning, while I was enjoying a quiet moment in the sunshine, I heard excitable talk coming from a group of R.A.M.C. men on deck nearby. A lively, humorous little red-headed fellow was regaling them with tales of his recent experiences.

"Something hit me, then I seemed to go down miles, and as I rose somebody grabbed my arm. I tried to shake them off but they locked their fingers in the strap of my watch, so I thought this is my finish, when suddenly a miracle happened, they let go!"

I remembered so well the security of that watch strap, it had seemed for a moment the one tangible thing in the world. But now looking at this cheerful little man, I was mighty glad its safety had not held me too long.

At last, in Malta, my brother William and I met. He found me in one of those grand old stone palaces where the Knights lived in the days of the Crusades, unchanged over the years. It was a great reunion, although so different from what I had anticipated.

All Distressed British Seamen like ourselves came under the charge of the port missionary. He was the pivot around which all work, other than naval, seemed to center in the harbor. With his untiring energy and extraordinary capacity for work, he had numerous duties. In fact, he was known as the hardest-worked, kindest man in Malta.

Skippers wanting fresh crew at a moment's notice, people perplexed about a host of different things and shipwrecked crews of every nationality sought his help. Though he never once mentioned he was tired, his task was not lightened by his very temperamental wife. People of all ranks used to come along to get a dose of his cheerful optimism, one of the great mainstays of those dependent on his care.

A good story was told about him. A certain gentleman of important standing, probably a little jealous of the chaplain's popularity, failed to present him when King George visited Malta. Later, apologies for this oversight were made and put down to the excitement of the moment, a lapse which had deprived our friend of a little talk with the King. But his cheerful reply was: "That's all right, my dear fellow, I speak with the King of Kings every day."

He arranged for William to spend all his free time with me down in Valetta at the Seamen's mission. He was able to get us many privileges including a visit on board the British submarine E.21. She had come in for repairs after her exploits with the Turkish fleet.

Every day saw the crew of some torpedoed ship land in Malta, people of every nationality and race utterly destitute. Where to get supplies to meet demand was always of grave concern down at the mission. Every day, the port missionary stood in the shade of a tree by a huge table laden with clothing, doling out garments to shivering men waiting in line. He always had a cheerful as well as a hopeful word, accompanied by a friendly slap on the back.

Sunshine, oranges, church bells, and goats are associated with those happy days in Malta, when William and I explored the island's unspoilt treasure spots. We delved into catacombs, reliving the lives of the early Christians; we felt at times like cave-dwellers ourselves. We saw the cave where St. Paul said his first mass after landing in what is now St. Paul's Bay, just as wild and rugged as the day that fiery saint had set foot there.

It was all very thrilling. If the goats and church bells reduced our sleep to a minimum, we were at least compensated by that exultation we felt partaking in something that had remained unchanged through the ages. And we tried to put aside the knowledge that William would soon bid goodbye to board a troopship for Salonika again.

The agonizing apprehension I felt as his boat, with its rows of khaki-clad figures singing and waving as she left Grand Harbour for the dangers lurking just outside, turned my blood to water for the rest of the day. Soon enough, we too would face that departure for home. However, the port missionary managed to reduce our sea traveling to the minimum; it was decided we should go overland through Sicily, Italy and France.

When the moment came, we found it difficult to say goodbye. Coming down the street to the mission, after some last minute leave-takings, I ran into a resplendent figure in naval uniform, who greeted me like a long lost relative. I was at a loss to identify this friendly man. Then some remark recalled him to my memory as the chief officer of the *Orinoco*, my very first ship as a stewardess. He had kindly helped me with the intricacies of signing the ship's Articles at the Board of Trade to become a full fledged "seaman."

He now had command, he informed me, not without pride. I must have happened along at the right moment, for he was longing to share some good news with someone from home, that he had had a son. I think, in spite of my being a woman, he found me appreciative. Our delight at renewed memories and the exchange of recent experiences was mutual, so I much regretted my inability to accept his hospitality for lunch, for we were due to sail that afternoon. He promised to come down to give us a parting cheer, as he was not sailing till the following daybreak.

I felt very important having so impressive a person all to myself to see me off, and was naturally proud when he gave my colleagues his rather flattering opinion of my character.

Next day, both he and his ship perished.

The little group of Distressed British Seamen, together with neutrals returning home on that Italian ship bound for Syracuse, was very mixed. But, with the friendliness that common danger engenders, we were drawn together irrespective of nationality. Soon after we all became acquainted, a young Danish ship's officer, also a Distressed Seaman, showed signs of attaching himself to me. Perhaps it was natural, as we were both the same age and younger than the rest. But my usual desire for aloneness had become more pronounced, so I found Alex's persistent presence irksome, though he was good to look at, attentive to a degree, and very naive at times.

The garlic-laden air of that dark little ship added seasickness to the fears that we felt on moonlit nights in wartime. The trip would have been a nightmare, had not my attention been distracted by a young Italian airman. Later, I learned he bore the famous name of Balbo. He and his companion sat in the dining saloon, their laughter as infectious as the first breath of spring. The radiance of youthful mischief on his face would be accentuated by the merriest laughter imaginable, as he stuffed spaghetti into himself as if into a void. The

absolutely carefree happiness of that laugh has always remained im-
printed in my memory.

Since Alex did not like garlic, I consumed enormous quantities
of salami, hoping to achieve a breath comparable to our boatman in
Malta, who nearly asphyxiated me each time I crossed the waters of
the Grand Harbour. But Alex was determined to bear my idiosyncrasies with fortitude.

The train to Rome was overcrowded with every class of people.
Peasants laden with innumerable parcels, soldiers, priests, gold-braid-
ed officers with beautiful Roman noses and a mixture of other Europeans. With great skill we managed to retain a few inches of seating
accommodation in our carriage but there was no room for Alex who
walked the corridor when he could steer a way through the medley,
looking sulkily into our compartment every now and then. I was glad
he was kept out without any effort on my part.

It was New Year's Eve. As evening drew near, I was not dis-
pleased to be wedged into my seat and dozing, undisturbed but for
the restless shiftings of my neighbors. An old priest got up and went
into the corridor; no sooner had he left his seat than Alex darted in
and took his place. He ignored our disapproving stares and sat looking as if waiting for doomsday.

When the priest returned, Alex ignored him, so he continued reluctantly down the corridor. Through half-shut eyes I saw Alex look
at his watch several times. Finally, tired of looking at him and feign-
ing sleep, I suddenly received a hearty kiss on the lips that I am sure
could be heard down the corridor. I jumped up in a fury but Alex explained in halting English, in that meek, well-bred way he had, that it
was the custom in his country to kiss people a happy New Year and
he had been waiting patiently all evening to do so.

Although I felt like shaking the very life out of him, I knew it
would be useless. So my companion and I made schemes to outwit
this persistent youth in order to preserve a shred of independence.

Rome at 6 a.m. on a winter's morning was disappointing, drab
and not a bit romantic. Later, I appreciated it tremendously and, in
spite of being handicapped by my wounded leg, was able, with the
guidance of a charming bersagliere who had attached himself to us, to
see all the places that hitherto had been but names. Alex showed signs
of a desire to kill that soldier and nothing seemed to exasperate him
so much as the Italian's debonair appearance first thing every morn-

ing, to conduct me on a sight-seeing expedition. But I think what most annoyed him were the gorgeous cock feathers trailing from the soldier's rakish hat. Alex would mutter: "Men in Denmark could not wear feathers!" Then he would perseveringly plod after us.

He was not sorry, I could see, when the time came to proceed on our journey to Paris. On a dry, frosty night, we all left the train to go through the passport and customs formalities at Modane. While I was explaining about the few gifts I had acquired in Malta, Alex rushed up to help me, continuing my explanations in his particular kind of English.

We were joined by a resplendently bemedalled English general, whom I had seen several times since we left Rome. Gallantly he offered to "see me through" and proceeded to address the customs officer in execrable French, to all of which that official listened with deference. Then, with an air of having got me out of a fix, he said: "Now let me help get your things back to your compartment."

I chuckled inwardly at this kind offer when I glanced down at my belongings, all in a bag made from a piece of old bed ticking. As I turned to thank the general, I found he had fled. He must have spotted my Dick Whittington equipment and realized I was only a Distressed British Seaman. What a glorious relief to travel without possessions!

Violet concludes here a fascinating account, her *Britannic* ordeal, complete save for any account of her homecoming. Despite her quite severe—and untreated!—wounds as well as her refugee appearance, it is symptomatic of this resilient and vivacious young woman that she never lacked for admirers, whether Alex, the tiresome Dane, flying officer Balbo, the dashing bersagliere, the pompous general at the Italian border and one other (unnamed) "companion" in Rome, probably a fellow nurse. Clearly, whatever the circumstances, Violet Jessop never lost any of her magnetic charm.

# 28

# Peace and Prohibition

I WAS SLOWLY RECOVERING from my injuries, which were more serious than first imagined. And because I needed to earn a living and my sea post would not be available until the war was over, I had the good fortune to secure a post with the London Branch of the Banco Español del Rio de la Plata of Buenos Aires.

Mathematics having been my favorite subject at school, I started working for the Credit Department. My consternation can be imagined when I realized I could no longer do even a simple sum. At the time, I did not connect this with the blow on my head. Later, when an X-ray was taken of a tooth, it was discovered that my skull had been fractured in a vulnerable part; luckily, it did not affect my memory. I was transferred to the Information Department, which was interesting and where my knowledge of Spanish was useful.

In those dark days of the war, I spent many a lunch hour roaming the neighborhood of Petticoat Lane in search of little luxuries for Mother, which I knew I was sure to find here, even if I had failed elsewhere. Here again I renewed my association with Jews which began during my sea service, though among a far different class. Yet the same characteristics were apparent, even here in their poorer fraternity. There was a living warmth down by the fish barrows, no less than in the sumptuous staterooms aboard ship.

Always the same humanizing smile, the same wide-awake friendliness and interest in everything. They drew nearer in my dark days and showed me they too had their sorrows and anxieties and were grateful for sympathy. They proudly showed off their khaki-clad sons on leave who gave a hand with the barrows.

I marveled at their healthy, well-clad children, at the discernment of their womenfolk while shopping, keenly scrutinizing every article, missing nothing with their X-ray glance which could even seem to bring a dead codfish to life. And how amused I always was by their well-meant warnings to "be careful" of my handbag lest it be stolen.

They were not without their own brand of diplomacy either. I decided to buy some particularly lovely plums. Remembering our good doctor, also a Jew, would be calling next day, I ordered a further pound, saying as I did so: "Give me nice ones, please, these are for Doctor Bernard; he is a friend of yours."

The man glanced at me, trying to hide the fact that he had not the faintest idea who Doctor Bernard was, yet replied: "Ah, the good doctor," and he picked out the very best plums on his barrow for me.

At sea, I've worked harder and longer for their rich brethren than almost any other class, giving them almost superhuman service. I tried to satisfy their exacting demands and they do like the best. I have had to endure their aggravating ways, and I don't think anyone can be more exasperating than they, barring of course, my own folk, the Irish. But like the Irish, it's their humanity that counts.

Armistice Day came, November 11th, 1918. It stands out in my memory for the dreariness of a morning that broke into a frenzy of uncontrolled exuberance which left me feeling so alone and cold. Every building poured forth its human content into the streets in vociferous confusion. People that one had hitherto known as very normal had a kind of madness in their eyes. Papers dropped from every window. Everybody had an insatiable desire to throw something out a window; the volume of that morning's business lay on London's pavements. Then the milling crowds were carried onward, leaving the streets strangely quiet and deserted.

My office colleagues had joined the throngs in the streets. It surprised me that normally placid people became, in one moment, hysterical children. I went into the manager's office with a letter I had been translating for him. We were the only two left in the building. There were tears in his eyes. We both wept openly as we discussed the contents of the letter. His old heart was torn by the news that his youngest son had just been killed in action during the same engagement as my poor Philip. We had our grief in common and to neither of us did that Armistice Day bring a message of joy.

Violet Jessop rejoined the White Star Line and went back to sea in June of 1920.

The *Olympic* had discarded her wartime camouflage and returned from Belfast, reconditioned for North Atlantic passenger service when I rejoined her after the war. But it was among an entirely new set of values that I found myself in 1920, or perhaps I should say a lack of values. Prohibition in the United States of America had revolutionized its people's morals—Americans made up most of our passenger list—and nowhere was this more noticeable than on board ship, which they now used as a means of circumventing what they had voted for.

All Americans aimed to travel some time in their lives, but here were people unused to voyaging, surrounded by ostentatious splendor, pathetic in their arrogance and not in the least embarrassed to be known as "bootleggers."

Perhaps the most pathetic of all were the ultra-fashionable who were forced to patronize shipboard to replenish their cellars. Coming back into the midst of all this, it struck me that here were people of every class and walk of life who were taking a holiday from their national conscience.

Incorporated into the many services performed by members of the victualing department, was the necessity to know the art of "dodging Customs." We were called upon as if it were part of our daily task, to help, advise, and often assist passengers to conceal their "hooch" as we drew near to New York.

It was all so fantastic. There were members of the Four Hundred, pillars of Wall Street, senators, lawyers, debutantes, card sharps, all with their minds on the same problem as we approached the shores of the United States. Under the circumstances, it was not surprising that often our men obliged, at a price, and even our women too. One ample-bossomed stewardess found she could carry off a quart of champagne in her "balcony," and no Customs official, however hardboiled, had the nerve to tap the offending bottle with his little metal mallet used for such purposes, so she got away with it.

Not quite so lucky was a small syndicate of stewards who ran quite a profitable business in liquor, until one day a coffin was needed in a hurry from the storeroom and their cache was discovered.

The Customs inspectors themselves were not beyond reproach. I have seen one take a bottle of stout from a steward who hoped to get it ashore to a compatriot, with such withering scorn that the poor fellow felt he was a criminal. The next day the Customs man was invited to participate in some refreshments laid out for Customs by the company; this was in a special cabin well supplied for the occasion, after the business of "passing" the ship was through. Probably that same steward cleared up the debris after the celebration.

One sailing day, a suite was booked in my section, and from an early hour arrived flowers in baskets and boxes, sheaves of orchids, pots of exotic palms, fruit and sweets, until the rooms overflowed into the passage. Nothing short of a fashionable wedding could account for such lavish offerings we conjectured, and with the curiosity that runs riot on such occasions, I waited to see the interesting parties arrive.

A few minutes before the ship was due to sail, a little, elderly, frog-faced man and a very fat, bejeweled, bow-legged woman waddled into the suite and surveyed the miscellany with beaming satisfaction. A crowd of well-wishers surged in after them, screaming good wishes at the top of their voices, trampling everything in their efforts to get near enough to shake hands with the chief bootlegger of the United States of America.

What struck me forcibly was the attitude taken towards all this by quite young girls of the better classes, who had everything they wanted in life but were drawn into the vortex because it was smart. One girl in particular I recall, because I had known her charming family for a number of years and had seen her develop into a beautiful debutante.

She was on her way to be presented at the Court of St. James by her aunt in London, and as family circumstances prevented her mother making the trip, I was asked to take special care of her on the voyage. One stormy day when the ship was kicking up her heels alarmingly and things were being smashed, I stowed away the most breakable articles in her stateroom. Later, I found her and a companion looking for something. From her description, I remembered the beautiful round, red leather box containing engraved perfume bottles.

"Oh, yes," I said, "your perfume set is in the wardrobe." To which she laughingly replied: "You sweet innocent, that's not perfume, that's whisky and gin and whatnot, without which we would not be welcome to any party."

Jessop's resumption of her stewardess life aboard the *Olympic* coincided with a radical change in the nationality and type of passengers who surged aboard the Atlantic Ferry just after the war. Mass immigration was over; Congress had eliminated it with a series of acts in the early 1920s restricting immigration.

In place of those traditional "huddled masses," Americans, in record numbers, began flocking to the piers. For the first time, mass tourism colored life aboard the North Atlantic liners. The majority of those adventurous parvenus were crowded down below, occupying former steerage cabins which had been repainted and (marginally) dressed up by the shipping lines; now they offered passage in a new class called tourist third cabin. These humble spaces were called roguishly by their new occupants the "white collar steerage" and it became an immensely popular and inexpensive means of crossing to Europe. Suddenly, everyone sailed abroad—farmers, salesmen, undergraduates, housewives and "the old traffic," recent immigrants who had prospered in the States and were anxious to see their villages again.

Up in first class country, Violet looked after richer elements of this new traffic, among them "the chief bootlegger of the United States." I wonder whether it was Al Capone but have not been able to discover whether the celebrated Chicago gangster ever sailed eastbound on the *Olympic.*

CHAPTER

# 29

# Tim Goes Missing

OWN THE LONG alleyway a huge wardrobe trunk on its truck moved waveringly forward. It was the kind of wardrobe trunk without which, at that period, no American woman would think of traveling. It hesitated, as passengers and friends crossed the path of its uncertain progress; now and then, around one side would peer a face—perspiring and apparently very sorely tried—but equally determined to carry on.

For Tim Nolan, first class bedroom steward, had endurance beyond question. His hair had whitened in its acquisition and he had the appearance of a venerable archdeacon, the contrariness of the Irish, the rosy face of a child and the soul of a vagabond.

It would take a mathematician to keep count of the good resolutions made and broken by Tim to refrain from a "drop of cheer" during one Atlantic crossing. He was very human and pleasant, though more discursive when he did break out again [fell off the wagon]. On those occasions, he was always conscious how near was the "boot" for him; but with the luck that attends children and drunkards as well as the aid of good friends, he managed miraculously to avoid this calamity.

We always noticed the onslaught of an attack by his irresistible habit of argument. He'd stand at the press in the pantry carving chicken at dinner (all bedroom stewards in those days had to be good carvers), a job he excelled at. But if he felt in the mood and decided it was a goose and not a chicken, the chef "was after giving him be-dad"; and he'd argue the point, watched disapprovingly by the chief steward, whose presence, at other times terrifying, he now ignored. In the end, he'd be relieved of his job, returning to his section of rooms to sulk and, out of spite, to become sober.

One of his longest suffering yet most loyal friends was the stewardess who worked with him. Generous to a fault and with discretion that would have done a diplomat credit, she always excused his waywardness, remembering his enormous family of girls who, though adored, made ever-increasing demands on his purse and were a constant source of dread.

He was lucky in many ways, not the least his good fortune in having nice passengers traveling in his section. Often people who knew him from previous crossings, or others who appreciated willing service and cheerful manners, were ready to overlook his occasional lapses.

But sometimes Tim drew a blank. A "terror" would book a cabin in his section and he would be awfully worried about his failing. He'd strive to hide it but could not relinquish the habit. Much thought would then be given to the subject. How best to have his little drop handy, so that he should not have to leave the section in case the "terror" rang?

Tim devised a plan that needed a knowledge of psychology. He sorted his passengers out in his mind. Having noted the lenient ones, he'd be guided by their habits. He knew whether they remained in their "sheds" (his reference to cabins) a good part of the day—the steward's nightmare—or were "regular folks" who made the deck their headquarters. In one of the latter's cabins, he'd hide a bottle of whisky, there to refresh himself at will while pursuing his daily tasks. When he managed this subterfuge and did not patronize the bar, his superiors were mystified; his jovial mood indicated that he was obviously drinking.

Success along that line was easy. Tim's next scheme was to make life more comfortable above stairs, to save himself from leaving his section for the distant glory hole when he needed a shave, sure to coincide with somebody ringing for him. How to bestow his gear for that purpose without detection? For no steward was allowed to keep anything personal in lockers or pantries. Indeed at inspection time, both were required to be completely empty. Why, one wondered, had they been built at all?

His good fortune deserted him one trip, when all had looked "set fair." He had deposited his little bag of necessities carefully behind the settee near the door in old Miss Lange's cabin. She was a Spartan lady of set habits who never took food in her cabin. Her early rising was the envy of the would-be energetics and the despair of the sailors who scrubbed the promenade deck.

Tim was at peace: His liquor well hidden, his bag handy and, to complete his well-being, he had Colonel Jones in cabin 143, who always had most entertaining literature to glance at in between jobs and who, like Miss Lange, kept on deck most of the day.

A beautiful Sunday morning, when the early risers' cabins had been cleaned, found Tim with the urge to smarten himself while waiting for the laggards to rise. As he made to enter Miss Lange's cabin, he met his stewardess laden with a breakfast tray, frantically making signs to him. He regarded the tray with apprehension, then with dismay as the stewardess said: "She's just rung for breakfast in bed, going to stay there all day as she feels a cold coming."

"But she was out just now when I cleaned her cabin," argued Tim.

"Well, she's come down since, but don't worry, I'll get your bag out when she falls asleep later," promised the stewardess.

Journey after journey, on some pretext or another, always found Miss Lange sitting up in bed, reading and very wide awake.

Tim haunted the corridor. Everything he possessed, from his shaving gear to his money, was in that bag. Hourly, he felt the bristles getting more pronounced on his chin. After two days of unsuccessful waiting, shaves with borrowed razors, nervous tension and vanished optimism, Tim resorted to "a double" at the pantry bar, probably two, and immediately showed it. Whereupon the stewardess, anxious to avoid complications, advised him to disappear, which he promptly did, nobody knew where.

Later, bells rang and kept on ringing for service, but no Tim appeared, rosy-faced and smiling. Glory holes were thoroughly searched without success. The stewardess, generally "in the know," knew nothing of Tim's whereabouts this time, and remembering his outlook on such occasions, was prepared for anything.

Another bell rang. It was old Colonel Jones, who decided he'd break his rule, as he had not slept well the night before, and take tea in his cabin. He had also taken a nap after lunch, a thing he laughingly admitted he had not indulged in for years.

A strange steward served him tea, critically observed by the colonel but without comment. He secretly knew the absent Tim's weaknesses though never a word had been exchanged on the matter.

Dinnertime came round and the colonel decided he would also dine in his cabin; still no Tim. The chief steward, a strict man, had to be told, for Tim was due at the carving wagon in the saloon that night.

About 10 p.m., the stewardess, by then very worried, made a last round to see if there was anything she could do in the absence of Tim. She ran into Colonel Jones on his way to his nightly bath; he stopped to commiserate over his good steward's disappearance, recounting his many excellent qualities and ignoring his bad ones.

Leaving him, the stewardess continued on to his cabin to straighten things up for the night. As she put her hand to the door, it was opened stealthily, revealing a figure that spluttered curses in a low and vehement tone.

It was Tim, his white hair standing on end with the force of his feeling, eyes popping like pigeons' eggs and glittering with fury. He was a sobered but injured person, raining down quaint and painful curses on Colonel Jones' innocent head, to the mystification of the stewardess.

"Where have you been?" she demanded.

The heated reply, "Sure, didn't you tell me to disappear and didn't I come into his room, knowing he was always out, and sure didn't I think the best place to disappear to and be quiet would be under his bed? I had a sleep and then didn't he come in as I was about to get from under the bed, and didn't he stay the whole blessed life-long day with me stewing under the draperies till I nearly chewed his boots up? Sure, wasn't I afraid I was going to sneeze every time I took a breath? It's me that'll be sober from now on, indeed I will."

We never knew just what Tim explained to the chief, but whatever it was, he got away with it.

A night later, Tim was on his way through the second class accommodation to third. He had been invited to see a real mermaid, stuffed of course. The owner, an ex-lighthouse keeper from the China coast, hoped to dispose of it to a London museum. On his way, Tim ran into the Bear Woman, one of a party of circus freaks traveling second class, who were returning from a tour of the United States. It took several people to convince Tim he was not still "under the influence" and "seeing things."

The combination of the mermaid (he could not forget her placid expression and dainty arms) and the Bear Woman did a lot towards keeping Tim on the water wagon for the rest of the year.

The misadventures of Tim bring us to the intriguing subject of drinking among the victualing staff aboard ocean liners. More than once, Jessop hints at it in the pages of her memoirs. Recall, if you will, Trole and Jackson on *Titanic's* sailing day who needed Dutch courage against the torment of moving Miss Townsend's cabin furniture; and Ma Maine's nightly bottle of stout as well as Ma Tims' gin bottle in her stocking top; remember too Jessop's reference to uncongenial cabinmates whose clothing bore unpleasant olfactory reminder's of their owners' "devotion to whisky and smoke."

Where did Tim and his fellows obtain their onboard bottles? There seems to have been a plentiful supply and I can only guess that it was either bought legitimately in the Pig & Whistle—traditional shipboard name for the crew's pub below stairs—or, during on-duty hours, cadged illicitly from friendly colleagues who dispensed drinks to passengers. Trole and Jackson, Violet suggests, merely made a call at the "pantry bar" for a double on demand. There is no evidence that the White Star Line discouraged or forbade crew drinking and much from Jessop's recall to indicate that a great deal went on.

Violet herself, despite her complaint in chapter 19 about excessive beer consumption among her fellow stewards, was no teetotaler. Her niece Margaret advised me her Auntie Vi was not only a dab hand at brewing a particularly potent tangerine liqueur but also enjoyed a dram till the day she died. Just after the second world war, when drink in the austerity-plagued United Kingdom was scarce, she used to smuggle bottles of grain spirits that she suspended cunningly beneath her uniform skirt, passing repeatedly through Customs without arousing the suspicion of the inspectors. She brought it home partly for herself and partly for Doctor Cree who had looked after her mother for years, and who could use it in his medical practice.

# 30

# World Cruise

I N THE FALL of 1925, Violet disembarked from the *Majestic*, left the White Star Line and stayed ashore for seven months. The following spring, she signed on with a new company, Belgium's Red Star Line, at one time allied with White Star under the American financier J. P. Morgan's International Mercantile Marine. Over the course of her service with the line, she would sail on five world cruises, the first over the winter of 1927-28.

Streamers, hundreds of thousands of them; passengers laughing and crying, calling goodbyes, throwing posies, a din that would deafen— all these things figured prominently the evening of that first world cruise of mine.

I, too, wanted to shout with joy and anticipation. All those places that from childhood I had longed to see, Japan, China, Siam, Java, represented history, mystery and love.

I stand unobserved and watch a boy and a girl say goodbye. She stands by her parents on deck. He, a student obviously, with a clear-cut face, stands anxiously on the dock. Is he thinking what I'm thinking? Will she be coming back, loving him, be the same girl he is sending off so reluctantly? She, too, is sweet in her way, and apparently demure. Strange how a demure face, which is somewhat unusual nowadays, attracts the opposite in men. I watch two men prowling with restless eyes. They have spotted the girl and, I feel sure, she shall receive their valued attention.

A great deal of shouting is taking place between members of one group, one part on the ship and the other on the dock. Next to those on deck stands a woman alone, very still and quiet. A slim-figured, gray-haired woman, who could not be called beautiful but is certainly arresting, she is superbly dressed. No one is seeing her off. She is interested and not a little amused by the antics of the crowd on the

dock but a little anxious and speculative about the crowd on deck. After all, five months is a long time to spend with the same people if
they turn out to be impossible at close quarters. This is the holiday
she has been wanting for years. A pity she could not have had this
chance ten years ago when the world was younger.

Here comes a fragile little old lady, a charming piece of Dresden,
with an independent tilt to her head as she graciously answers a boy
with a telegram who has been paging her on deck. She waves her hand
to a crowd of well-dressed people on the dock who are all sad to see
her go. She looks as if nothing would keep her back from hiding her
straightened circumstances, in a cheap cabin, a little, hot inside cabin
on a world cruise, where she can housekeep for five months within
her diminishing means, and without having to accept hospitality from
her more fortunate friends. I'm going to like her, I make a mental
note; it's a good sign, those carefully darned gloves. A well-ordered,
well-balanced brain usually accompanies them.

A woman comes running who does not seem to approve of anything she has seen up to now. She moves to the rail where her friends
are gathered in a group below, evidently with the idea that in unity
there is strength. They, I feel sure, hope that she will not change her
mind at the last moment, as she so often does, and leave the boat.

Ah, here comes what I feel sure will be the life of the party! See
how his father makes room for him at the rail. This young man, if I
am not very much mistaken, is going to be one big character on this
trip. Yes, I feel sure we will see and hear much of you, young fellow,
say, until Shanghai, reaching your peak around Calcutta and sinking
into lethargy about the time we reach Athens, where you won't care
when or why the Acropolis was set on that hill.

A bit of excitement around the gangway to make way for late arrivals, but such jolly arrivals. An obviously delightful family, so pleased
to be here, a little apologetic for the delay to the purser who nevertheless reassures them with one of his most winning smiles. They are
grateful for his understanding, breathing a sigh of relief that the awful weather up Boston way did not prevent them from coming on the
trip they had so wanted to do. Now they are here and they like the
look of everything, earning for themselves "good starting" points
which will entitle them to willing service every time.

No, they are not a bit concerned about their baggage—lots of it,
unfortunately—but what can you do with so large a family, asks

Father in reply to polite enquiries from the baggage master, who is young and anxious to get a start and get better acquainted.

Here we are, all nice and friendly already. A group passes, talking in those high-pitched voices people affect when trying to get better acquainted, hiding the fact with much friendly banter. Yes, I thought so! They surge into the sitting-room of a man's suite, who has obviously come with the idea of showing the world a thing or two. There is much clapping of backs and patting of strangers' shoulders, with sidelong glances to see how far it is possible to go at this early stage.

Much ringing of cabin bells for lots of cracked ice, dozens of glasses, as many as the steward can carry, of ginger ale. No, they have everything else, thank you, with a knowing wink at Uncle Sam's unsuspecting back, and 'everything else' proceeds to be disgorged from various places in alarming amounts, considering Uncle Sam's hatred of the stuff.

"Sounds like a Christmas party and all," says young Peters, the bellboy, as he answers the bell for the dozenth time. But he changes his mind when he goes inside the cabin again.

"Looks like the night after the big storm," he comments and thinks privately. "Wonder how the chief is going to make the glasses go round if so many go west on the first night!"

This won't do at all, day-dreaming and making up stories. So much remains to be done before the fateful hour of sailing. Midnight and a bit—to whit twelve-fifty—sees us pull away. That bit tacked on-to the midnight hour is funny, is it not? It's to pretend you have sailed on one day, whereas the Company longs to cling as near as possible to the other, and nobody knows who is the gainer.

Now we are looking all merry and bright, the pantry's bell-board radiating twinkling little friendly calls to get acquainted. A variation can be detected in these bells: Some ring lingeringly, others incisively and others hesitatingly, as if perhaps it's a bit soon to ring. I take a quick look and gamble on the first to be answered. After all, I cannot respond "first come first served" to this array of bells; the board is plastered with anxious summonses.

I knock on a door and Madam bids me enter. I do so into a cabin I don't recognize, almost bare in its emptiness. Where is the furniture? A sound comes from behind me and I see the steward, doubled in two, removing a screw from the last piece of movable furniture to be taken out of Madam's sight in order to make room for her lug-

gage. I catch his eye as he unfolds himself and he telegraphs me a
warning with an agonized entreaty for me to do my best. He seems
to say, "After all, she is your own sex, and anyway I'm fed up."

Madam, smiling most graciously but as distantly as a goddess in
a Shinto temple, does not address me. Madam is royal; that is, her
husband was a Portuguese prince of the blood royal when he was
alive. Madam thinks it is incompatible with royalty to talk to me herself. Every carefully modulated word she utters is spoken for her by
her sister. The latter is a faded lady who does not at all understand the
workings of royalty and is bored stiff anyway; but she submits meekly because her passage has been paid for and she is glad to get away
for the winter. She does not even seem to mind if her royal sister does
insist on dropping hints at times that she is a maid and not a relation.

Yes, of course I will arrange her flowers as I stagger out with a
dozen boxes prominently labeled "Her Serene Highness." There are
a few violets in a tumbler placed beside an unframed photograph of a
heavy, uniformed, much bemedalled man that tells me she still loves
his memory.

Little Joe Van Wallendael, our newest bellboy, is trundling a
truck up the alleyway in a resigned, apathetic manner. The truck is
full of parcels of every shape and size. He looks at them with a pained
and hurt expression. They have no right to come in such quantities
and he wonders why people want to send each other parcels by the
truckload anyway. It's going to make a lot of work for all poor bellboys to get rid of roomfulls of torn paper and string, which will surely blow back again as soon as it is thrown overboard. Whoever
throws it away will surely do so on the weather side, and then the
chief officer will send a report to the chief steward and everybody
will be very cross.

It is said that the darkest hour is just before the dawn. It seems
true to me just now, as I hear in the distance the echoing cheers that
speed us on our way. There are a few out there who will go on cheering until the police remove them.

This surely must be the darkest hour, I think, as I struggle to fix
the contents of an ordinary flower market into the few vases available,
while the hot air parboils the lot. We must start off well, we must have
hot air to make things comfortable. It does not matter if it is mild
outside; it is December and we must have hot air, says the chief electrician.

My two stewards come in. That is, they wedge themselves through the debris and drop onto a stool in the corner. In silence each searches for his fags [cigarettes]. They are still speechless. The night watchman puts his nose around the corner. He reflects that, as things are, he stands a good chance of a few shillings to do the early scrub down for these two. He utters one or two platitudes, shifting from one foot to another but avoiding looking in my direction and my pile of rubbish waiting to be dumped. He might be asked to dump it. He waits a little longer and gets what he wants, ambling away in time to see that Cabin 30 has sneaked into Cabin 58 and locked the door.

I'm through at last, breathing my last breath of salt air before turning in. Billy, the bandy-legged deck boy, has just come up with sandwiches for the officer of the watch. I remember Billy as a fair-haired youngster, small and stocky, when he came to us first with his broad smile. I'll swear he hasn't grown one inch and his fair hair, blue eyes and broad smile are still the same. But there is a change nonetheless. Billy was a kid then; now he is a responsible member of the deck department and everybody from the skipper down recognizes it. I am told that he goes off the deep end now and again in Antwerp. He gets drunk on a few glasses of beer and insists on taking his landlady, a giant of a woman, out to a cabaret show. Yet, studying that boyish figure as it disappears up to the bridge, I wonder if anyone is maligning him.

So ends our sailing day from New York on our first world cruise.

# CHAPTER

# 31

# At Sea

DAWN. A BEAUTIFUL soft dawn is breaking, chasing away the winds of the night. The soft air from the Caribbean caresses my face, bringing with it green, earthy smells.

In a few minutes will start that serenade of bells, a proper carillon, for breakfasts in bed. But I am going to look at Morro Castle and get my first view of that beautiful historical place that acts as sentinel to Havana Harbor. You can almost smell the damp of ages from those old, old stones as the ship steams slowly by; you dream of the ghosts of Spanish grandees haunting it at dusk, when they must look with haughty disdain and not a little amusement at some of our modern perversions.

There go the bells, ringing like mad. They are all so very hungry, anxious to see everything and yet reluctant to get out of bed, I think, as I stoop to lift a handkerchief for a languid hand that cannot reach it.

"This cruise is going to be such a thrill," she says in tired tones as I draw the curtains.

"Yes," I agree, "it's going to be marvelous," trying at the same time to forget my night with three hours rest. "It has already begun to be wonderful," I continue, as I point out the beautiful outlines of the castle coming now through her window.

"How perfectly wonderful," she echoes, glancing at herself in the hand mirror which she keeps in her wall rack. "Wonderful," she continues as she busily colors her lips and gently pats her hair.

As I leave the stateroom, she is still murmuring something into her mirror. Morro Castle smiles back in benign forgiveness.

I go to the pantry. From it come sounds of hectic movement, rising in volume as I descend into a maelstrom of moving, jostling humanity. The chief, good soul, looks on in helpless impotence. What is to be done with the mob of sweating, swearing, screaming men, snarling out orders until they bring down the wrath of that overpatient man? Many of them are new to the ship; they'll be quite different when they get acquainted. The pantry cat stalks majestically across the deck and, strangely enough, does not get hurt by the hundreds of moving feet.

Old Ben, the dishwasher, smiles to welcome me. He works so quietly and patiently in his corner day after day. Few notice him, yet everybody howls when he is absent for a few moments. They even forget to give him his food at times. He is rather old and has only one eye, and a very meek manner besides. He started life gently in a country parsonage and has never really learnt to push, so the world rushes past him. He does not blame them as they jostle and push him further into his greasy corner.

He knows what they are up against, knows that they are fighting because their daily bread depends on it. He knows they are not fighting for themselves; they are not the ones who want steaming hot toast at the other end of the saloon or a red-hot omelet with a soft inside. But they run the risk of being dismissed at the slightest provocation.

I catch my breath as the ship's nose is turned into the Panama Canal. How many memories does it revive for me of a dear, kindly friend and a hot, happy journey in his company, over the very ground where now is stretched this most stupendous feat of engineering. Marvel of marvels, no mosquitoes, but it is stiflingly hot and unbearably damp.

Watching someone greet another from home when they are miles from it themselves always touches me deeply. Over the railing, I look at those United States Navy boys down on Balboa Quay as they drift down to the ship, all stiff and starched in their immaculate whites. Such smart figures they are with their straight backs and boyish faces, and with what hungry eyes they look at the ship that has just come from "way back home." This look never leaves their eyes as they chat and laugh with compatriots around the ship as she prepares to slip out into the Pacific.

The last sight I have of land is of a row of dozens of eager young faces standing stiffly to attention as the strains of *The Star Spangled Banner* float to them, still with that longing in their eyes.

# 32

# The Jinrikisha Man

YUWA, THE JINRIKISHA man is at his usual corner, one alert eye on the after-gangway, looking for me. Such calm, uncomplaining patience can be found only in a Japanese rikisha man.

I am hoping to escape for a few hours' leisure; it is indeed heavenly compared to the turmoil of ship's life. No recriminations because I am late, just an understanding nod. There is a lot Yuwa knows and never needs to be told. He knows, for instance, when he sees me coming down the gangway whether I am tired or not. Generally, I am tired when I tuck myself into his rikisha, and he will start off at a brisk trot without any questions and drop me off at a place we both know.

Today, I am going to wander with Yuwa's guidance in and out of old pottery shops, the more tumbledown the better. We are going to choose a brazier. One of those huge blue ones I shall always associate with Japanese men sitting around on their elevated, matting-covered platforms, transacting business in eager staccato tones, warming their hands over its embers, ignoring the surrounding icy atmosphere.

Yuwa was both mystified and intrigued when I first told him of my quest and the use I intended to put it to. He looked pleased when I told him it would look wonderful in a garden in England. Yet I saw that he had doubts about it being the most advantageous place for a brazier but he dismissed his doubts with a nod; Westerners ask for and do so many strange things. Besides, we are good friends.

I see him now in my mind's eye. Day after day, his shabby little rikisha would be in its corner at the dockside, hung with two frail paper lanterns, which were, however, never so frail that they perished in a storm of rain. And what storms had not Yuwa weathered with his lanterns! His square, high-cheeked unemotional face with its tightened skin would show the faintest spark of pleasure at the sight of a favorite fare—for I suppose rikisha men have their likes and dislikes, although they never betray emotion over tips. This spark of pleasure in Yuwa's face was betrayed by his eyes alone. They were very sad, tired eyes generally, although I have seen them light up once with a cold gleam like polished steel at an unexpected insult.

Yuwa had a damaged hand. On busy days, one would notice that his rikisha swayed a little, his hand hurting and his grip uncertain. But for that one drawback, he was the best rikisha man I ever hired, the fleetest-footed of an army of fleet-footed men. The soft pad of his small feet on the road at night, beating in time with the soft crunch of the wheels, was a restful experience. He would bring you with a grand flourish to your destination, where you alighted, exhilarated by the drive through the keen night air of a Japanese winter. These winter nights were not good for Yuwa. His hacking cough would guide you to the bamboo enclosure where the rikisha men wait for fares, playing games or chatting in their sharp accents.

Yuwa and I were good friends, dating from a day long ago when I introduced to him a particularly nice fare, telling her she would be well looked after and could rely on being taken to the best lacquer shop in Yokohama. Yuwa's eyes sparkled. He loved lacquer and knew I loved it too, having taken me on various expeditions to buy my favorite pieces.

One day he told me his story. Since childhood, he had worked in a famous lacquer factory in Kyoto, the home of beautiful lacquer. His father and his grandfather had both worked at the same craft. As he grew older and more accomplished in his work, he did many choice pieces, some of them exhibition pieces or offerings for the Imperial Palace. He took on the finest work, tracing the delicate designs.

There was one wonderful piece he had worked on for a long time; it had not been ordered by anyone and could be bought. One day, a party of tourists passing through the factory stopped to admire it. Among them was a rich man, so fascinated by the piece Yuwa was working on that he asked to purchase it. Then and there he paid the large sum demanded.

There was, however, still much work to be done on it, so the purchaser arranged for its delivery on board a steamer bound for America as soon as it was finished. Yuwa's master promised that it should be put on board by the very workman himself, for it could be in no safer keeping on its journey to Yokohama.

Yuwa had one other mission in Yokohama, more important even than the delivery of his precious lacquer. He was going to the Yoshiwara where the "Aphrodites" of Japan are segregated. There, a fragile little "Lotus Flower" had gone to sacrifice herself for a ruined father, deeming it her duty so that he might survive.

It is said that in Japan love seldom enters into the marriage contract. But love had touched Yuwa's heart when, as a lad, he had been apprenticed to the lacquer craft. The daughter of a wealthy merchant, she had often stopped in passing to praise the youth's work, thereby inspiring his devotion. She often went to admire his work and, despite his deep humility, he imagined that he was pleasing to her too.

The rich merchant failed in his business, and his daughter stopped visiting the lacquer factory. By tactful questioning, Yuwa learnt that she had chosen the way, common among the dutiful daughters of Japan, to become a voluntary slave in the "Quarter," defiling her body but not her heart.

For Yuwa, his mission in life started that black day. Every yen was saved and every economy made, no matter how long it took to buy his Lotus Flower from her slavery. It took many long years. His love did not diminish even though he could not deny that her beauty was fading.

The day came when the last installment was ready to be delivered in exchange for her freedom. So, it was with a double purpose that he set off on that September morning, wondering which errand to execute first. He decided on his love. His hard-earned money would be a source of worry until it was paid over. His beautiful lacquer piece would be safe enough with him and he would carry it with him until he had safely recovered his loved one.

Great peace and contentment filled him as she trotted alongside him on her wooden sandals. It was like a dream to Yuwa, whose life hitherto had been one long nightmare of sacrifice. Everything was so beautiful for him that day.

Then there was a low, distant, ominous roar, growing louder and nearer, and then oblivion for a while.

All the world knows what happened to Yokohama on that September day in 1923. But nobody cared much, in the midst of so much horror, for a distracted little man with a mutilated hand, scratching and digging with his one free hand, praying to the gods of his ancestors to help him extricate his beloved Lotus Flower from the wreckage. At last, weary and spent, he found her, bleeding and crushed almost to a pulp, but to him more dear and precious than ever.

Day after day he watched by her side up in the hills where the rescued were taken, making the tedious journey on bruised and aching feet, then returning to the scene of the tragedy to search for his lost handiwork, the precious lacquer without which he dared not return to Kyoto and his honorable firm. The devastating fire that had followed the earthquake could not have spared his treasure. Yet he did not give up hope and at last came upon a fragment. He knew that design, which contained his own work, a tiny spray of cherry blossom entwined with bamboo, symbols of beauty and manly strength.

That tiny piece showed him that hope was dead. He could not return to that honorable firm in Kyoto and expect them to understand that his own precious mission had caused him to put the delivery of the lacquer in second place. He would be condemned, of course, and if, out of pity, they allowed him to remain in the works, his hand was so badly damaged that he could not hold a fine tool for any length of time without losing control and feeling.

He felt an outcast, yet knew that if he had to choose again he would not have chosen differently. His Lotus Flower lived, although hopelessly maimed, and it was for her that he plied his jinrikisha up and down the streets of Yokohama without complaint.

Yuwa had been for days at the beck and call of a young acquaintance of mine, his nimble feet flying up and down the streets, to the fashionable Grand Hotel, and then to some other less reputable place, then back to the ship, warmed by the promise of a reward which would enable him to get food for his loved one. The day we sailed he got his reward, his fare employing him almost until sailing time.

I always liked bidding farewell to Yokohama from the deck, no matter how early the hour of our sailing, and usually with the cold, bleak wind blowing in the face of the few on the dock, some of whom had contributed to a pleasant stay for us and appreciated a farewell wave.

Yuwa had just been paid. I could see him clutching a note with an ecstatic look on his usually expressionless face, and his eyes smiled at me as the ship pulled away. Somehow I did not feel confident about that transaction, knowing a little about the man who paid. Later, this blade laughingly told me that he had substituted a cigarette coupon for a note and given it to that "coolie boy" who had pulled him around to all the sights. I couldn't understand how any rikisha man, however trusting, could be taken in so easily, until I saw one of those wretched coupons myself.

A year elapsed before we returned on another world cruise. I did not see Yuwa. I was told that he had died a month after we sailed, two weeks after his Lotus Flower had faded away. He had just sat, drooping and coughing in his bamboo waiting pen at the corner of the street. Through all those chilly nights, he had waited for fares, crushed with anxiety and, when one day he was told she had gone, speaking his name, he grieved silently. All had been taken from him and he had nothing else to live for.

His thin, cold body was sitting waiting, when a neighborly coolie tapped him on the shoulder to answer the call of a fare. But Yuwa had gone to join his ancestors.

# 33

# The Baroness

W HEN I FIRST saw her, I could not help wondering how anyone could get so out of shape. There was no semblance of what the baroness might have been as a girl, or even a young woman. Her clothes were a mixture of past and present finery; neither they nor her nails were ever clean and fresh.

Crowning all this was the most gorgeous array of jewels, of which she was inordinately proud. She had traveled around the world with us several times, collecting the best each country had to offer. She returned from Agra, that famous city of gems, with some priceless piece, kept for her special temptation by a wily owner.

This would be locked away in one of her innumerable trunks, never really unpacked from the time she came aboard. It would be carefully stowed amongst priceless brocades from Japan and filthy underclothing which she was too mean to have washed, but would do so herself at odd moments when she was annoyed with somebody, or more often they with her. On these occasions she would demand, with a regal air, complete privacy, which we were only too happy to grant.

She loved gossip and friendliness, yet was the loneliest of figures, in spite of many acts of generosity towards her fellow passengers and the crew. For underneath that grotesque exterior beat a very warm and kindly heart, ready at all times to aid a cause and, indeed, very often she was the one to suggest some act of kindness.

I remember one sunny Christmas morning off the coast of California. One of our sailors, while opening an iron door for air on the ship's side, was washed overboard by an unexpected wave and never seen again. The baroness was so deeply moved that a relative could not have shown more sorrow, both for the lost man and his family, for whom she at once generously headed a list for a fund to be collected.

It was difficult to reconcile this side of her nature to the other: Suspicious of almost everybody, vain to a degree, and the worst glutton imaginable.

Food was her all important consideration and, when something went wrong, she raised all kinds of storms, with much interviewing of the chief steward who ultimately would end up saying, "Give her anything to keep her satisfied." A sigh of relief would go up from the dining saloon when word went around that she was taking dinner alone or in company with her canaries, which she loved like children. She was a lonely woman in spite of her reputed vast wealth.

One of her most irritating habits was to mislay things and immediately call me. Then she'd accuse somebody of theft, at the same time making me promise not to tell the purser, to whom such things must always be reported. On one occasion it was her handbag, containing several valuable pieces of jewelry, which she said she had brought down to her cabin as we approached Singapore, where no one from ashore was allowed on board without a permit.

I suggested that she might have left it by her chair on deck, and for my pains was rewarded with a sarcastic and emphatic reply. I decided to say no more but a shadow of suspicion fell upon me and everyone else.

Still, I was getting used to it by now. She continued to maintain that she had seen a certain lady, whose private character she censured, looking guiltily about; she went on to suggest that I should ask this woman if, by any chance, she had mistaken her cabin, which I refused to do.

Later, when all had gone ashore to dine at the famous Raffles Hotel, I saw her come furtively down the opposite alleyway to that which she normally used. Not wanting to appear unconcerned about her loss, I asked whether she had found out anything about it.

"Yes," she said delightedly, "I found it by my chair on deck." When I remarked that it was a good thing I hadn't complied with her request to approach the woman she suspected, she became furious, said that I was most insolent and dismissed me there and then from serving her in the future. It was very sad, because I was the only person who had any patience with her, and she knew it.

So I was not surprised when, an hour later, she rang for me for some small service. I am sure she had feared that I would betray many of her confidences.

For example, she had taken a very great liking to a young doctor, actually proposing marriage because she liked him and could help him financially; she knew that he was not well off and very ambitious. Besides, such a marriage would ensure that her family, whom she distrusted and disliked, would not inherit the bulk of her fortune when she died. She had been sad, her vanity shocked, when the doctor gallantly declined.

When we arrived in Egypt, she insisted on going to Cairo with the other passengers. She was not very well at the time, although I was not supposed to notice it. And when she returned, I could see she was really ill. I welcomed her back, which seemed to please her, and made an excuse for taking her temperature. To my horror, it stood at 103.

I speedily found the doctor and my friend Nurse Margaret, a perfect nurse with a refreshing personality. We all used our persuasive powers and got the baroness down to the hospital, where she could be properly watched and cared for. She, to my surprise, as though trying to smooth over past injustices, left all her priceless things in my charge.

Down in the ship's hospital, for three days and nights, we took turns watching over her raging illness. Sometimes her poor, swollen face would try to smile, although she hardly knew us. On the fourth day, during a wave of general indisposition on the ship, when doctors and nurses were called for many times a day, she died.

That night, I went down to the hospital and offered a prayer by her side. I realized that a poor, stormy, undisciplined but very big-hearted woman had passed away, dying a very lonely death in the kind of place she would most probably have hated, utterly dependent upon those whom she had most harassed and suspected.

As if to compensate for everyone else's neglect, Nurse Margaret decided that she would lay her out to the best of her ability. When Americans lay out a corpse, it is so splendid that one almost loses sight of the fact that it is a dead body. All she regretted was that the ship's hairdresser, when approached, did not seem anxious to oblige and, indeed, found a great number of appointments in his book that day. Nurse Margaret told me that, in her part of the world, hairdressers did not in the least mind dressing the hair of corpses. Knowing my aversion to make-up, she said to me: "Don't you ever let me get buried without a hairset and my full share of lipstick, or I'll haunt you for the rest of your life!"

However, her plans were frustrated. She had to go to another case before the baroness was embalmed, and it was left to me to arrange her for the last time. As an especially large casket was needed, we had to wait for the carpenter. Even then, we could not get her in very well, as she had become almost rigid. One arm kept coming up in a most menacing manner, as if protesting at her treatment, as in life she had protested at so much. Having done my best, I covered the casket, which lay on the deck, with a white sheet, so that the captain on his rounds could take a look at her.

The death had not yet been mentioned on board and, late that night, a well-intentioned stewardess came down to the hospital with a small offering for another patient. Passing through the alleyway where the sheet-covered casket lay, she stubbed her toe and fell over it. Fearing that she might have disturbed whatever lay beneath, she lifted the sheet. Whereupon, the baroness's arm shot up admonishingly, to the absolute horror of my colleague, who was seen running wild-eyed until she gained the deck, her hair on end and teeth chattering.

# Tom's Downfall

TOM SUMMERS WAS our youngest recruit. Small for his age, he was fourteen and a bit, "nearly fifteen," he always added with pride when the matter was mentioned.

I had seen him for the first time one cold and dreary morning in Antwerp, prior to the start of another world cruise as I made my way by cab to the ship. I noticed the new clothes, new suitcases and heavily laden kitbags which he and another clean-faced kid were dragging along, obviously fresh recruits from the training ship. Dumped here in a strange land among people whose language they could not understand, they looked bewildered as they trudged along.

As I looked at their patient faces, I felt dismay that a commercial enterprise would have the power to govern these children's destinies, to take them from the security of their homes to a life of servility among strangers, just to satisfy the demand for boys in buttons!

Tom and I became great friends. He confided in his shy way that he was pleased to have been detailed to my deck, as he had never been to sea before. "You couldn't exactly call a training ship being at sea, Miss, could you?" he added. He was my shadow for a while, until I told him that he must give everybody a share of his valuable service. He was the most willing youngster imaginable, and looked such a child as he started his day by scrubbing his particular pantry in his diminutive trousers and singlet. There was something infinitely pathetic about him, a lonesome look, as if he would like to be near someone friendly but was too shy to do so.

On world cruises, we used to have grand times together in port when all the passengers had gone ashore. Tom had not chummed up with anyone then and kept very much to himself, probably because the other boys were so much bigger. He'd do the work of two men, scrubbing and cleaning, covered in a big apron which reached to his feet, probably loaned to him by the largest steward on the deck. When he was fairly well advanced with his work, he would come along to see how I was getting on with mine, chatting the while about his training ship, which he loved, and about himself.

On one occasion he picked up a film magazine which I had laid down and remarked, "You know, Miss, I think my mother was an actress. Of course I'm not sure, but I heard one of the officers say something about it one day on the training ship." Then he continued: "I never saw my father and mother. I think they died when I was very little. That's one thing I envy kids, having a mother and father they can go to." All of this was said while he was polishing a porthole screw.

I asked him, without seeming to be curious, whether he had any relatives.

"No," he replied, "there's only Mrs. Brewster that comes to fetch me sometimes, and takes me home with her. She's not exactly a relation, at least I don't think so. She's very kind to me but of course she has kids of her own and she's not very well off." After a silence he'd disappear to his pantry to do a bit more polishing.

Tom loved a fair, and when we returned from our cruise, he would save every penny for the great kermess in Antwerp. I'd see his radiant face in company with one or two other youngsters, watched over by their good Flemish landlady, Madame Van Rossen, a woman of ample form and, to judge by her care of these boys, of ample heart as well.

She was the proprietress of one of the more respectable cafes on Antwerp's waterfront, where she wielded fierce authority over a turbulent clientele. With the youngsters, however, she was different, showing them a truly motherly side, keeping an eagle eye on them while allowing them to retain that manliness which they had suddenly assumed when thrown alone into a foreign country. The birds of passage that come to Antwerp concentrate mainly on the waterfront and remain there during their stay in port. They seldom go further afield to seek other sights and pleasures than those afforded by the port's cheap and noisy cafes.

How Madame Van Rossen came to acquire the guardianship of Tom and his two companions I never was told. But from bits of gossip picked up here and there, I was able to guess. I believe the old mussel vendor on the corner, a great friend and admirer of Madame

Van Rossen's, had a good deal to do with it. Everyone knows everyone else near the docks and the moving population is very soon cata-
loged. The appearance one evening of three fresh-faced youngsters
who lacked the cocksure mannerisms affected by youths already
trained on a liner made old Madame of mussel fame take notice.

It was not surprising that, when she saw the boys pause as the
sound of music and laughter and English drifted through half-open
doors, the mussel vendor should hurry across to her good friend,
Madame Van Rossen. Moments later, Madame Van Rossen entered
the door whence came the music and asked the owner for the loan of
a pot. Turning with feigned surprise, she saw the three young boys
being jocularly greeted by some compatriots. With assumed relief, she
beckoned the boys and told them that somebody down the road had
been eagerly seeking them.

Now, Tom and his companions had never been eagerly sought by
anyone, with the exception perhaps of the officer-in-charge on their
training ship. So this novel experience caused them to fall out of that
popular music cafe so rapidly that they almost fell into the *petit salon*
of Madame Van Rossen before they knew what was happening. There
then ensued questions and answers, and much motherly advice given
in broken but telling English. From then on, Tom and his mates
made their headquarters at Madame Van Rossen's; no matter where
else they went or whatever they had to do, they were in duty bound
to report at some time or other to that good lady.

In a few months we left for American waters to make short cruises; their main purpose was to enable thirsty Americans during Prohibition to get their thirst assuaged. Tom was eagerly looking forward
to these cruises and all the novelty and fun they would mean to him.
By the time cruising started, he had pretty well been run off his feet.
Bellboys usually don't have enough real work to do. There has always
seemed to exist a management conspiracy to keep them free of man-
ual work with the idea that they will then be free for passengers' service. The system has exactly the opposite effect, however.

When these short cruises started from New York, Tom was put
on a regular job that meant a terrific amount of running about, all day
and sometimes far into the night. He came less often to pour his troubles into my ears. I could see that he was too harassed to want to talk
to anyone, assisting stewards to carry drinks from bar to cabins all day
long. It was a pity. He was too young to start life like that, and in such

an environment. Sometimes I would meet him, looking pathetically young and miserable, his bewilderment growing day by day; even his meal times were interrupted by demands for service.

It was on one such occasion that something happened to mark a turning point in Tom's life. It was the day before we were due back in New York. The ship was a madhouse. All the second-rate artists comprising the Entertainments Committee were doing their utmost to outdo the passengers. Parties were in progress everywhere, wild parties where the number of broken glasses and smashed pieces of furniture were taken as proof that it was a "swell" party, and women had lost all sense of decorum.

Young Tom came up for the hundredth time with a message and was told by an overworked, harassed steward to deliver it himself. I happened to be passing at the time Tom knocked at the door of the stateroom, and a chorus of strident voices called "Come in!" I saw Tom go in and almost immediately come out, his face scarlet. Ignoring me, he flew down the stairs, leaving the door open in his haste. It was just being closed as I passed and I beheld the most revolting sight of my life: A room full of stark naked people in the extreme stages of intoxication.

From that time there was a distinct change in Tom. He seemed to put aside his pleasing, happy ways, and became sullen and brooding, never speaking unless addressed and very often giving a curt reply. Everybody was too busy to notice much and too tired to bother, but I often wished those youngsters had a man, a capable, understanding man, deputized to deal with them when they were up against such things and to explain to them that life was not as vile as it appeared.

My heart ached for Tom, but it was difficult to approach him. He avoided me, of all people, perhaps because I had been the recipient of so many of his aspirations. He seemed to fear I might condemn him for witnessing what he could not avoid. I hoped that the approaching world cruise would, with its changing scenes and varied interests, help him adjust.

The cruise did brighten Tom up considerably, and I was delighted to see him take an interest in sport again, now that his days were less arduous. He came to see me in Honolulu to tell me, with a touch of his old enthusiasm, that he was going surf-bathing. One of the native divers was going to teach him to use an outrigger board and he was breathless with expectation. He now seemed his normal self and often went ashore with the crowd of sports enthusiasts for the inevitable game of cricket, played at every available port. If I did not always care for the company he kept, at least there was safety in numbers.

Other, sadder things occupied my mind for some considerable time after this and several annual world cruises passed.

There was a Mediterranean port which was used towards the end of a world cruise as a clearing station, where the fit and medically un-fit were evaluated before proceeding to New York with its rigorous health laws. A sorry group of medical outcasts left the ship there for home and, it was hoped, treatment.

I always avoided the deck on days when these groups left us, not even wanting to know who among the crew were marked to go, so depressing it all seemed to me. But on this particular day the sun was shining behind brilliant white clouds and the port was a most en-chanting sight, making me forget how tired I was and drawing me out to lose myself in thoughts of home now that April was here.

I suddenly caught sight of a group of men being conducted off the ship by a young official from the consul's office, and I knew at once what it meant. Among the unfortunates, the diseased throw-outs, was my once sunny-faced Tom. I came in from the deck before he could catch sight of me. At least I could spare him the pain of be-ing a witness to his sad farewell to us.

"Booze cruises" they were called, short, frantic voyages to escape the stric-tures of prohibition. Thousands of Americans thronged the ships each week, impatient to get beyond the three-mile limit where the bars would open to non-stop business. The pace of drinking and carousing increased as the re-turn to New York loomed.

Violet showed deep concern for the loss of innocence that she felt younger crew members suffered aboard ship. I suspect there were many Toms in her life, lonely, green boys who looked to her for comfort and guid-ance. Violet was a motherly soul who felt a proprietary concern for those she thought needed her protection.

Other shipmates recalled her special affection for them. Shortly after *The Only Way to Cross* was published back in the early seventies, I had a letter from Vernon Finch, a retired steward living in Vancouver. He had sailed with Jessop on board *Belgenland* and excerpts from his letter bear witness to the special esteem in which Violet was held by everyone on board:

"She had given so much comfort and care to so many during her lifetime . . . She was so like a mother to us younger members of the ship's company. No doubt memories of bellboys who perished on the S.S. *Titanic* and the frightened ones on the *Britannic* made her so forgiving when at times we disappeared to have a smoke in the glory hole when we should have been on duty . . . She would not tolerate any word or conduct from anyone which went against her strict code of living and everyone respected her for this. During the daily inspections at sea, the captain or the officers would always have a few words with Violet . . . She was a remarkable woman who loved the sea and ships as very few women ever can, and I only regret that I did not know where to contact her when she was still alive."

It was about this time, "in her late thirties," Margaret Meehan had suggested, that Violet Jessop's marriage took place. Have we a hint of it in the wording that introduces one of the paragraphs near the end of this chapter: "Other, sadder things occupied my mind for some considerable time," she writes obliquely. Might this have referred to her engagement, wedding and subsequent unhappiness? We shall never know.

# EPILOGUE

S O VIOLET JESSOP'S manuscript ends. Clearly, Violet cherished the earliest years of her employment, especially the first years with Royal Mail and subsequently with White Star.

What we do gather from the final, episodic chapters is Violet's enchantment with long cruises, idyllic passage to the Far East and back, the very antithesis of service across the stern, gray Atlantic. Five consecutive annual world cruises—from 1926 through 1931—obviously appealed, despite prolonged absence from home. She loved the exotic and she loved a bargain; she brought back with her a rich profusion of ivories, statuary and porcelain, even a giant clam shell that still serves as a bird bath in the Meehan sisters' London garden.

Moreover, she found *Belgenland* a happy ship, perhaps even as happy as her prior favorite, *Olympic*. In chapter 19, the one in which she devotes so much time to castigating her fellow stewards, she suggests that the best "social harmony" she had thus far encountered had been aboard the Red Star vessel because of its "mixed nationalities crew." Those mixed nationalities apart, I suspect that *Belgenland* was also fondly remembered because of its global deployment, golden days spent drifting from one adventurous port to another. Itineraries of that kind perpetuate a roseate luster to ships on which one has served.

In 1935, Violet returned to her first company once more, Royal Mail Line, serving on board *Alcantara* until the outbreak of war. During the Second World War, Violet remained ashore, working in a censorship office at Holborn, reading and snipping Spanish-language correspondence. In 1942, her mother died; Katherine Jessop was 82 years old.

After VE-Day, when Violet's wartime employment ended, she entered her 58th year with no pension in prospect for her approaching retirement. So she obtained a menial post at a government office in Acton, wearisome, ill-paid clerical work in which she was joined by her sister Eileen. Once that stint was over, Violet was hired for factory work at Sanderson's, the great wallpaper manufacturer located nearby in Ealing.

Then the sea called one final time. Resumption of Royal Mail's South American service in 1948 meant that, although strictly speaking she was overage at 61, Violet could sign on for a last, two-year stint of "Brazil Mail"

221

runs to South America aboard the *Andes*. On the last few voyages, she over-lapped with her niece Mary Meehan who embarked on the *Andes* as one of the ship's telephonists.

Violet swallowed the anchor for good in 1950. Mary, who had also de-cided to come ashore for employment, took a job in a Mayfair estate agency. It was there that she got wind of a thatched cottage in the Suffolk village of Great Ashfield that was for sale. Violet decided that she would sell the Ealing house that she and her mother had shared at 22 Vallis Way, hard by Ealing Common. She hoped that the sale would pay for the cottage as well as leave her with some leftover capital as well. She would need every shilling she could raise since her state pension amounted to no more than a few pounds each week. Violet made the move to her new country home and, on the land surrounding the cottage, raised hens to provide additional income.

In later years, when Violet no longer sold eggs, the Meehan family did what they could between them, helping her both practically and financial-ly. Additionally, Violet's brother Patrick sent a monthly stipend to his older sister from Australia.

Another brother, Jack, came back to England and made an extended visit to Maythorn in 1956. He was a skilled carpenter and swiftly put the cot-tage's attached piggery into sound condition; Violet's plan—never real-ized—was to grow mushrooms there to provide additional income. Shortly after Jack returned to Australia, the Meehan's parents, Eileen and her hus-band Hubert, retired and moved to the Suffolk village of Hartest, only eigh-teen miles away on the other side of Bury St. Edmunds. Throughout the sixties, the two sisters met regularly, traveling by bus to meet for a shopping day together in Bury or visiting each other at home.

Violet never forgot her brother Patrick's generosity. In gratitude for his financial help, Violet left him half her estate. His only daughter, Marilyn (now Skopal) shares in the ownership of her Auntie Vi's memoirs.

If we remember Violet's admiration for the wild flowers of the pampas as well as the city gardens of her youth, it is not surprising that in retirement, she put her green thumb to good use; she became an enthusiastic and tire-less gardener. She was fortunate in being able to hire a part-time gardener, a fellow pensioner who helped her landscape and plant. Between them, they filled the land fronting the cottage with such a profusion of bulbs that in the spring, she was surrounded by a riot of daffodils, crocuses and tulips. Rose bushes flourished and she also grew vegetables. Later on, after she had given up her hens, Violet let out the field as pasture for a neighbor's horse; the animal became one of her great favorites.

But the most relentless perennial at Maythorn was continuing financial shortfall. A fitted pigskin dressing case, complete with tortoise-shell combs and brushes as well as silver-stoppered crystal bottles, had once been the gift of an admiring passenger; presciently, he had recommended not mono-gramming it in the event she ever wanted to sell it. Now it *was* sold, courtesy of Margaret Meehan, to a well-known Bond Street shop from whence it had come, realizing sixty precious pounds for Violet.

She hoped too for additional income from the sale of her memoirs, which had languished untouched since the mid-thirties.

Despite her limited income, Violet decided, in the mid-nineteen-fifties, to take up driving. She arranged for some lessons and found a second-hand baby Austin that she could afford. That car made for a marvelous extension of her mobility. Margaret Meehan recalls being amazed at her Auntie Vi's competence behind the wheel, especially her reaction time to oncoming traffic, the alert response of a far younger woman. But ultimately, the vehicle was destroyed in an accident: A young man drove out of a lane into the side of her car. Luckily, Violet was unhurt but the poor little Austin was a writeoff. Rather than try and replace it, she kept the insurance money and made do with buses.

I sometimes wonder how Violet adjusted to retirement, how she fared after exchanging the close camaraderie of shipboard for the isolation of a cottage in the depths of rural Suffolk. Was that grass as green as she had anticipated? Might her chosen exile, however bucolic, have proved an unsettling contrast to her former peripatetic existence as part of a tight-knit, sociable crew? Certainly, Eileen and her husband helped fill the void when they also moved to Suffolk. But telephone communication between Violet and Eileen was impossible, alas; her younger sister was nearly completely deaf, legacy of childhood rheumatic fever in Argentina and a mastoid operation.

If Violet Jessop did find Maythorn lonely, she never spoke of it; I expect she made the best of things and soldiered on. Then too, perhaps I overestimate her attachment to past shipmates. When the time came to sign off from the *Andes* forever, she may have felt surfeited with shipboard life. Perhaps she relished the prospect of rest, retirement and a patch of garden, however remote. As it was, looking after a flock of laying hens kept her extremely busy.

Though Violet made several local friends in Great Ashfield, family gatherings at the cottage were impossible since only one overnight visitor could be accommodated at a time. Christmas and Easter reunions had, perforce, to take place at Eileen and Hubert's house in Hartest. Nieces Margaret and Mary came to see her whenever they could get away from their London jobs, meeting her either at Maythorn, Bury St. Edmunds, or Hartest. Near the end of her life, the Meehan sisters found a flat on their London street that boasted what they thought might be a suitable garden for their Auntie Vi but by then, her health had deteriorated. "I think," wrote Margaret recently, "she would have said no to any move from Maythorn."

As she aged, Violet took to sleeping downstairs on her sitting room sofa; the cottage's steep staircase was more than she cared to essay each night. For weekly groceries, she managed to catch a bus from nearby Daisy Green into Bury St. Edmunds. And when that became too much, a local mobile grocery van provided her with necessities.

In the spring of 1971, she suffered a fall. Her hip was not broken but she lay helpless on the floor overnight. Luckily, a neighbor who was her closest friend, found her the following morning and summoned an ambulance to take her to the hospital in Bury.

There she lay for the few weeks remaining to her. Margaret and Mary rushed down from London as soon as they heard news of her admission to the hospital. They found Vi in good spirits; she told her nieces how amused she had been when a young nurse suggested she might be more comfortable putting her teeth in a glass overnight; Violet had to explain that "it would be very difficult because every tooth I have is mine!"

Mary remembers to this day her last sight of their Auntie Vi, her face framed in a mob cap (by then her hair was gone), the pleasing lilt of her voice unchanged and her unforgettable eyes "two great orbs of blue."

Violet Jessop died of congestive heart failure in May of 1971. Thanks to the kindness of the local vicar, she was buried in the Hartest churchyard where she lies close to her sister Eileen.

I have saved one last anecdote that Violet shared with me on the day that I visited her less than a year before she died. She told me that one night, about a fortnight earlier, there had been a violent thunderstorm. Often, when lightning struck telegraph wires down the line, her telephone would ring erratically and she had learned to ignore it.

But very late that night, it rang and rang in earnest. Violet got up from her sofa bed and went into the hall to answer it. A woman's voice came through the ear piece.

"Is this Violet Jessop?"

"Yes," responded Violet. "Who's calling?"

"Is this the Violet Jessop who was a stewardess on the *Titanic* and rescued a baby?"

"Yes it is," answered Violet, increasingly irritated by the mysterious stranger. "Who is this? What is it you want?"

The woman laughed. "I was that baby," she announced abruptly and hung up. She never called back.

The call utterly mystified Violet. Perhaps, I hazarded, it could have been a prank played by someone in the village; but Violet reminded me that until my arrival two weeks later, she had told no one about her role aboard *Titanic*, least of all about rescuing a third class passenger's baby. Could the woman actually have been the baby grown up? It seems unlikely that she would have been able to find out the name of the retired stewardess who had held her through that bitter night fifty-eight years earlier and then tracked her down to a cottage in the depths of the countryside. Moreover, if the caller were indeed genuine, why call after midnight and why hang up?

I had thought that this puzzling telephone call should close the saga of this particular *Titanic* survivor. Here was a tantalizing voice from the past—

bogus but curiously well informed—that summoned up for the elderly stewardess/nurse a haunting remembrance of that long-ago disaster.

But I prefer another chance juxtaposition of images. Recently, I sat entranced through a New York City Ballet performance of Balanchine's *The Nutcracker.* Towards the end of the first act, little Marie lies asleep atop her ruffled white bed as it glides magically through a snowfall toward an enchanted forest. In an instant, my mind's eye summoned up a parallel vision, that of another girl on a bed. Only this was no theatrical fantasy, this was desperately ill young Violet, fighting for life amid a torrent of white oleander blossoms in a Buenos Aires hospital garden.

Who among that staff could have guessed the momentous events in which their apparently doomed young patient would participate in years to come?

# APPENDIX I

## Jessop's Ships and Voyages

| COMPANY | VESSEL | DURATION | DESCRIPTION |
|---------|--------|----------|-------------|
| Royal Mail | Orinoco | 10/28/08 - 12/28/08 | West Indies |
| " " | Oruba | 02/03/09 - 04/09/09 | " " |
| " " | Oruba | 04/14/09 - 06/14/09 | " " |
| " " | Danube | 07/09/09 - 06/14/09 | River Platte |
| " " | Clyde | 09/15/09 - 11/15/09 | West Indies |
| " " | Clyde | 12/22/09 - 02/21/10 | " " |
| " " | Clyde | 03/16/10 - 05/16/10 | " " |
| White Star | Majestic | 09/28/10 - 10/20/10 | New York |
| " " | Majestic | 10/26/10 - 11/17/10 | " " |
| " " | Adriatic | 11/30/10 - 12/22/10 | " " |
| " " | Adriatic | 01/04/11 - 01/29/11 | " " |
| " " | Oceanic | 03/15/11 - 04/05/11 | " " |
| " " | Oceanic | 04/12/11 - 05/03/11 | " " |
| " " | Oceanic | 05/10/11 - 05/31/11 | " " |
| " " | Olympic | 06/14/11 - 07/05/11 | " " |
| " " | Olympic | 07/12/11 - 08/02/11 | " " |
| " " | Olympic | 08/09/11 - 08/26/11 | " " |
| " " | Olympic | 08/30/11 - 09/16/11 | " " |
| White Star | Olympic | 09/20/11 - 09/22/11 | Intended New York (*Hawke* collision) |
| " " | Olympic | 11/29/11 - 12/16/11 | New York |
| " " | Olympic | 12/20/11 - 01/06/12 | " " |
| " " | Olympic | 01/10/12 - 01/31/12 | " " |
| " " | Olympic | 02/07/12 - 02/28/12 | " " |
| " " | Olympic | 03/13/12 - 03/30/12 | " " |
| White Star | Titanic | 04/10/12 - 04/15/12 | Intended New York |

(Sails eastbound as passenger aboard Red Star's *Lapland*)
(*Olympic* enters Harland & Wolff for refit following disaster)

| COMPANY | VESSEL | DURATION | DESCRIPTION |
|---------|--------|----------|-------------|
| White Star | Olympic | 06/05/12 - 06/22/12 | New York |
| " " | Olympic | 06/26/12 - 07/13/12 | " " |
| " " | Olympic | 07/17/12 - 08/3/12 | " " |
| " " | Olympic | 08/07/12 - 08/24/12 | " " |
| " " | Olympic | 08/29/12 - 09/14/12 | " " |
| " " | Olympic | 09/18/12 - 10/06/12 | " " |
| " " | Oceanic | 11/13/12 - 11/30/12 | " " |
| " " | Oceanic | 12/04/12 - 12/21/12 | " " |
| P & O | Malwa | 02/28/13 - 06/14/13 | Australian Mail |
| White Star | Olympic | 07/23/13 - 08/09/13 | New York |
| " " | Olympic | 08/13/13 - 08/30/13 | New York |
| " " | Olympic | 09/03/13 - 09/19/13 | " " |
| " " | Olympic | 09/24/13 - 10/11/13 | " " |
| " " | Olympic | 01/21/14 - 02/11/14 | " " |
| " " | Olympic | 02/18/14 - 03/11/14 | " " |
| " " | Olympic | 03/18/14 - 04/04/14 | " " |
| " " | Olympic | 04/08/14 - 04/25/14 | " " |

(Violet Jessop went ashore for training as a V.A.D.)

| COMPANY | VESSEL | DURATION | DESCRIPTION |
|---|---|---|---|
| White Star | Britannic | 11/12/16 - 11/21/16 | Intended Moúdros |

(Distressed British Seaman Jessop was repatriated 1/6/17 and worked in a bank until she signed on again with the White Star Line in the summer of 1920.)

| COMPANY | VESSEL | DURATION | DESCRIPTION |
|---|---|---|---|
| White Star | Olympic | 06/25/20 - 07/15/20 | New York |
| "        " | Olympic | 07/21/20 - 08/11/20 | "        " |
| "        " | Olympic | 08/18/20 - 09/04/20 | "        " |
| "        " | Olympic | 09/08/20 - 09/25/20 | "        " |
| "        " | Olympic | 09/29/20 - 10/16/20 | "        " |
| "        " | Olympic | 10/27/20 - 11/13/20 | "        " |
| "        " | Olympic | 11/17/20 - 12/04/20 | "        " |
| "        " | Olympic | 12/15/20 - 01/05/21 | "        " |
| "        " | Olympic | 03/09/21 - 03/26/21 | "        " |
| "        " | Olympic | 04/06/21 - 04/27/21 | "        " |
| "        " | Olympic | 05/04/21 - 05/21/21 | "        " |
| "        " | Olympic | 05/25/21 - 06/11/21 | "        " |
| "        " | Olympic | 06/15/21 - 07/20/21 | "        " |
| "        " | Olympic | 07/06/21 - 07/23/21 | "        " |
| "        " | Olympic | 08/03/21 - 08/20/21 | "        " |
| "        " | Olympic | 08/24/21 - 09/10/21 | "        " |
| "        " | Olympic | 10/05/21 - 10/22/21 | "        " |
| "        " | Olympic | 10/26/21 - 11/11/21 | "        " |
| "        " | Olympic | 11/30/21 - 12/17/21 | "        " |
| "        " | Olympic | 12/21/21 - 01/06/22 | "        " |
| "        " | Olympic | 02/08/21 - 02/25/22 | "        " |
| "        " | Olympic | 03/01/22 - 03/18/22 | "        " |
| "        " | Olympic | 03/02/22 - 04/08/22 | "        " |
| "        " | Olympic | 04/12/22 - 04/29/22 | "        " |
| "        " | Olympic | 05/02/22 - 05/20/22 | "        " |
| "        " | Olympic | 05/24/22 - 06/10/22 | "        " |
| "        " | Olympic | 06/14/22 - 07/01/22 | "        " |
| "        " | Olympic | 07/05/22 - 07/22/22 | "        " |
| "        " | Olympic | 08/23/22 - 09/09/22 | "        " |
| "        " | Olympic | 09/13/22 - 09/30/22 | "        " |
| "        " | Olympic | 10/04/22 - 10/21/22 | "        " |
| "        " | Olympic | 10/25/22 - 11/10/22 | "        " |
| "        " | Olympic | 11/22/22 - 12/09/22 | "        " |

(*Majestic* was the new Hamburg-Amerika Line's *Bismarck,* handed over to White Star as a spoil of war in 1922)

| COMPANY | VESSEL | DURATION | DESCRIPTION |
|---|---|---|---|
| "        " | Majestic | 02/27/23 - 03/10/23 | "        " |
| "        " | Majestic | 03/21/23 - 04/06/23 | "        " |
| "        " | Majestic | 04/10/23 - 04/27/23 | "        " |
| "        " | Majestic | 05/02/23 - 05/18/23 | "        " |
| "        " | Majestic | 05/23/23 - 06/08/23 | "        " |
| "        " | Majestic | 06/13/23 - 06/29/23 | "        " |
| "        " | Majestic | 07/04/23 - 07/20/23 | "        " |
| "        " | Majestic | 08/22/23 - 09/08/23 | "        " |

| COMPANY | VESSEL | DURATION | DESCRIPTION |
|---|---|---|---|
| White Star | Majestic | 09/12/23 - 09/28/23 | New York |
| "         " | Majestic | 10/03/23 - 10/19/23 | "         " |
| "         " | Majestic | 11/14/23 - 11/30/23 | "         " |
| "         " | Majestic | 12/04/23 - 12/21/23 | "         " |
| "         " | Majestic | 01/02/24 - 01/18/24 | "         " |
| "         " | Majestic | 01/23/24 - 02/09/24 | "         " |
| "         " | Majestic | 04/09/24 - 05/02/24 | "         " |
| "         " | Majestic | 05/07/24 - 05/23/24 | "         " |
| "         " | Majestic | 05/27/24 - 06/13/24 | "         " |
| "         " | Majestic | 06/18/24 - 07/04/24 | "         " |
| "         " | Majestic | 07/09/24 - 07/25/24 | "         " |
| "         " | Majestic | 08/06/24 - 08/22/24 | "         " |
| "         " | Majestic | 08/26/24 - 09/12/24 | "         " |
| "         " | Majestic | 09/17/24 - 10/03/24 | "         " |
| "         " | Majestic | 10/07/24 - 10/24/24 | "         " |
| "         " | Majestic | 10/29/24 - 11/14/24 | "         " |
| "         " | Majestic | 11/19/24 - 12/05/24 | "         " |
| "         " | Majestic | 12/08/24 - 12/23/24 | "         " |
| "         " | Majestic | 03/18/25 - 04/03/25 | "         " |
| "         " | Majestic | 04/22/25 - 05/08/25 | "         " |
| "         " | Majestic | 05/13/25 - 05/29/25 | "         " |
| "         " | Majestic | 06/02/25 - 06/19/25 | "         " |
| "         " | Majestic | 06/24/25 - 07/09/25 | "         " |
| "         " | Majestic | 07/14/25 - 07/31/25 | "         " |
| "         " | Majestic | 08/11/25 - 08/28/25 | "         " |
| "         " | Majestic | 09/01/25 - 09/18/25 | "         " |
| "         " | Majestic | 09/23/25 - 10/09/25 | "         " |
| "         " | Majestic | 10/13/25 - 10/24/25 | "         " |

(Seven months ashore without a ship or a company)

| COMPANY | VESSEL | DURATION | DESCRIPTION |
|---|---|---|---|
| Red Star | Belgenland | 05/24/26 - 06/07/26 | "         " |
| "         " | Belgenland | 06/11/26 - 07/05/26 | "         " |
| "         " | Belgenland | 08/06/26 - 08/30/26 | "         " |
| "         " | Belgenland | 09/03/26 - 09/27/26 | "         " |
| "         " | Belgenland | 11/23/26 - 05/09/27 | World Cruise |
| "         " | Belgenland | 05/13/26 - 05/09/27 | New York |
| "         " | Belgenland | 06/10/27 - 07/04/27 | "         " |
| "         " | Belgenland | 07/15/27 - 08/10/27 | "         " |
| "         " | Belgenland | 08/13/27 - 09/05/27 | "         " |
| "         " | Belgenland | 09/12/27 - 10/03/27 | "         " |
| "         " | Belgenland | 10/07/27 - 10/31/27 | "         " |
| "         " | Belgenland | 12/02/27 - 05/12/28 | World Cruise |
| "         " | Belgenland | 05/25/28 - 06/16/28 | New York |
| "         " | Belgenland | 06/22/28 - 07/14/28 | "         " |
| "         " | Belgenland | 07/20/28 - 08/11/28 | "         " |
| "         " | Belgenland | 08/17/28 - 09/10/28 | "         " |
| "         " | Belgenland | 09/14/28 - 10/08/28 | "         " |
| "         " | Belgenland | 10/12/28 - 11/05/28 | "         " |

| COMPANY | VESSEL | DURATION | DESCRIPTION |
|---|---|---|---|
| Red Star | Belgenland | 12/03/28 - 05/12/29 | World Cruise |
| "        " | Belgenland | 05/17/29 - 06/10/29 | New York |
| "        " | Belgenland | 06/14/29 - 07/08/29 | "        " |
| "        " | Belgenland | 12/04/29 - 05/11/30 | World Cruise |
| "        " | Belgenland | 05/16/30 - 06/09/30 | New York |
| "        " | Belgenland | 06/18/30 - 07/07/30 | "        " |
| "        " | Belgenland | 08/08/30 - 09/01/30 | "        " |
| "        " | Belgenland | 09/05/30 - 09/29/30 | New York |
| "        " | Belgenland | 10/03/30 - 05/09/31 | "        " |
| "        " | Belgenland | 12/02/30 - 05/09/31 | World Cruise |
| "        " | Belgenland | 06/12/31 - 07/05/31 | New York |
| "        " | Belgenland | 07/08/31 - 07/05/31 | New York/Halifax |
| "        " | Belgenland | 09/04/31 - 09/27/31 | New York |
| "        " | Belgenland | 10/02/31 - 10/29/31 | New York |
| "        " | Belgenland | 10/31/31 - 11/23/31 | "        " |

(Half a year's layoff, doubtless due to the Depression)

| | | | |
|---|---|---|---|
| "        " | Belgenland | 06/17/32 - 09/18/32 | New York/Cruise |

(Another long layoff, five months ashore)

| | | | |
|---|---|---|---|
| "        " | Belgenland | 02/12/33 - 03/26/33 | West Indies Cruise |
| "        " | Lapland | 04/12/33 - 09/23/33 | Mediterranean Cruise |
| "        " | Lapland | 06/03/33 - 07/01/33 | "        " |
| "        " | Belgenland | 07/28/33 - 09/23/33 | "        " |
| "        " | Westernland | 10/06/33 - 10/31/33 | New York |
| "        " | Westernland | 11/08/33 - 11/29/33 | "        " |
| "        " | Westernland | 12/01/33 - 12/23/33 | "        " |
| "        " | Westernland | 01/26/34 - 02/30/34 | "        " |
| "        " | Westernland | 02/23/34 - 03/20/34 | "        " |
| "        " | Westernland | 03/23/34 - 04/17/34 | "        " |
| "        " | Westernland | 04/20/34 - 05/14/34 | "        " |
| "        " | Westernland | 05/18/34 - 06/11/34 | "        " |
| "        " | Westernland | 06/15/34 - 07/10/34 | "        " |
| "        " | Belgenland | 07/25/34 - 09/14/34 | Mediterranean Cruise |

(Another long layoff, ten months ashore)

| | | | |
|---|---|---|---|
| Royal Mail | Alcantara | 07/15/35 - 07/18/35 | Jubilee Naval Review Cruise |
| "        " | Alcantara | 07/27/35 - 09/02/35 | Brazil Mail |
| "        " | Alcantara | 09/07/35 - 10/14/36 | "        " |
| "        " | Alcantara | 11/02/35 - 12/08/35 | "        " |
| "        " | Alcantara | 02/28/35 - 02/03/36 | "        " |
| "        " | Alcantara | 02/21/36 - 03/30/36 | "        " |
| "        " | Alcantara | 04/18/36 - 05/25/36 | "        " |
| "        " | Alcantara | 06/13/36 - 07/20/36 | "        " |
| "        " | Alcantara | 07/31/36 - 08/04/36 | Cruise |

| COMPANY | VESSEL | DURATION | DESCRIPTION |
|---|---|---|---|
| Royal Mail | Alcantara | 08/08/36 - 09/14/36 | Brazil Mail |
| " " | Alcantara | 10/03/36 - 11/09/36 | " " |
| " " | Alcantara | 11/14/36 - 12/21/36 | " " |
| " " | Alcantara | 01/22/37 - 03/01/37 | " " |
| " " | Alcantara | 03/20/37 - 04/26/37 | " " |
| " " | Alcantara | 05/15/37 - 06/21/37 | " " |
| " " | Alcantara | 07/10/37 - 08/06/37 | " " |
| " " | Alcantara | 09/04/37 - 10/11/37 | " " |
| " " | Alcantara | 10/30/37 - 12/06/37 | " " |
| " " | Alcantara | 12/29/37 - 02/07/38 | " " |
| " " | Alcantara | 02/18/38 - 03/28/38 | " " |
| " " | Alcantara | 04/16/38 - 05/23/38 | " " |
| " " | Alcantara | 06/03/38 - 06/08/38 | Weekend Cruise |
| " " | Alcantara | 06/11/38 - 07/18/38 | Brazil Mail |
| " " | Alcantara | 08/06/38 - 09/02/38 | " " |
| " " | Alcantara | 10/01/38 - 11/07/38 | " " |
| " " | Alcantara | 11/12/38 - 12/09/38 | " " |
| " " | Alcantara | 01/20/39 - 02/27/39 | " " |
| " " | Alcantara | 03/11/39 - 04/17/39 | " " |
| " " | Alcantara | 04/29/39 - 06/06/39 | " " |

(Jessop leaves the sea until three years after the war, working ashore in the censor's office, vetting the Spanish mail.)

| | | | |
|---|---|---|---|
| " " | Andes | 09/29/48 - 12/20/48 | Unknown |
| " " | Andes | 01/17/49 - 02/28/49 | Brazil Mail |
| " " | Andes | 03/01/49 - 02/28/49 | " " |
| " " | Andes | 04/19/49 - 07/24/49 | Unknown |
| " " | Andes | 07/25/49 - 11/07/49 | Brazil Mail |
| " " | Andes | 01/17/50 - 06/05/50 | " " |
| " " | Andes | 06/20/50 - 12/21/50 | " " |

At the age of 63 years, just before Christmas of 1950, Violet Jessop signed off *Andes* and retired. She had pursued her career since 1908; forty-two years of life at sea, interrupted by two world wars and two shipwrecks, were over.

The foregoing has been compiled from Violet Jessop's four seaman's discharge books or, as each is labeled on the cover, *Continuous Certificate of Discharge*; representative pages are reproduced elsewhere. Those blue-bound volumes are about the size of a passport; on their pages, every British seaman's ship was documented and he or she was rated with a stamped VERY GOOD at voyage's end. (A voyage, in seamens' parlance, was a return trip, from home port outbound to destination and back again.) Not surprisingly, the pages of Violet Jessop's books are consistently festooned with VERY GOOD's, one each concluding each of her more than 200 voyages.

In setting up the foregoing log, consecutive *Olympic* crossings or *Alcantara* journeys to Brazil could merely have been lumped together. But I think that listing every voyage separately conveys not only the extraordinary scope of Violet's sea time but also her complete life. In 1912 and 1916 respectively, she served only briefly aboard doomed *Titanic* and *Britannic*—"New York and Moúdros Intended"—

and it is understandable that those notoriously incomplete voyages preoccupy us. But they skew the overall picture, shortchanging the bulk of a long career. We should be reminded of those other years of service where Violet Jessop performed with equal dedication. Reproducing the full log redresses that imbalance.

Violet tended to serve on vessels for long, continuous spells, including 60 not quite consecutive voyages on *Olympic*, 39 on *Majestic*, 38 on *Belgenland* and 29 aboard *Alcantara*. But regardless of which vessel she signed on, it was unquestionably a demanding life. Weekends and holidays were things of the past. From 1908 until 1913, for instance, she was at home in England for only one Christmas. Though they tended to be rougher, consecutive Atlantic crossings had the advantage of allowing more frequent time at home between voyages. When *Olympic* sailed westbound for New York, depending on the weather, about seventeen days would pass before she would tie up again in Southampton's Ocean Dock. Turnaround time there would vary, from as little as four days to a week, more than sufficient time for Violet to sign off and hasten up to London on the train to see her beloved mother and sister.

But when she transferred to the Red Star Line in 1926, Antwerp rather than Southampton became her home port. Voyages to New York on slower *Belgenland* consumed three and a half weeks. With only a four-day turnaround in Antwerp, there was time for no more than a hurried ferry ride across to England and back for brief visits between trips. But worse was in store: That immutable pendulum of Antwerp/New York service was interspersed annually with a world cruise, one each year from 1927 until 1931.

*Belgenland*'s languid, global circumnavigation consumed six months, from early December until mid-May of the following year. World cruises were (and are to this day) testing marathons, for stewards and stewardesses in particular. For half a year, day after day, cabins had to be made up, trays carried and cleared, errands run and all the hundreds of chores that made up a stewardess' day completed. There was no respite, no day off and no layover between crossings as with North Atlantic service. Moreover, as indolent months passed aboard world cruise ships, ennui mounted and tempers frayed. Passengers became restive and irritated, new friendships were ruptured and what had enchanted on a dining saloon menu at the start of the cruise began to cloy.

And for Violet, there would be no immediate home leave throughout additional New York trips to follow. After *Belgenland* tied up in Antwerp at the end of the world cruise of 1926/27, for instance, note that Jessop remained on board for two additional voyages before being granted a paltry eleven-day leave in early July; a week and half off after seven month's of seven-days-a-week work. It cannot be said too often, Jessop's life was demanding; those mute columns of dates from her *Continuous Certificates of Discharge* tell the tale.

(Sadly, the log is not quite complete. No documentation exists of several voyages made at the start of the First World War, specifically Violet's eastbound *Olympic* crossing when HMS *Audacious* came to grief, documented in chapter 25. An entire two-year book is missing. Jessop's first book ends in April 1914—well before war broke out the following August—and the second begins with *Britannic*'s fatal voyage of November 1916.)

# APPENDIX II

Excerpts from a letter from Violet Jessop to Mrs. Emery. In it, she refers to the British film "A Night to Remember" which premiered in 1958.

Maythorn, July 29, 1958

Dear Mrs. Emery

How very kind of you to write to me. I was interested to learn of your family connection with Captain Rostron of the *Carpathia*. You said you thought the film long. I think that was done to impress.

The *Californian* was within sight all the time and therefore was the real cause of calmness on the *Titanic* as we all expected a ship so near to come straight away to our assistance. Of course, nobody realized she had stopped her engines. I think the *Carpathia* did a magnificent job as she had to alter course, was an old boat, and steamed full speed through the ice fields right to us.

But the main cause of all the loss of life was the failure of the Board of Trade to require a sufficient number of lifeboats for all. It was terribly difficult to make people get into the boats and leave their menfolk behind. After we had done all we could below stairs, we went up on deck and were just standing back watching a young officer trying to persuade emigrants to go into the boats. As he could not make himself understood (they were mostly Poles, Russians, etc.), he asked us to give a good example and get in. That is the reason why I am alive today.

I think Pinewood [Studios] did a wonderful job in recreating something that happened so long ago and if I disagree with a lot of things—such as the scene where it would appear the third class were locked in, and the behavior of some of the crew—it is only because to a person like myself who was there it seems like undue criticism.

I now greatly regret not having accepted Mr. MacQuitty's [the producer] several invitations; if I had seen some of the sequences, I could have pointed out discrepancies. I begged Miss Coffin [the costume director] when she interviewed me and later sent various questionnaires not to put women on board in the very beflowered, beplumed hats of the period as American women (and they were mostly Americans) would never wear street hats on board, and look what met your eyes at the Captain's table! Everything except the kitchen stove on their heads!

My failure to accept the invitation was due to the fact that I could not leave my chickens as I was alone then, and chickens are more demanding than passengers of those days—if that is possible. I find the days are not long enough so it is very difficult to get sufficient quiet and calm to rewrite the book but if ever it is published, I'll send you a copy.

All good wishes.

Sincerely,

Violet C. Jessop

# Bibliography

Boyd-Smith, Peter *Titanic from Rare Historical Reports,* Brooks Books, Southampton 1992

Bullock, Shan F. *A Titanic Hero, Thomas Andrews, Shipbuilder,* Seven C's Press, Riverside 1973

Eaton, John P. and Haas, Charles A. *Titanic, Triumph and Tragedy,* Patrick Stephens, Wellingborough 1986

- *Falling Star,* Patrick Stephens, Wellingborough 1989

Gracie, Col. Archibald *The Truth about the Titanic,* Mitchell Kennerley, New York 1913

Lord, Walter *A Night To Remember,* Henry Holt and Company, New York 1955

- *The Night Lives On,* William Morrow and Company, Inc., New York 1986

Lynch, Don & Marschall, Ken *Titanic, An Illustrated History,* Madison Press Books, Toronto 1992

Marcus, Geoffrey *Maiden Voyage,* George Allen and Unwin, Ltd, London 1969

Maxtone-Graham, John *The Only Way to Cross,* Macmillan, New York 1972

- *Olympic and Titanic,* Patrick Stephens, Wellingborough 1983

- *Crossing & Cruising,* Charles Scribner's Sons, New York 1992

Reade, Leslie *The Ship That Stood Still,* edited by Edward de Groot, Patrick Stephens, Sparkford 1993

Thayer, John B. *The Sinking of the S.S. Titanic,* Privately Printed, Philadelphia 1940

Wade, Wyn Craig *The Titanic, End of a Dream,* Rawson, Wade Publishers Inc., New York 1979

Watson, Arnold and Betty *Roster of Valor: the Titanic-Halifax Legacy,* Seven C's Press, Riverside 1984

For a cassette recording of the tune *Titanic*'s gallant bandsmen last played—Archibald Joyce's *Songe d'Automne* with piano accompaniment and then without—please send a check for $15 payable to Crossing & Cruising, to John Maxtone-Graham, 117 West 78th Street, New York, NY 10024, postage and handling included. Overseas readers please include a dollar draft for $18 or a sterling check for £12.

# Index